THE THEATER OF GOD

ROBERT PAUL ROTH

THE THEATER OF GOD

Story in Christian Doctrines

Fortress Press   Philadelphia

All Scripture quotations in this publication are from the Holy Bible, New International Version. Copyright © 1973, 1978, International Bible Society.

"Soli Deo Gloria" is taken from "The Dry Salvages" in *Four Quartets* by T. S. Eliot. Copyright © 1943 by T. S. Eliot. Renewed 1971 by Esme Valerie Eliot. Reprinted by permission of Harcourt, Brace, Jovanovich, Inc., and Faber and Faber Ltd.

"The Walking Song" is taken from *The Lord of the Rings* by J. R. R. Tolkien. Copyright © 1954, 1965 by J. R. R. Tolkien. Copyright renewed 1982 by Christopher R. Tolkien, Michael H. R. Tolkien, John F. R. Tolkien, and Priscilla M. A. R. Tolkien. Reprinted by permission of Houghton Mifflin Company.

Copyright © 1985 by Fortress Press

All rights reserved. No part of this publication may be reproduced, stored in a retrieval system, or transmitted in any form or by any means, electronic, mechanical, photocopying, recording, or otherwise, without the prior permission of the copyright owner.

Library of Congress Cataloging in Publication Data
Roth, Robert Paul.
    The theater of God.

    1. Story-telling (Christian theology)   I. Title.
BT78.R67   1985   230'.01'8   84-48725
ISBN 0-8006-1841-6

1274B85   Printed in the United States of America   1-1841

Soli Deo Gloria

These are only hints and guesses,
Hints followed by guesses; and the rest
Is prayer, observance, discipline, thought and action.
The hint half guessed, the gift half understood, is Incarnation.
Here the impossible union
Of spheres of existence is actual,
Here the past and future
Are conquered, and reconciled.

T. S. Eliot
Four Quartets

Contents

Prologue	ix
1. Methodology and Argumentation —stage directions	1
2. Narrative Hermeneutics —a Greek chorus	6
3. Narrative Ontology —the play's the thing	20
4. Reality and the Fantasy Metaphors of Creation —and God said	45
5. A Beginning Scientific Prescript on Understanding Life's Origins —a flashback	55
6. Reality and the Tragicomic Metaphors of Redemption —the cosmic *eucatastrophe*	64
7. The Tale of the Dragon and the Lamb —the meaning of atonement metaphors	78
8. Christ and the Trinity —obscene action in the flies and the wings	88

Contents

9. Baptism and the Church
   —going back to the beginning again 116

10. The Bible and Preaching
    —the sacrament of the Word 139

11. Eucharist and Service
    —liturgy and the action of Christ's passion in the global city 156

12. Into the Ages of the Ages
    —the inevitable sequel 174

Index of Scriptural References 185

Index of Names 187

Index of Subjects 191

Prologue

In *Story and Reality*, an earlier work, I explored five themes—evil, love, holiness, hope, and meaning—that run through all of literature in order to indicate the reality of story.

> Philosophical abstractions, whether monistic, dualistic, or pluralistic, fail to convey reality as it is experienced. We have therefore turned to story as a vehicle more suited to carry the rock of Sisyphus. We are not saying that reality is ultimately illusory as stories are fictional. We are saying that reality is multifarious, that it includes many realms, that some are empirical and some are not, some are historical and some are not. Moreover, there is a sickness unto death that runs through all reality, whether it is historical or not, empirical or not. And against this sickness there is a holy warfare which is dedicated through suffering to bring health and wholeness to the entire creature. The nature of reality is therefore dramatic. There are persons in conflict and reconciliation in view.

Now with less restraint and modesty, in fact with unabashed audacity, I want to explore what it will do to Christian theology if we substitute story as a category in place of all the philosophical metaphors and scientific models. I want to see what the doctrines of creation, redemption, Christ, the Trinity, baptism, the church, the Bible, preaching, the Eucharist, service in the world, and eschatology will look like cast in the shape of story rather than any of the analogues previously used in the history of theology. The only disclaimer I wish to make is that this is an experiment in thought. Experiments sometimes fail. This is no exception. But I have unfettered my imagination just to see what will happen. Naturally it is presented at times in anecdotal style.

Story is here regarded as the fundamental category of reality. It is not the same as a philosophical root metaphor, nor a scientific model, but it must do the work in the whole scheme of theology that these analogues have

Prologue

formerly tried to do. Plato's ideal form, Aristotle's substance, Leibniz's monad, Descartes's matter and mind, Hume's impression and idea, Whitehead's experient occasion are all analogues that are intended to be elemental, irreducible, and universally applicable. Yet they are inadequate to include mystery, conflict, absurdity, surprise, and climax. These latter are elements in reality which can be embraced by story.

It is true that story is not a simple or elemental analogue. It has component parts, and in this respect it resembles scientific models. But models are used by scientists for operations in limited spheres of observation without claim to be universal. The model of atomic structure, to be sure, does have universal application to all observed matter, but it says nothing about the shape of families or nations or historical sequences. Story, on the other hand, is a category that informs us about the behavior of gases as well as the conflict between Christ and Satan. Nature, history, heaven, and hell can all be conceived in terms of the struggle for reconciliation. There is climax in the fulfillment of a DNA molecule just as there is climax in the history of a culture.

Precisely what is the category of story? It is simple. There is nothing abstruse about story. We all know what stories are. They have beginnings and endings. They are sequential occurrences in places and times. They have persons in the drama who act and are acted upon. There are props or settings which support, shape, and limit the action and passion of the story. There are plots with anticipation, conflict, climax, and resolution. Everybody and everything has its story. Story is the nature of reality. Reality is story.

And now before the play begins, I give my thanks to Carol Garman, Harold Rast, and Davis Perkins for their cheerful help. From Margaret, my beloved wife, encouragement and smiles gave me the strength to pen these lines. And when at last the curtain falls I pray that God will gently say, *"Plaudite, amici, comedia finis est."*

Lake House of the Golden Dragon   Robert Roth
Easter 1985

1

Methodology and Argumentation

—stage directions

Melanchthon said a good theologian must have language, logic, and the Spirit.

If we want to bring clarity and conviction to any issue, we must use language without equivocation, yet also not univocally. Sometimes a word will be taken with meanings not intended. At other times a word will have multivalent meanings and we pauperize it by restricting its meaning to one, simple, empirical, or historical sense.

For example, the same words in different contexts often have different meanings. If I say, All who squawk are ducks; Dr. Merriweather squawks; therefore Dr. Merriweather is a duck, I mean one thing if Dr. Merriweather is the name of my theology professor and another if Dr. Merriweather is the name of my pet duck. If I say he went up, I mean one thing if I refer to walking up the stairs, another if I mean climbing the ladder of success, and still another if I mean ascending to heaven. Up can refer to physical place, social status, or transfer from one level of being to another. Thus it is irresponsible to use language univocally when its richness requires a variety of meanings. Take the word Christ, an important word for Christians. To Pilate, Christ as the king of the Jews was a possible threat to Caesar; to Herod, Christ as the Son of David was surely a threat to his throne; to the disciples, Christ as the Son of man was the fulfillment of a prophecy. Jesus as the Christ was all three of these but in different ways than any of the people who knew him realized. That is why Jesus always had to answer questions about himself indirectly. A literal meaning will never work, because Jesus is always more than we take him to be.[1]

On the other hand, totally different words may have the same meaning in different contexts. For this reason translation is possible, and translation is largely the task of the pastor in preaching. For example, I am a sailor and I have five children whom I taught to be sailors. We sail in regattas with snipes. This is an equivocation. To some a snipe is a marshland bird, but to me it is an international racing class sailboat. My children learned the fresh, crisp language of the sea. They learned how to skipper and win races too; all but one. My youngest daughter fell in love with a horse. In a weak moment I bought her that horse, a magnificent chestnut American saddlebred. But the night before the horse was to be delivered he got into a fight with his stablemate and received a terrible gash in the side. I thought I had better tell Sonja about it before she saw the wound. She was, of course, dismayed and excited, and she burst forth with a torrent of questions about how it happened and especially where the wound was. I tried to tell her, but I did not know horse language; I did not know the words for the exact parts of a horse's anatomy. So I finally said in the language of boats, "Sonja, your horse has been stove in amidships along the chine of the starboard beam." She said, "Oh, Daddy, you mean three hands below the withers on the right flank."

The translation was perfect. The language was precise and we both knew exactly what we meant. The church has been translating the gospel into various languages and idioms from the beginning. This is how the language of the Logos came into the writings of John and Paul. This is how the doctrine of the Trinity was shaped by the language of Plato and the sacrament was transubstantiated by Aristotle. These translations worked more or less for former cultures, but they no longer work for us because we live in an age of empirical science. We cannot speak of causal sequences in the language of today and mean the same thing that Paul and Jesus did when they spoke of salvation. I suggest, therefore, that we couch our meanings in the language of story because story language reaches across cultures and down through the centuries. Otherwise we will reduce the gospel to mere history, or mere anthropology, or mere sociology, or mere natural philosophy.

Connected with the right use of language is the correct use of reason. The theologian must be careful of logic. The story is told of a man in a mental hospital who said to the doctor, "I am dead, you had better call the undertaker." The doctor was puzzled for a while, but then he decided to use logic to convince the man that he was not dead. He took a needle and jabbed it into the patient's thumb and squeezed until the blood came out. Then he said, "Do you see, you are bleeding. That proves that you are alive." But the patient said, "Nonsense, that does not prove that I am alive. It proves that dead people bleed!" You see, the patient may have been wrong about being dead but he was not stupid, and he knew logic better than the doctor. We may be forgiven for being a bit crazy when we proclaim the gospel through preaching and the sacrament, but we will not be allowed stupidity. Logic is a tool helpful for conceptual ordering of the things of reality, but logic does not say anything really about those things.[2]

When words are put together to convey thoughts the outcome can be puzzlingly ambiguous. The little word "is" can have as many as five different meanings when it is used as a copula to connect the same subject with the same predicate. Take the Bible as the object of thought and connect it with the concept of inspiration. The connection between Bible and inspiration can involve predication, class inclusion, implication, identity, and equivalence. Here are five sentences, all of which connect with the same verb "is" the same two objects of thought: Bible and inspiration. But there are subtle differences of meaning among them all.

1. *The Bible is inspiring.* This sentence says something about the Bible but it also says something about people who read the Bible. It says the Bible is a kind of book that brings inspiration to its readers. The word "inspiring" predicates the quality that the Bible is inspiring literature.

2. *The Bible is inspired.* This sentence says something about the Bible in itself regardless of who reads it. It says the Bible is a kind of book that belongs to a class of inspired literature. It says nothing about its readers, but it classifies the Bible as a member of a class of inspired books.

3. *The Bible is inspirational.* This sentence says something by implication. It may not always be so but it is implied that if you read the Bible, you will find it inspirational.

4. *The Bible is inspiration.* This sentence can mean that the Bible is identical with the Word of God as given by the inspiration of the Holy Spirit.

5. *The Bible is inspiration.* This sentence, which is identical with sentence number 4, thus demonstrating most effectively the ambiguity of language, can mean that the Bible is equivalent to inspiration for the reader. This meaning is quite different from the meaning in sentence 4. It says that reading the Bible is sheer inspiration. Again, as in sentence 1 compared to sentence 2, there is a shift of meaning from an objective statement about the Bible to a subjective reference to the reader of the Bible.

Not only must we be careful to shape our sentences so that we will bring out these subtle nuances for the sake of accuracy and clarity but also we must avoid other kinds of ambiguity that result in confusion and contradiction. A single predicate may be connected with a variety of subjects by means of the simple copula "is," and because the sentences look similar we may be tempted to think we can interchange one subject for another without changing meaning or value. Thus we say (1) the Bible is the Word of God, (2) the gospel is the Word of God, (3) the sermon is the Word of God, and (4) Christ is the Word of God. In each case the concatenation of words brings a different meaning to the phrase "Word of God." Certainly we cannot substitute Bible or sermon for Christ and mean the same thing. Also we do not give equal authority to all four subjects unless we want to mess up our priorities.

Confusion of meanings arises when words have similar appearance. Thus we have seen that to say the Bible is inspired is to say something descriptive about the reader of the Bible. What is inspiring is not necessarily inspired. A sound is audible because people hear it, but a war is not desirable because people desire it. Adjectives do not mean the same thing when applied to individuals as when applied to classes. A good artist is not always a good person.

There are many fallacies in argumentation due to prejudice, intimidation, carelessness, haste, neglect, and sheer perversity. Christians must be precise in the use of reason because it is a God-given tool.

But besides precise and intelligent use of language and logic the Christian must have the Holy Spirit, as Melanchthon said. This is where distinctively Christian theology begins. Without the Spirit our words about God and our destiny always mean something different from what the Spirit makes them mean. We do not know how to talk, we do not know how to pray, but the Holy Spirit intercedes for us and turns our talk around, turns our wrong prayers into holy words that are pleasing to God. Our problem is that of Valentin the clown. He was on a dark stage standing under a streetlamp. Down the street was a row of houses, all dark. The only light was the streetlamp. Valentin was not dressed like a clown with baggy trousers and a funny nose. He had ordinary clothes, but he was a clown nonetheless. He went round and round under the lamp, obviously looking for something. A policeman came and asked, "Did you lose something?" "Yes," said the clown, "I lost the key to my house." The policeman joined the search. Around and around they went under the light. Finally the policeman grew weary and said, "Are you sure you lost it here?" "Oh, no," said the clown, "I lost it over there," and he pointed to the dark side of the stage. With total exasperation the policeman said, "Why on earth are you looking for it here?" "Because," said the clown, "there is no light over there."

This is our problem. If we look in the wrong place, we gather the wrong data. We are trying to find God and we want a miracle of light to show us where he is. The ancient Jews and the current charismatics are alike. They both want a sign to prove they have the Spirit. They want the kind of sign that will prove directly in broad daylight that the power of God is theirs to use. They want the key to heaven, and with it they want to get a treasure trove on earth of health and wealth and political power. So they talk about being born again by the power of the Spirit so they can claim his gifts.

Here is the equivocation. What they mean by being born again and what Scripture says are two different things. Current talk about being born again must therefore be distinguished from biblical talk about being born anew. People who talk about being born again want God to be at their beck and call. They want a God who will intervene on their behalf. They think that God is very close to them, that he is busily programming all history and personally intervening both to punish and to reward our human actions and decisions. Although they would not use the word, for them God is always meddling in history and in our personal lives. They think of him as interrupting with punishment or chastisement or training to some and protection or healing or rewards of wealth and power to others.

The story of the New Testament is different. Here it is revealed that God is free and we are free. He made us in his own image and therefore he does not meddle. He delivers us up to our freedom, and if in our freedom we choose to be sinners, this means he delivered us up to our own sin (Rom. 1:29). He does not stop us, he does not intervene. His wrath is not a thunderbolt from heaven; his wrath is the hurt we bring to ourselves when we seize for ourselves his holy fire. And if we are sinners, then we must be born anew, we must be remade, re-created now in the mold of Christ rather than in the mold of Adam. And this involves a process, an age-long development which begins in baptism but continues everlastingly into and through the age of the ages, *aiōn tōn aiōnōn*. We are born anew to be molded and fashioned in the image of Christ, to be filled with the whole fullness of deity bodily (Eph. 3:19).

The unregenerate self, like Ibsen's Peer Gynt, goes to live with the Trolls trying to be sufficient to self, only to find that the person who seeks himself or herself alone becomes just that—himself alone or herself alone. And the button molder must come to melt the person down so that the person can start all over again. Against this ultimate death we must go through the death to self in order to be molded anew in the image of Christ.

NOTES

1. A great many books have been published in recent years on the errors of literalism. Among the most helpful is Robert W. Funk, *Parables and Presence* (Philadelphia: Fortress Press, 1982).

2. Cf. Alfred J. Ayer, *Language, Truth and Logic*, 2d ed. (New York: Dover Publications, 1936).

2

Narrative Hermeneutics

—a Greek chorus

We live in a story-shaped world. Reality is story. We cannot reduce reality to an idea or a thing or a manifold of impressions or an all-embracing God or a process of sentient occasions. The root metaphors of the grand philosophies in the past have proven inadequate because they have not recognized that reality includes radical changes in being, irreversible movements in time, trivial and magnificent absurdities, comical and tragic incongruities, and mysteries beyond resolution. There is in reality a plot which carries persons and props to a meaningful conclusion, but the meaning is full of surprises and there is not a sufficient reason for everything. Indeed, the deepest meaning is a mystery that is celebrated because its satisfaction is precisely in its awesome power to delight us in repetitions that are never the same. Hence reality is a story that keeps going on.

What will happen to the doctrinal formulation of the Christian faith if story is used as the category of reality? What will happen if we stop talking about creation in terms of the philosophical category of causality, if we abandon Aristotle's efficient cause, material cause, formal cause, and final cause? Modern science has already abandoned the last three; I suggest we abandon the first one as well.

I am not suggesting we quit asking etiological questions. I am proposing we enlarge our quest about origins to include mysteries that cannot be found in any rational or empirical chain of being. What will happen if we describe the Trinity not in terms of a hypostatic union but rather from the perspective of dramatic action in a plot? What will happen if the two natures of Christ become two characters in a play about a single person, as with the Duke and the friar in Shakespeare's *Measure for Measure*?

These are questions that deserve to be asked in an experimental way for all the doctrines of the church, but before we can do this we must establish a hermeneutic. During the twentieth century two approaches to scriptural interpretation prevailed until about 1960: historical analysis and dialectical theology. Historical analysis used scientific critical tools to locate the text in its original setting. Original texts were sought among extant manuscripts through methods of textual criticism. Dates, places, and authors were identified by criticism of forms and by tracing the redaction of editors, with the help of archaeological evidence. But historical analysis left us with an embarrassment of riches, a sterile erudition which lost the forest for the trees. Who can preach about J, E, D, and P, or Q, the L source, and M?

The other approach to scriptural interpretation came from Karl Barth and his dialectic between the Word of God and the text. The concern is for God's message speaking from the Bible across the ages. Systematic theologians from Emil Brunner to Gerhard Ebeling have echoed this affirmation of the priority of God's Word in the text over the context in which it is given. Biblical theologians like Walther Eichrodt found that message in the Old Testament to be the concept of God's covenant with Israel.[1] Gerhard von Rad found it to be the history of God's mighty act of deliverance.[2] Rudolf Bultmann said it is the message of self-understanding (*Selbstverständnis*).[3]

But with the 1960s came the cry from Walter Wink that biblical criticism is bankrupt and from Brevard Childs that biblical theology is dead.[4] Since then a variety of alternatives have been proposed, with none as yet reaching ascendancy. The problem is that on the one side history is too relative to provide authenticity, and on the other side dialectical theology is too dogmatic to account for the reality of the human situation. The result is that some have sought religious satisfaction by turning inward. If the Word no longer speaks either as history or as theology, then there is appeal to the Spirit.[5] This accounts for the quest for personal experience in the rise of many new cults.[6] Others have pushed the appeal to history to the extreme. This is what Wolfhart Pannenberg and Jürgen Moltmann are doing with their assertion that history itself reveals God.[7] The historical process is known through Jesus, and although we do not know the end, hope is possible because God's future is invading the present. Political hermeneutics is closely associated with this view in the liberation theology of Gustavo Gutiérrez and Dorothee Soelle.[8] Another tack has been taken with the construction of a new metaphysics in the naturalism of process thinking from Alfred North Whitehead. This is an appeal to nature and creation. It is a turn outward, and it involves both the sophistication of process thinking and the simplistic talk of God as nature, in either case resulting in an optimistic affirmation of the world.[9] Finally, Paul Tillich tried to revive an old metaphysic, Platonism, by providing, in a method of correlation, essentialistic answers to existential questions.[10]

From Germany and France, however, two separate schools have arisen that seek a new hermeneutic in the analysis of language. Ernst Fuchs and Gerhard Ebeling in Germany have examined the power of the word to create.[11] Language has the creative power to make things new. They call this *Sprachereignis,* which means a language event. This is objectively given through communication, and this must therefore be distinguished from *Spracherlebnis,* which is a subjective experience. In France a similar reaction against the subjectivism of existentialism has arisen with the help of language analysis. Ferdinand de Saussure, Claude Lévi-Strauss, Roland Barthes, and Paul Ricoeur have sought meaning in symbols and metaphors which are the stuff of language and the building blocks of stories.[12]

The structural analysis of language has an exceedingly complicated vocabulary. Perhaps this in itself will inhibit this hermeneutic from achieving general acceptance. Furthermore, it is not clear where structural analysis finds its philosophical base. Robert Detweiler, in *Story, Sign, and Self,* tries to relate structural analysis with the phenomenology of Edmund Husserl.[13] *Phenomenology* is the descriptive study of essential being as intuited by human consciousness apart from logic and empirical experience. It suspends the commonsense perception of the world in order to bracket out unessential elements of a thing and thus discover its *eidos,* or essence. Reality is seen, therefore, to include more than the actual, the empirical, the literal. *Structuralism* is the analysis of language which is formed by the human mind, which thus in turn forms culture and the world in which we live. The stories told in cultures are shaped by the structure of the mind which has a quality that is innovative and free and cannot be mechanized but that is also appropriate and coherent and structured, not just a heap. Therefore Noam Chomsky says, in *Language and Mind,* that language has an innate mental, deep structure beneath the surface structure of its variable grammars.[14] Language has a universal grammar which requires certain kinds of sentence structure and rejects others. For example, the sentence "John was persuaded to leave" remains meaningful if "persuaded" is substituted by "forced," but it becomes a non-sentence if substituted by "tired," though not meaningless if substituted by "too tired." Thus both phenomenology and structuralism are linked to linguistics and both seek to probe beyond the literal and empirical by a transformation to a deeper reality.

Edgar V. McKnight, in *Meaning in Texts,* tries to associate structuralism with the existential philosophy of Wilhelm Dilthey and Martin Heidegger. In *Being and Time,* Heidegger says, "Only as long as Dasein *is* . . . 'is there' Being."[15] Yet paradoxically Being "determines entities as entities."[16] Thus from Heidegger the new hermeneutic says there is a relationship between Being and language which is equiprimordial. Being is the condition of language, yet without language Being is nothing. But at the same time language is earlier than its ground, earlier than Being. Although speech is not Being, only in speech is Being spoken out.

This eidetic relationship between Being and language, says McKnight, has value in that if a text is viewed as literature, "reference will not be made to real, verifiable historical factors, but to something else, to perspectives on the world, to various poetic experiences or effects, to life, and to God.[17] When biblical narratives are read as literature, not only as history but as an art form, systematic theology is not bound to a literal reading of the text. Narrative hermeneutics thus involves the reader creatively in using the text as a "language event" for the present time. "History provides the elements of narrative, but worlds of personal meaning—social, religious, theological—help create and structure the text and may be discerned in the text."[18]

In the past we have used philosophical structures to understand texts, but sometimes we have abandoned them to engage in a direct encounter with the sacred, taking God as the object of our religious experience. Philosophical objectivity was always inadequate because it lacked the subjective dimension of personal involvement. Direct subjectivity was also inadequate because it was obscurantist and wishful. Now in narrative hermeneutics the reality of the gospel is seen as story, and both objective and subjective dimensions are embraced. We are not concerned to reduce everything to a set of propositions, nor do we want to concentrate only upon subjective experiences. We are, rather, concerned descriptively about the account of the story of faith. Both the abstraction of philosophy and the concretion of history are set aside for the moment while we look at the tale that is told. History is not abandoned, because there is much in common between story and history. They are both episodic and sequential. The narrative of Scripture has much within it that is historical, but stories are not the same as history. We need to recognize elements of the nonhistorical and see them to have reality that is given, not just subjectively invented.

For example, Genesis 1—11 mixes the historical and the nonhistorical by relating events with both human and divine causation. This raises the problem of explanation. Confronted by surprise and novelty and mystery, we seek to explain events. The etiological question has found several different kinds of answers. A study of the career of this questioning reveals that truth is multiform. There are various satisfactions. Thus there are philosophical, psychological, sociological, historical, and scientific answers. The explanations depend upon the way the questions are asked. And science itself has various kinds of explanations according to what we are looking for and what satisfies us. Science is not a single unified system. It is a method of searching. Some explanations are operational, as in physics and chemistry; some are genetic, as in biology; some are statistical and probabilistic, as in quantum mechanics and sociology. All seek for causes that will fill up the sequences and leave no gaps. And while there may seem to be no gaps, and while these various explanations may satisfy us each in its own way, there are other dimensions in the concatenation of events which cry for recognition. None of these quests have room for mystery, surprise, humor, irony, or absurdity. Yet reality is full of these oddities. How can we talk of explanations for things that can find no place for either the holy or the ridiculous? History looks for causes, but history describes people and events which are enmeshed in comedy and tragedy that transcends ordinary causes. Stories provide, then, a position from which we can look at the world anew. Stories will heighten our sensitivity to see the world as it really is, and stories will lift us heuristically beyond the present world so as to create a new reality. Stories construct an alternate world. The process of interpreting the text of a story is a process of anticipating a new world.

Paul Ricoeur, in "Biblical Hermeneutics,"[19] says that metaphor is not grounded in resemblance as merely an ornament of discourse, as the rhetorical tradition has always said. Metaphor establishes reference through mimesis as "world disclosure." It therefore offers new patterns of reality. Metaphors are "semantic innovations." They "say something new about reality." The transforming power of metaphor is the ability to precipitate a conflict of interpretations of a semantic unit (the sentence) and thereby destroy literal meaning (resemblance) and initiate a new view of reality (difference). The metaphor is heuristic fiction; it finds a new reality which differs from facts of literal reality.

Exegesis must have levels because being has levels.[20] The literal is only one level of meaning. The literal is what it is, but we can move through it to another reality or realm of being because God imagined it so. "In my Father's house are many rooms" (John 14:2). Reality is therefore metaphorical. It is reachable only through similes, metaphors, and symbols which cannot be taken literally but which truly embrace the reality we seek.[21] The problem with modern exegesis is that it allows as real only what can be historically verified, yet it tries to talk also about "acts of God" which can be accepted only by faith and cannot be verified.

Paul Hanson has shown, in *Dynamic Transcendence,* how the prophet in Second Isaiah viewed his own historical situation by using the exodus as a window. The story of the exodus was not shaped singly by a great storm on the sea, but by a host of intertwining forces, historical and cosmic. Among the forces were Egyptian social structures and their mythic reification, the customs and beliefs of early Hebrews, the Northwest Semitic cosmogonic myth, political realities of the Late Bronze Age, and immediate historical happenings. All these forces and happenings occur together, but they are perceived differently by those to whom and around whom they happen. Thus the Egyptians did not see what the Hebrews saw at the exodus because they did not have the Hebrew confessional heritage. A "revelation" was given to the Hebrews so that the same historical data, now by the force of metaphor, lifted the Hebrews to a new realm of reality. For this kind of revelation there had to be preparation. This was done by the covenant with Abraham. "This is to say, happenings experienced as insignificant by other observers (i.e., the Egyptians) were experienced by the Hebrews as redemptive because, when viewed from the perspective of the confessional heritage, they were recognized as relating to earlier events as subsequent points along a purposeful continuum."[22] The new revelation not only confirmed the old confessions but amplified and deepened them. And just as the escape over the Red Sea is the metonymical episode for the whole "act of God" in the past, so now in Isaiah we can read Cyrus's deliverance as a new metonymical episode. And indeed the exodus, for Paul in 1 Corinthians 10, becomes a type for Christ and his deliverance from death.

The interplay of historical events with different levels of meaning is like the synchronic and diachronic dimensions in plays and novels. In *A Midsummer Night's Dream* the story of Oberon, Titania, and Puck is interwoven with the story of Bottom and Quince, and Flute, and these stories are interwoven with the story of Hermia, Lysander, Theseus, and Hippolyta. Bottom never saw what Puck was doing, yet they interacted in such ways that the final denouement resolves all the disastrous and comical twists and turns of the play. But the resolution is different for each group of characters because they live in different worlds. Bottom does not understand magic potions and Puck understands them too well.

Narrative analysis builds on linguistic analysis by moving from extensive sentence structure to story structure.[23] Sentences have subjects, predicates, and modifiers. Likewise stories have agents, objects, and helpers/hinderers. Different names are given to these components by various analysts.[24] Some refer to the components as actants which include senders, receivers, and adjuvants/opponents. Thus there is a story in every sentence just as there are sentences in every story. There is conflict. There is a binary situation which moves in time to a climax and denouement, not necessarily a solution but a resolution; not a conclusion but a completion, bringing the story to satisfying fullness and resolving the conflict by mediation. Stories have the function of providing mediating factors for fundamental contradictions. Thus the contradiction becomes a tolerable paradox. Reality and truth are fundamentally paradoxical. There is conflict between opposing realities. All the world, and especially human life, is contrapuntal. Some analysts say this is because of the binary nature of the human mind. There is in the nature of things a tension between chaos and order, monster and God, male and female, father and son, wet and dry, cold and hot, raw and cooked, and so forth. The conflict is not resolved but is mediated. The purpose of mythmaking is to describe the creation of the world with its differentiations and antagonisms, its changes and limits, and also to provide hope through an awesome sacrificial mediation which makes our condition not only tolerable but redemptive.[25]

The resolution is always unexpected. Reality has a surprise ending. "Behold, I make all things new." "The kingdom of God will come as a thief in the night." Stories therefore have excitement, but this is because of the quality of unexpectedness, not the fact of it. We read stories over and over again, and we are equally and increasingly thrilled even though we know what comes next, and the outcome. C. S. Lewis said:

> We do not enjoy a story fully at the first reading. Not till the curiosity, the sheer narrative lust, has been given its sop and laid asleep, are we at leisure to savour the real beauties. Till then, it is like wasting great wine on a ravenous thirst which merely wants cold wetness. The children understand this well when they ask for the same story over and over again, and in the same words.[26]

Roland Barthes provides an analysis of the structure of the story of Jacob wrestling with the man at the River Jabbok. It will serve to illustrate what I have been saying about narrative hermeneutics and the surprise ending.[27] Barthes calls the man who wrestles with Jacob an angel. The story is about a conflict that is resolved with an ironic and unexpected turn. According to structural analysis, stories have senders and receivers with an object sent, and helpers and opponents with a subject who is the hero that resolves the conflict.

$$\text{sender} \rightarrow \text{object} \rightarrow \text{receiver}$$
$$\uparrow$$
$$\text{helper} \rightarrow \text{subject} \leftarrow \text{opponent}$$

In this story God, as sender, brings Jacob to the object of crossing the River Jabbok into Canaan. Jacob helps the action by using his weakness. With his hip hurt he demands a blessing. He had used his weakness before to demand a blessing from Isaac, and this is a type of the struggle between weak Israel and mighty Canaan. God then as angel is both sender and opponent. He is his own adversary. And Jacob as receiver is his own helper.

$$\text{God, the sender} \rightarrow \text{River, the object} \rightarrow \text{Jacob, the receiver}$$
$$\uparrow$$
$$\text{Jacob, the helper} \rightarrow \text{Jacob, the subject} \leftarrow \text{Angel, the opponent}$$

Barthes calls this story an example of an "extortion folk narrative" in which God not only defends the river against the trespassing hero but supplies the blessing when he is "defeated." This is the surprise, the scandal of God being unable to win: "The man saw that he could not overpower him" (Gen. 32:25).

This is the way Barthes reads the story of Jacob and the angel. But he himself says he wants to open all possible meanings. Rather than definitively reduce the text by a confining explication, we should recognize that a text may have literal and symbolic meanings, and each has its own system. None should exclude or take precedence over another. In the spirit of this exegesis I suggest we look at the story in a completely different way.

Barthes sees Jacob as the hero-subject who seeks his destiny in Canaan.

For this he must struggle with God. Suppose we make God the hero-subject; the story is then about God, who wants to help Jacob find his destiny and his God. If God is the subject of the story, then Jacob becomes the dispatcher and God the receiver. Jacob is seeking God for himself and his family by crossing the river. He is also his own adversary. God is the helper who received the glory in the conflict. The story is about God in conflict with his creature, but although the creature is wounded, he is not destroyed, and ironically he is finally blessed. But the blessing is given only after God enters into a struggle with his creature on the creature's level as a man.

Jacob, the sender → River, the object → God, the receiver
↑
God as man, helper → God, the hero-subject ← Jacob, the opponent

When the story is read in this light it can be seen as an adumbration of the scandal of the cross. We have seen how Paul read the exodus story as a type for the resurrection. The literal leads to the analogical, which is not another idea but another reality.

Robert Funk shows how a structural analysis of the parables of Jesus can provide not only more than one reading of the text but also a clue to the best reading by means of a proper understanding of metaphor. If the structure of the parable of the good Samaritan is shaped by a *determiner* and *respondents,* the parable may be read as a story either about the Samaritan or about the victim, depending upon who is considered to be the *determiner* of the action in the story. *Determiner* here refers to semantic action, not necessarily to dramatic action. And if the parable is read as an illustration of the virtue of being and doing good to one's neighbor, then the Samaritan is the determiner and the victim is the respondent. The point of the story is the moral of neighbor-love as contrasted by the callous behavior of the priest and the Levite. On the other hand if the victim is the determiner of the meaning of the parable, then it becomes a story about the scandal of a Jew who has become a helpless victim. In his inability to resist he receives mercy from his mortal enemy, a Samaritan. Now the parable is not about virtue, a timeless abstraction, but it tells a story about what it means to receive unmerited mercy. Now it is a story that belongs with all the other parables of Jesus which tell of the grace of the coming kingdom. And best of all, the story "does not suggest that one behave as a good neighbor like the Samaritan, but that one become the victim in the ditch who is helped by an enemy."[28] Thus the parable tells us that in the kingdom mercy is always a surprise. All of this means that stories may indeed be used to illustrate eternal verities or in a rhetorical and ornamental way, but when they are read with a hermeneutics of metaphor they become vehicles that carry us beyond the literal to the story of reality itself. In short, they do not sew us into a cocoon of fixed truth but they invite us to become participants in the opening drama that is being disclosed.

A multiple reading of a text has merit. In the Middle Ages the exegetical method was the quadriga, the fourfold meaning of the text, which moved from a literal reading to an analogical meaning such as we have seen Paul do with the exodus story. A tropological or moral meaning was added to the literal and analogical meanings, and finally an anagogical or eschatological significance was determined. This method was grossly abused and justifiably abandoned by Luther during the Reformation. It had the merit, however, of letting us look at the text in more than one way, and it recognized the possibility of different realms of reality. It is true that we abuse a text if we make it serve a moral. Its beauty or its truth should be autonomous. But, as Kierkegaard said, we must pass through the first order of immediate sensibility in order to reach a second order of vision; and this involves moving from the aesthetic, through the ethical, to the religious.[29] When the quadriga was replaced by the plain, simple, single grammatical and historical sense of the text, we became limited to meanings that could not reach beyond our humanity.

Perhaps it would not be wise to try to revive the quadriga, but certainly it is helpful to look at a text from a variety of perspectives. Samuel Beckett's enigmatic play, *Endgame*, provides an illuminating example. This play, taken literally, is nonsensical absurdity.[30] It is scarcely a story at all, since nothing happens until the end. Four characters speak and seem to interact, but they do not carry forward an obvious plot. One of the actors, Hamm, is blind and bound to a wheelchair. Another, Clov, is bound to Hamm as his servant. Hamm is sensual, domineering, self-indulgent, untidy. Clov is rational, submissive, servile, orderly. They depend on each other as the heart and the head in a complete personality. Perhaps this is the clue. The two characters are really one person. Moreover, the other two actors, the parents of Hamm, are really not his parents but are his memory. Perhaps we have intimations here that will help us to understand both Christology and the Trinity.

Analogically *Endgame* is the story of a single person who is going through the process of deteriorating until he finally ends in death, when the heart and mind release each other. But on still another level the play can be read anagogically as the type for the deteriorating destiny of the whole human race. And finally the play can be read as a moral analysis of how one meets death, and as such it becomes a satirical admonition. Certainly all of these readings are possible, and none excludes another, but each adds to the richness of the play's reality.

If my thesis is correct—that reality is story—then there must be in reality a struggle against that which would frustrate its destiny, against that which would make reality something other than what it really is, either into a distortion or into nothing. We shall see what the content of this means when we discuss the adversary in the christological story, but in the present hermeneutical discussion it is helpful to notice that mythmaking is always in need of renewal. The story reality is always under attack.

Mircea Eliade says that the Greeks gradually emptied their mythical stories of their sacred and divine character until they were considered only of culturally exemplary value and of no metaphysical truth or religious value. Xenophanes (ca. 565–470 B.C.) criticized Homer and Hesiod in this way. Thus "mythos" was contrasted with "logos" and later with "historia." The original, true, and sacred story is thus "attacked," and either reduced or replaced by an abstract metaphysics or a demythologized history.[31] It is interesting to see, however, that story still remains in the most abstract philosophy and in the most scientific historiography. Whitehead's sentient occasions are "adventures of ideas" and Toynbee's *A Study of History* is a tale of beginning and ending.[32] Moreover, after all the demythologizing is done new myths are born and old myths are revived because cultures inevitably rise by living out their myths.

Eliade says,

> Myth narrates a sacred history; it relates an event that took place in primordial time, the fabled time of the "beginnings." . . . In other words myth tells how, through the deeds of Supernatural Beings, a reality came into existence, be it the whole of reality, the Cosmos, or only a fragment of reality—an island, a species of plant, a particular kind of human behavior, an institution.[33]

Myths usually presuppose original perfection that has been spoiled. To restore origins the present reality must be destroyed. This is the fundamental meaning in the drama of Christian baptism in which we die with Christ to be reborn in the Spirit (Romans 6). On a cosmic scale, this is the story of the flood in retrospect and the horror tale of fire at the end in eschatological prospect. Millennialism arises when there is a reaction "against the terror of history with the energy that only the extremity of despair can arouse."[34] Even the invention of bad stories proves the thesis. And when bad stories prove deceptive or inadequate, we tend to debunk them and settle for more rational and historical solutions. Eliade says that since Augustine the main church tradition has tried to reduce eschatological tension by the triumphalism of the church, but the sects have always kept it alive. In modern times a secular millennialism arose both among Nazis who expect a final battle between the elect Aryans against the hosts of evil Jews, and among Marxists who expect a final battle between the elect proletarians against the evil bourgeoisie. At this point it should be said that the deluding fantasies of millennialism can be corrected more fruitfully by a *theologia crucis* than by a *theologia gloria,* by a church that meets the crises of history with suffering service rather than pompous power.

The purpose of myth is to restore what has been lost in time. Time erodes our lives, and the work of myth is to return to origins and renew what time destroys. But simple storytelling alone does not accomplish this. The story must be ritualized. As Eliade states:

> The apodictic value of myth is periodically reaffirmed by rituals. Recollection and re-enactment of the primordial event help "primitive" man to distinguish and hold to the real. By virtue of the continual repetition of a paradigmatic act, something shows itself to be fixed and enduring in the universal flux.[35]

The transcendental world of gods, heroes, and mythical ancestors is accessible because ritual abolishes profane, chronological time and recovers sacred time.

It is important that we have a proper understanding of time. Perhaps we should speak of a proper understanding of times, because just as there are realms of being in the spatial dimension, so there are many sets of sequences in the temporal dimension.[36] In this connection Claude Lévi-Strauss observed that myth and music are both languages which, in their different ways, transcend articulate expression while at the same time, like articulate speech, require a temporal dimension in which to unfold.[37] But myth and music need time only to deny it, that is, although time passes for the listener, he or she blots out the external passing of time and is oblivious to it. This is like the time of dreams which have their own pace apart from the time that elapses during sleeping when the dream occurs. Time itself is not denied, but a particular sequence is bracketed out so that we can experience another. We do not enter into timelessness, because there is no such thing, only the deluding threat of it. Thus it becomes evident that the nature of time is multiple. There are many times and the diachrony of one time may be the synchrony of another, and vice versa. C. S. Lewis explores this aspect of reality in *The Chronicles of Narnia,* which relate the adventures of children through a prolonged period that involves only a split second in their normal sequence of time.[38]

Ritualized myths transport us into another time sequence, or perhaps we may also say that they bring another time sequence into our ordinary time. But myths decayed when rationalists pointed to their anthropomorphism. Euhemerus in the third century B.C. said that the gods of myths were only ancient kings deified. Since men are not gods, the myths must be discounted. And the stories that speak of gods in human form must also be discounted, since the gods are not human. Since the Greek myths had cultural value, even though they did not survive in worship, we still preserve them in the arts. The demythicization of Greek myths did not leave a religious vacuum, however, because new stories emerged among the Pythagoreans, the mystery cults, the Neoplatonists, and the Gnostics. Then came the unique story of Christianity.

The Christianization of myth is the most fascinating story of all. How was it possible for the Christian story to contend with and supplant all the competing myths of the first century, and how will it be possible for

Christianity to continue in the face of new myths that are being born? Judaism historicized seasonal festivals and cosmic symbols of the Canaanites by connecting them with important events in the history of Israel. Passover, which celebrated deliverance from slavery, was associated with the harvest of the first fruits, and Tabernacles, which celebrated the wandering in the wilderness, was associated with the second harvest. The story of the God who creates and sustains us in nature is also the story of the God who redeems us in history. And Judaism gave the church its allegorical typology, for so the Old Testament is interpreted in the New. The story of the coming of Christ in the babe of Bethlehem is the fulfillment of "the hopes and fears of all the years." Nostalgia for nature and yearning for life in winter solstice and spring festivals were absorbed and sanctified by the Christian celebration of Christmas and Easter, with the added heightening of eschatological hope.

Not all stories are good. Some stories are inadequate or misleading or deceiving. By their fruits you shall know them. Stories may tend to crystallize an intolerant situation and make it accepted when it could be otherwise. This is why Karl Marx called religion the opiate of the masses. The Chinese myth of the Will of Heaven for centuries supported a Confucian stratification of society, and people therefore became locked into an oppressive feudalism. The new myth of Marxist historical determinism and scientific progress has shattered the old myth, and the mythicized history of the "Long March" under the leadership of Mao Tse-tung has become the cultic replacement for incense at the altar of Buddha. But the "Long March" will not fulfill the needs of a yearning people, because ultimately we do not live by bread alone. A more adequate and uplifting story will prevail, just as the Judeo-Christian story of the creation of Eve, as the equal of Adam and his partner, is more edifying for us all than the story of Pandora, who was given by Zeus to harass men for their pride. The stories that are fully satisfying and edifying will prevail over the stories that are discriminatory and destructive.

The stories that are true, in the sense of being a description of reality and not a wishful twist of it, will prevail over stories that are told only to serve what is taken to be true. Moralistic and propagandistic motives will always corrupt the truth and result in bad storytelling. Count Leo Tolstoy provides a classic example of not only deterioration in artistic expression after reaching his peak in *Anna Karenina* but misunderstanding the nature of reality when he "got religion" and sought through his stories to effect conversions similar to his own. This is not to say that his moral view of life was altogether wrong. Life and reality have a radical distinction between good and bad. Nor is this to say that Tolstoy came to his moralistic position suddenly. There are intimations of it in *War and Peace* and in *Anna Karenina* long before he wrote *Resurrection*, just as there were intimations, as Thomas Mann observed, in Richard Wagner's *The Flying Dutchman* and *Tannhäuser* before he openly declared his Christian faith in *Parsifal.*[39] But the kind of story that reality is is always different from our human construction of it. This is due not only to the sinful corruption we make of our comprehension and apprehension of reality but also to the surprises given by God, the author of reality. This is why some stories are better than others. Some stories have a closer approximation of what God is saying as he tells his story.

NOTES

1. Walther Eichrodt, *Theology of the Old Testament* (Philadelphia: Westminster Press, 1941).
2. Gerhard von Rad, *Old Testament Theology,* 2 vols. (New York: Harper & Row, 1962-65).
3. Rudolf Bultmann, *Faith and Understanding* (London: SCM Press, 1969).
4. Walter Wink, *The Bible in Human Transformation* (Philadelphia: Fortress Press, 1975); Brevard Childs, *Biblical Theology in Crisis* (Philadelphia: Westminster Press, 1970); and Brevard Childs, *Introduction to the Old Testament as Scripture* (Philadelphia: Fortress Press, 1979).
5. Cf. Thomas J. J. Altizer, *The Gospel of Christian Atheism* (Philadelphia: Westminster Press, 1966).
6. James and Marcia Rudin, *Prison or Paradise? The New Religious Cults* (Philadelphia: Fortress Press, 1980).
7. Cf. Wolfhart Pannenberg, *Revelation as History* (New York: Macmillan Co., 1968); Jürgen Moltmann, *Theology of Hope* (New York: Harper & Row, 1967).
8. Gustavo Gutiérrez, *A Theology of Liberation* (Maryknoll, N.Y.: Orbis Books, 1973); Dorothee Soelle, *Political Theology* (Philadelphia: Fortress Press, 1974).
9. Cf. John B. Cobb, Jr., *A Christian Natural Theology* (Philadelphia: Westminster Press, 1965).
10. Paul Tillich, *Systematic Theology,* 3 vols. (Chicago: University of Chicago Press, 1951–63).
11. Cf. Gerhard Ebeling, *Word and Faith* (Philadelphia: Fortress Press, 1963); Gerhard Ebeling, *The Word of God and Tradition* (Philadelphia: Fortress Press, 1968); Ernst Fuchs, *Zum hermeneutischen Problem in der Theologie* (Tübingen: J. C. B. Mohr [Paul Siebeck], 1965).
12. Ferdinand de Saussure, *Course in General Linguistics,* ed. Charles Bally and A. Sechehaye (London: Peter Owen, 1964); Claude Lévi-Strauss, *The Raw and the Cooked* (New York: Harper & Row, 1969); Roland Barthes, *Elements of Semiology* (Boston: Beacon Press, 1970); Paul Ricoeur, *The Symbolism of Evil* (Boston: Beacon Press, 1967); and Paul Ricoeur, *The Rule of Metaphor* (Toronto: University of Toronto Press, 1977).
13. Robert Detweiler, *Story, Sign, and Self: Phenomenology and Structuralism as Literary-Critical Methods* (Philadelphia: Fortress Press, 1978).
14. Noam Chomsky, *Language and Mind* (New York: Harcourt, Brace and World, 1968), 30.
15. Martin Heidegger, *Being and Time,* trans. John Macquarrie and Edward Robinson (Oxford: Basil Blackwell, 1973), 212.
16. Ibid., 6.
17. Edgar V. McKnight, *Meaning in Texts* (Philadelphia: Fortress Press, 1978), 273.

18. Ibid., 274.
19. Paul Ricoeur, *Semeia*, no. 4 (1974), 75–106.
20. Cf. William F. Lynch, S.J., *Christ and Apollo: The Dimensions of the Literary Imagination* (New York: Sheed & Ward, 1960).
21. Cf. Brian Wicker, *The Story-shaped World: Fiction and Metaphysics: Some Variations on a Theme* (New York: University of Notre Dame Press, 1975).
22. Paul Hanson, *Dynamic Transcendence* (Philadelphia: Fortress Press, 1978), 31.
23. Cf. Detweiler, *Story, Sign, and Self*, for analysis of linguistic structure into phonemes, morphemes, sonemes, sentences, paragraphs, and passages of discourse.
24. Cf. Vladimir Propp, *Morphology of the Folktale*, 2d ed. rev. (Austin, Tex.: University of Texas Press, 1968); Barthes, *Elements of Semiology*; A. J. Greimas and J. Courtés, *Semiotics and Language: An Analytical Dictionary* (Bloomington, Ind.: University of Indiana Press, 1982).
25. Cf. Claude Lévi-Strauss, *Structural Anthropology* (New York: Basic Books, 1963); Edmund Leach, ed., *The Structural Study of Myth and Totemism* (Tairstock, 1967); Geoffrey S. Kirk, *Myth: Its Meaning and Functions in Ancient and Other Cultures* (London: Cambridge University Press, 1970).
26. C. S. Lewis, "On Stories," in *Essays Presented to Charles Williams*, by C. S. Lewis (Grand Rapids: Wm. B. Eerdmans Publishing Co., 1966), 103.
27. Barthes, *Elements of Semiology*.
28. Robert W. Funk, *Parables and Presence* (Philadelphia: Fortress Press, 1982), 34.
29. Cf. Søren Kierkegaard, *Stages on Life's Way* (Princeton: Princeton University Press, 1945).
30. Samuel Beckett, *Endgame* (New York: Grove Press, 1958).
31. Mircea Eliade, *Myth and Reality* (New York: Harper & Row, 1963).
32. Cf. Alfred North Whitehead, *Adventures of Ideas* (New York: Macmillan Co., 1933); Arnold J. Toynbee, *A Study of History*, abridgment by D. C. Somervell (New York and London: Oxford University Press, 1967).
33. Eliade, *Myth and Reality*, 5.
34. Ibid., 68.
35. Ibid., 139.
36. Funk, *Parables and Presence*, 67ff., suggests that Jesus' view of the coming kingdom requires more than one framework of time. Also, of course, there is the famous treatment on this subject by Oscar Cullmann, *Christ and Time* (Philadelphia: Westminster Press, 1950).
37. Lévi-Strauss, *The Raw and the Cooked*.
38. C. S. Lewis, *The Chronicles of Narnia*, 7 vols. (New York: Macmillan Co., 1950–56).
39. Cf. Thomas Mann's introduction to Leo Tolstoy, *Anna Karenina* (New York: Random House, 1939), xv.

3

Narrative Ontology

—the play's the thing

Methodology on meaning is not enough. People want to know if stories are true in reality. Hence we must move beyond a narrative hermeneutics and establish an ontology. We may find fictive characters in imaginative stories interesting, intriguing, even valuable. Their value may be a necessity for the full and proper understanding and use of the ordinary world. We may need them to turn our attention and open meanings. But if these stories involve only meanings and values, we can put them aside. Are there stories that compel us to acceptance, belief, decision, or action? Are there stories that have a truth claim upon us which must be acknowledged whether or not we perceive it, desire it, or accept it?

A great many people have recently been discussing the power of metaphor to reach reality. Almost all of these people are biblical scholars or literary critics, not systematicians. If they are philosophers, they are interested in the analysis of language and not in ontology. They do, however, point in the direction systematic thinking must go, and they give us tools and vehicles to help us on our way. The scholars I refer to are advocating a radical reversal of what is primary and secondary with regard to reality. They are saying that the language of metaphor is primary and the language of logical discourse is secondary.

The old point of view may be represented by scholars such as David Friedrich Strauss, Adolf Jülicher, Joachim Jeremias, and Rudolf Bultmann. Strauss said that myth is the narrative embodiment of an idea.[1] Myth is the story about the "other side" told in terms of "this side," but in relating a myth, one is really talking about the historic reality of being human in this world. Thus the "other side" does not refer to another world but refers to a side of this world which helps us get a clearer idea of reality. Bultmann had the same notion.[2] The nature of reality is not that of a story but an idea. Bultmann wanted to demythologize the gospel by stripping away all myths and legends peculiar to the first century that are not essential to the kerygma. The story is reduced to a message and the message becomes a changeless idea. Jülicher had the same idea when he said that parables are stories that point to timeless truths as metahistorical models.[3] And Jeremias says that parables are located in Jesus' own historical experience as visual aids to defend a proclamation delivered before them and without them.[4] All these notions are considered wrong by the new group of scholars.

Mircea Eliade may introduce the new group with his contention that myth narrates a sacred history and reenacts by recitation and ritual so that origins can be experienced and present mysteries resolved.[5] The celebration of Passover or of the Eucharist brings to life a story that has not only origins but a present reality that thrusts us into the future. Time in such a view is real, and reality is not a timeless idea but a living story. Paul Ricoeur's concern is with primary symbols, and for him myth functions as a symbol representing a primary aspect of experienced reality.[6] Poetic diction is primary, and ideational language with structured concepts is secondary. We speak primarily of metaphors and stories and secondarily of ideas and concepts about them; we do not speak of metaphors and stories which illustrate or lead us to more basic ideas and concepts. The ideas are about stories rather than the stories being about ideas.

For more than thirty-five years Amos N. Wilder has been quietly making this point, but never more clearly and forcefully than in his recent publication, *Jesus' Parables and the War of Myths*. He says that metaphor does not point to something completely other than itself, such as a theme or a concept or a moral or an idea or an institution. Metaphor points to something that is both itself and not itself, and it has the power to transform. "Now we know that a true metaphor or symbol is more than a sign, it is a bearer of the reality to which it refers. The hearer not only learns about reality, he participates in it. He is invaded by it. Here lies the power and fatefulness of art. Jesus' speech had the character not of instruction and of ideas but of compelling imagination, of spell, of mythical shock and transformation."[7] Wilder thinks that in the New Testament there is an unconscious assumption by Jesus and his hearers that all of life has the character of a story and a plot, and therefore more justice should be done to the mythopoetic structure of the gospel with its claim to provide a dramatization of existence.[8]

If we wish to make an ontological claim for story, we must deal with the connection between stories as story and reality as story. Both stories and reality must come out right. We have an inescapable and incontrovertible compulsion that this be so. All literary criticism looks for this inner integrity in stories. All human consciousness requires an ultimate satisfaction. Aristotle said a play is the imitation of an action. A play then must meet the test of relevance. It must have the integrity and satisfaction that we both experience and demand of reality. No work of literature can ignore what Samuel Johnson meant by "life," that is, the human situation: reality.

The literary critic Herschel Baker makes this point in a comment on *Measure for Measure*. His comment is entirely wrong, but in making it he shows the necessity for relating story to reality. I quote it at length both to underscore the relationship and to show how a proper reading of the play gives us a proper reading of reality.

> It is not that we require an easy calculus of triumph for the good and disaster for the bad, but that a play reveal—or permit us to infer—a necessary connection between what happens to a man and the kind of man that he is. When this requirement is evaded, as it seems to be evaded, for example, in the last act of *Measure for Measure*, we are baffled and uneasy because we feel a lack of moral sequence. Conversely, when the conduct of the action, however painful, satisfies our moral expectations we are forced to yield assent. Thus, although the conclusion of *King Lear* is as harrowing as anything in drama, we accept it, in our anguish, because we recognize its dreadful logic.[9]

What Baker is rightly looking for is the essential identity between the story and reality. What he missed in reading *Measure for Measure* is that in reality there is more than retributive justice; there is also redemptive grace. Lear brought his doom down upon himself, but Angelo received a transforming forgiveness. The story of Lear is great both because it is magnificently told and because it grasps for us an aspect of the story of reality. The story of Angelo perhaps is not told with such elegance, but it reaches for a deeper and fuller grasp of reality, the story of an unexpected reversal through mercy.

The Bible is the story of God that satisfies both of these needs, the need for moral integrity and the reversal of grace. In the Bible, God makes demands that fulfill our moral expectations, and God is satisfying because he always does what he says. Yet this trustworthy character does not always do what we expect; he surprises us with grace.[10] Here is revealed through story the paradoxical ontology that reality is metaphorical. It both is and is not what the words say. Because of this nature of reality, parables have the power to reveal its story quality. Things might be just the other way around from what we expect. Hence parables with their surprise show opposition to all forms of idolatry and absolutism.[11] As Paul Ricoeur says, parables work on a pattern of orientation, disorientation, and reorientation.[12] This illustrates the conflict motif. Because there is in reality a cosmic conflict, the story resolution of the conflict requires a movement from an intolerable position in time to one of acceptance. This movement introduces the surprise of the extraordinary in reorientation, and that is what redemption is all about.

Our compelling need is to be assured that we are talking about reality. Although the metaphor of story may amuse or edify, we will not be satisfied if we know that it is merely decorative or rhetorical, nor will we rest with the language of games.¹³ Therefore we shall have to delve deeper into the philosophical discussion of what we mean when we say something is real.

THE SEARCH FOR REALITY THROUGH PERCEPTION

Philosophers seek reality, but in modern times critical honesty limits them to saying about reality only what they can truly know. Hence ontology is limited by epistemology. Occam's razor is applied with unrelenting discipline from Immanuel Kant to Ludwig Wittgenstein. We must speak of that which we know; but of that which we do not know, therein we must remain silent. Knowledge is limited to human experience as it comes to us through the senses and the processes of the mind. Thus Descartes doubted the reality of everything, but he could not doubt his self-consciousness. His purpose was not simply to doubt; he wanted to prove the real existence of the extramental world, and to affirm it as mathematical in the scientific sense that was later to develop through Newtonian physics. We not only think and are aware of our thinking, we also think of other things. Descartes tried to affirm this external world as true, as perceived with objective reference and validity, and he finally resorted to the veracity of God. But simply to call in God is an assertion, not cognitive proof.[14] We want to know the reality of creation, but the minute we refer to reality *as creation* we assume a creator and that is precisely the relationship which is in doubt.

Although Descartes appealed to human consciousness, he retained the ancient and medieval notion that reality is fundamentally substantial. He invoked a dualism which intended to account for the reality of both mental and physical things. Then, of course, he had to explain how they are related and interact.

Kant tried to answer this by what he called his Copernican revolution in epistemology that shifted the center of knowing from external objects to the human mode of cognition. Kant's problem was the same as Descartes's: how can we know reality to be what it is? Or as Kant put it: how are synthetic *a priori* propositions possible? Can the propositions of mathematics, science, and metaphyscis be universally and necessarily valid? For Kant, the process of cognition begins with the sense data which are the given manifold of experience that impinges upon our consciousness from without and is apprehended by sense intuition. Then the imagination (the imaging process) reproduces the sense intuitions as concepts for understanding. Finally, the understanding makes judgments on these concepts according to their quality, quantity, relation, and modality.[15]

Besides asserting the knowability of all objects of experience, Kant denies the ability of the mind ever to know nonsensible reality. "Concepts without percepts are empty; percepts without concepts are blind." The only world we can seek to know is the given world of sense. Pure theoretical knowledge of God is impossible, because "no one has seen God at any time." But then, can we have any necessary and universal *a priori* propositions about this world of sense? Can we say causality is a universally valid principle of physics and can we say really that five plus seven equals twelve? Is this a synthetic proposition with necessary validity that is more than a mere analytical tautology?

To know the sense world at all, for it to enter into our consciousness, it must conform to our cognitive faculties. Thus all natural objects have certain common characteristics because our minds are so constituted. The categories of substance and causality, for instance, are universally applicable to all objects of experience. But for Kant, substance was not hypostatized spatial stuff. He understood the substance of things to be an interpretive concept in terms of which we must apprehend the element of permanence in the given space-time order of impressions which make up the real world. And causality is not a force or conveyance of "something" from one physical object to another, but it is the necessary order of sense impressions in a spatiotemporal series which we cannot reverse or alter. Kant assumes the internal continuity of all things in a Newtonian world of one total time and space.

This is the Kantian claim for a Copernican revolution in epistemology. Hitherto it had been supposed that all knowledge must conform to objects, and that God brings them into purposeful order, either by a Platonic push from below or an Aristotelian pull from above. Now Kant said that objects conform to our mode of cognition, and God is not needed in the process. By this construction of our way of knowing, however, Kant divided the world into objects of experience and objects in themselves *(Dinge an sich)*. Since the thing in itself is not a sensible object of experience, nothing can be said of it with positive certainty. The universal categories are valid for use only with objects of experience. Kant thus proves the *a priori* universality of the propositions of mathematics and physics, but of God, freedom, and immortality nothing can be known, since these are not objects of the senses.

Kant maintains that we have a "transcendental unity of apperception" or a universal scientific mind which gives rules to the experience of phenomena. Sense objects do not hit us willy-nilly. We receive them and sift them and understand them in a fixed order. This irreversibility is the law of cause and effect. Here Kant is not a revolutionary. He belongs with the philosophers of the "Great Chain of Being" who affirm the principle of sufficient reason which says there is an internal continuity of all relations.[16] It is bound up with the old idealistic argument which is the same in Anselm's one absolute truth, Aristotle's plenitude of being, and Plato's one in many *(simile in multis)*. Newton also had the idea of a single worldwide time with no gap between cause and effect. In this view, cause is not just a logical method of description. In the unity of nature, causality is constitutive of events.

Somewhat earlier David Hume denied the absolute hypostatization of time, and somewhat later Albert Einstein said time is relative to its space reference and vice versa. Causality therefore need not show temporal succession or contiguity from one space-time frame of reference to another. Post-Newtonian physics does not require the kind of necessity and universality Descartes and Kant sought.

Hume offered a theory far more radical and revolutionary than Kant's. He said ideas are not representatives of external objects. Perceptions and objects are interchangeable, since they both denote "what any common man means by a hat, a shoe, or a stone, etc." All mental states are on the same footing, and this also holds for their temporality as "perishing existences." They perish because no perception can ever recur. Then how do we know that what we perceive now is identical to what we perceived before?

The problem for Hume is not whether bodies exist apart from the mind and continue in their identity when not perceived, but how we come to believe in their continued and distinct existence. The answer is that the perceptions in succession resemble each other and the imagination mistakes a succession of perceptions for the continuous, uninterrupted presence of an unvarying perception. When we think about this, however, we also know that we are imagining, and so we mistakenly invent the representative version of the theory of ideas—we distinguish objects and perceptions as if they had a double existence. The identity or continuance is ascribed to objects, and interruptedness and multiplicity to perceptions (now called representations). But the truth, according to Hume, is that our consciousness of the identity of an object does not arise in spite of but in explicit reference to the multiple perceptions of the object. Because we later perceive the object to be the same as the one it was before, we say it has identity or continuance. Identity and multiplicity are opposed but not as contradictions, rather as correlatives mutually requiring and demanding each other.[17] Again we find reminiscences of the *simile in multis* of Plato.

WHITEHEAD'S SOCIETY OF OCCASIONS

The purpose of this review of philosophical theories of perception is to obtain a grasp of reality. The direction of Kant and Hume leads us to an egocentric predicament which ends in the absurdity of solipsism. Franz Brentano tried to avoid this in his early writings but became lost in subjective skepticism in later life. According to Brentano's early view, when one thinks of a unicorn, there is produced an immanent or intentionally inexistent unicorn. This intentionally inexistent unicorn is an actual intentionally inexistent unicorn, an entity in addition to the one who is thinking. But according to Brentano's later view, his reistic view, when one thinks about a unicorn no intentionally inexistent unicorn is produced and there is no actual entity other than the person thinking. "Es gibt ein Gedachtes" says no more than "Es gibt ein Denkendes."[18]

How can we avoid this subjective skepticism and its resultant absurdity? I take it to be an absurdity, that is, if the only reality we can grasp is the self. This is what happens when we think of reality as apprehensible only through the individual perceiver. What happens when we think of experience in social terms? And furthermore, what happens when we think of reality in terms of communication?

The philosophy of Whitehead should commend itself to a story theology in the light of these questions because it is a colossal metaphor.[19] Whitehead advocates a grand reversal with regard to the reality of matter and form. In ancient Greece, for both Plato and Aristotle, form is real, actual, limited, and perfect; matter is unreal, potential, unlimited and infinite in unreal possibility. For Whitehead, matter (now called events) is real, limited, actual, and complete. Form (now called eternal objects) is unlimited, infinite, incomplete, and infinite in real possibilities. Notice that reality pertains in Whitehead to both events and the form they take as they perish in time to become eternal objects.

Whitehead repudiated all forms of materialism and the Aristotelian subject-predicate substantial philosophies. He also attempted to solve the body-mind problem and overcome the Cartesian bifurcation by means of his concept of organic prehension. He described reality as a society of occasions. Time is epochal, occasional, but when its atomic epochs are temporalized, time is a *quanta continua*, both divisible and continuous. This fits well into the new physics of relativity, affirming a multiplicity of space-time systems. The unit of reality for Whitehead is the temporal-spatial event which is an ingression of an eternal infinite hierarchy of possibilities. Actuality is therefore limited and finite. The event is not a primal static substance or datum, but an organism that becomes and perishes. It passes from non-being-potentiality into being-actuality and into non-being objective immortality. Time is constantly perishing. The event-organism has two routes of passage: physical and mental. Thus there is for Whitehead neither the stuff of matter nor mind, but rather physical and mental functions of the actual occasion.

The aspects of materialism that Whitehead refined away are the following: (1) We no longer apprehend matter at an instant. If we did, our present perception would be static with no activity in it. Modern physics supports this when it says that we cannot tell what an electron is at an instant. (2) There is no simple location in space or in time. We cannot say what a particle would be if we had no field of energy within which it could move. Energy and matter are mutually transformable. (3) There is no absolute routine for material things. Materialism said dead matter follows a routine while live matter does not, but the new physics shows that the absoluteness of physical laws is only the statistics of an average effect. Moreover, electrons appear in physics to have no individuality. They seem to have indeterminacy but they are absolutely equivalent. If two electrons were to interchange, no change would take place and no energy would be involved. Finally, Whitehead asserts that this pattern is no different in physics, biology, and psychology. Habits in psychology are no different than laws are in physics. There is the problem of entropy, however, which physics describes as the cooling of all forms of energy. In *The Function of Reason,* Whitehead argues that there must be a contrary constructive tendency in nature which physics does not explain. Entropy taken by itself contradicts creativity. Experience shows that there is an everlasting process of creativity at work realizing all possible values.

The ultimate reality in Whitehead's metaphysics is the actual occasion that has a duality of objective and subjective poles. The potential objectivity is always in process of becoming real (actual). The actual occasion has a subjective aim, or "lure for feeling," which makes it self-creating. In its objective pole it is data felt or potential for feeling; in its subjective pole it is an experiencing entity, a "feeler." Actual entities are guided in their function of self-creation by their ideal of themselves. In their lure for feeling they can embrace as part of their own essence any other entity.[20] This means that there is a relatedness or connectivity in nature which goes beyond the discrete contiguity described by Hume. The feeling or emotional tone of the actual entity need not be conscious. Consciousness, in fact, arises only in the highest forms of such occasions. Sympathy is the literal structure of the world, however, and everything has a feeling for the feeling of others, and nothing is self-sufficient. Besides the immanence of the past in the present in the passage of occasions there is also a contemporaneous togetherness among occasions. Relativity is organic throughout the universe. Organic connection is the mutual sustenance of all things. Thus a thing is where it is and when it is in the universe because of what it is. This is the ground of order. It is the causal efficacy of organic relations. There is no such thing as a thing in itself. A thing is always *for* something. A book is for reading; God is for the world, and the world is for God. To speak of God's aseity is to speak nonsense.

We may characterize Whitehead's metaphysics as a philosophy of a "feeling universe," a pan-aestheticism running the gamut from electrons to God. And the way of knowing is experience, which is perception, whether sensuous or non-sensuous, conscious or unconscious, of the actual and not of the representative of the actual. The question arises now how particular occasions are related causally. For Hume, causal efficacy was derived from presentational immediacy; for Whitehead, causal efficacy and presentational immediacy are two modes of symbolic reference.[21]

We may say there have been three conceptions of causality: (1) cause is greater than effect, (2) effect is equal to cause, and (3) effect is greater than cause. When cause is greater than effect all effects are ultimately derived from a First Cause according to the principle of Plenitude and Sufficient Reason. This involves an absolute determinism and denies free will and the responsibility of the individual agent. The second view says that all effects follow from the causes in mechanistic order. Here again determinism sets in. The third view is Whitehead's notion of emergent novelty whereby the effect contains the identity of its cause plus some new increment. Thus in the process of the universe there is an immanence of the past in the present so that the past is present with something added. This addition is *causa sui*. This self cause is the equivalent of the doctrine of free will, and this notion of free will is a product of a determinism of causal efficacy plus novel creativity. But the notion of innovation is always a novel increment creating itself in terms of relatively limited alternatives. The self-caused increment is organically related to the past which gave rise to it. In no instance does free will mean unrelated realization. We are our brother's keeper, and our brother includes every entity in the universe. There is no independence in Whitehead's view of organic relativity. All innovations are relative to certain conditions set up in the past. Novelty is a realization in terms of greater relevance. Free will is therefore a product of identity and difference. The identity is accounted for in terms of efficient causation, and the difference is accounted for in terms of final causation. The identity has reference to the iron hand of the past reaching into the present, and the novelties have reference to unrealized potentialities whose relevance is likewise grounded in what has been in the past together with future possibilities. Thus the innovation is spontaneous and accountable to the subject, but the spontaneity is relative. This doctrine emphasizes both the unity of nature and its creative evolution. It explains the self-identity of enduring objects in a way not dreamed of by Hume, Kant, or the phenomenologists.[22]

Whitehead's idea of causality is an attempt to transcend Hume's notion of cause as the mere succession of antecedent and consequence related as cause and effect by sheer custom and habit. Hume ruled out the notion of necessary efficaciousness in causality. Kant could not rest with mere habit, because this played as much havoc with scientific universal laws as it did with Leibniz's Principle of Sufficient Reason. Therefore Kant conceived a notion of causality whereby the mind provides the category of cause that organizes the space-time manifold. The category is a criterion, a perspective, a form which the mind imposes on its unorganized experiences. It is a transcendent imposition on the data of reality. But Kant's notion of causality was rejected by Whitehead because it bifurcates nature and ultimately finds rationality only in the mind of human beings and not in the experient occasion. Therefore he described causality as the vector structure of nature moving in the opposite direction from Kant's process, that is, from object to subject rather than from subject to object.

Since contemporary events happen in causal independence of each other, this causal independence is a ground for freedom. The novelties are solved in isolation but always relative to a graded relevance of possibility. And these possibilities bring them into relationships of differing kinds of social organization. By reason of their prehension, actual occasions involve each other and such a unity of occasions is called a nexus. There are many different types of nexus, ranging from galaxies, regions, persons, enduring objects, incorporeal substances, living organisms, to simple events.[23] When a set of actual occasions are mutually immanent in each other we can speak of a nexus of occasions.

The apparent gap between the living and the nonliving nexus can be explained by the greater mutuality of purposes in the living organisms. In a living society the co-ordination of organic mutual sustenance intervenes so that thwarting prehensions do not cancel each other out as they do in inanimate enduring objects. "Life is the co-ordination of the mental spontaneities throughout the occasion of a society."[24]

We come now to the notion of valuation in the creative advance, and subsequently to Whitehead's idea of God. We have seen that the creative process is that transition by which one occasion enters into the birth of another instance of experienced value. Actuality is enjoyment and enjoyment is experiencing value. Each epochal occasion is a microcosm of the universe in this valuation. Each occasion has the nature of perceptivity. Though it is without reflective consciousness, it is the self-value of its own microcosmic apprehension. It enjoys itself. We have also shown that the actual occasion has two sides: its mode of creativity causing itself, and its creaturehood or its caused actuality. These are not two entities but one—a self-creating creature. But in the creative process the actual is synthesized with something not-actual. Process is fusion of Being with Not-Being. The novel consequent must preserve some character of identity with the ground of its past out of which it arose, and it must also have some contrast. All aesthetic experience is feeling arising out of realization of contrast under identity.[25]

The epochal occasion also has two poles: physical and mental. The physical occasion has two possible routes of passage. One is toward another physical occasion, and the other is toward a mental occasion. The most individual actual entity is a definite act of perceptivity. There is an ordered route of occasions of perceptivity. Some are blind physical occasions and some are self-conscious mental occasions. In the case of human beings, there are routes of mental and physical occasions in connection. Hence we speak of mind and matter as components of the human organism. In mere mental occasions the physical pole is minimal; in mere physical occasions the mental pole is minimal. In the nexus of the human organism there is a mutuality of mental and physical occasions. When this mutuality is disrupted, when prehensions fail to co-ordinate themselves with the environment, the human organism becomes sick, either mentally or physically. Total disruption means death.

Value enters with the realization of greater possibilities of organic mutuality. There must be a ground for the ordering of this mutuality of values, and there must be a noncontingent ground for the contingency in the world, and that ground is Whitehead's referent for God. God's purpose or subjective aim is attainment of value. In other words, God's purpose is a striving toward the highest actuality feeling. Apart from God, the formative elements of creativity and ideals would fail in their functions. God's ordering has caused the world. The actual world is the outcome of the aesthetic order, and the aesthetic order is derived from the immanence of God.[26] This may be called Whitehead's aesthetic argument for the existence of God. But it is only half the story, because God is also created by the world. God is as much a product of the creative process in the world as he is the producer of the process. God and the world require each other. You cannot say simply God is cause and world is effect. Both require each other.

God is therefore also the actual attainment of the process of valuation, having overcome evil with good. He is both the process of creativity itself and the consequent valuation. He is not the world, but he is the valuation of the world. God is thus not the transcendent creator of the biblical story, but by valuation he is the harmonizer of self-creating creatures. God is both the final act of completion of all possible values and also the creative process in realizing these ideals. "There is a kingdom of heaven prior to actual passage of things and there is the same kingdom finding its completion through the accomplishment of this passage."[27] This duality comprises God's Primordial Nature and his Consequent Nature. In his Primordial Nature, God is the "conceptual realization of value." He is "the concrescence of unity of feelings including in their data all eternal objects." In this mode of functioning God is "free, complete, primordial, eternal, actually deficient, and unconscious." In his Consequent Nature, God originates with physical experience derived from the temporal world. This side of his nature is finite and limited. Here he is the actual realization of value, and it belongs to the nature of the actual that it is finite. In this nature, God is "determined, incomplete, consequent, 'everlasting,' fully actual, and conscious."[28]

What shall we say then from the perspective of story theology about Whitehead's process philosophy? Is the philosophy of actual occasions in process adequate both for an understanding of our world and for the translation of the gospel in terms of it? Can we use it for constructive theology in the way Augustine used Plato and Thomas Aquinas used Aristotle? I think the answer must be yes and no. There is so much in Whitehead's scheme of things that is intriguing to a story view that we must ask if it is not also beguiling.

The grand metaphor of experient occasions is a story packed with "adventures of ideas." There is room in Whitehead for freedom, for love, for future. Time is a process of valuation. There is organic connectedness in the actual occasions which means that everything comes on cue. There is a sympathetic aestheticism in Whitehead's universe which means that the world is a play in which the plot has an integrity that grips with a depth of feeling. There is freedom in the process such that the future brings surprises and turns in the plot which are truly innovative but are not unrelated to the previous action of the plot. There are varieties of organic relationships or nexus which means that there are possibilities for many different plots, sub-plots, and sub-sub-plots woven and interwoven among each other. The process of valuation is congenial to the need in stories to bring everything to a satisfying conclusion, and there is no need to rest with simplistic melodrama in Whitehead's scheme.

Indeed there is so much in Whitehead that readily supports a story view of reality that we are tempted to adopt his scheme uncritically. Or we might say, with some necessary modifications. One modification would have to be with regard to the presence of evil in the world. Process philosophy, as Whitehead and his followers have articulated it, is notoriously inadequate in its recognition of the reality of evil. This deficiency, however, is not fatal, and it could be corrected if the metaphysics of process were written explicitly with a story view.[29] Our critique, however, cannot be so simple. There are two areas of serious defect which make it impossible to adopt process philosophy as the intellectual construction of story theology. The first concerns the relationship between process thought and science, and the second concerns Whitehead's doctrine of God.

One of the most attractive features of Whitehead's philosophy, its congeniality with modern science, is precisely its vulnerability. Just as the relationship between Aristotle and Ptolemy's *Almagest* brought collapse to Aristotelian philosophy and theology, so postmodern physics will bring serious question, if not collapse, to Whitehead's scheme of process without beginning or ending. Scientists today talk about the beginning of space-time and matter-energy with a "big bang" and the ending of space-time and matter-energy in black holes. They speak of the implosion of the universe when the gravitational force overcomes the other three forces which from the beginning have held the universe on an expanding vector: electromagnetic waves, the "strong force" that holds elements together, and the "weak force" that brings radioactive disintegration. Science is constantly changing because of new evidence and new perspectives. The very thing that is essential and commendable to science, shifting paradigms, is embarrassing and destructive to philosophical systems.

It is precisely for this reason that I advocate a story theology in place of every philosophical scheme because it will do successfully what philosophy pretends to do but fails to do. Philosophy pretends to account for all constancy and change in the universe, including God. Science makes no such pretense. It limits its talk to what it can measure. Reality goes beyond commensurable data, and the various philosophies have tried to deal with that but without success. Story as a category is open enough and flexible enough to allow for the changing sciences within the plot. Any radical shift in a scientific model only adds to the excitement of the story that is being told. And beyond this, story can embrace the mystery of reality that eludes the sciences.

The problem of God is more serious. For Whitehead, God is the process of love which entertains all ideals, urging each to finite attainment in due season. This sounds good so far. God's infinity is constantly acquiring finite realization in the creative advance. This is very different indeed from the God of Thomas Aquinas who is fixed in perfection as *actus purus*, but there is nothing that I can see in Whitehead's changing, growing God that is contrary to the living God of the Bible. God is indeed magnified by what he does and what he makes. His constancy is in his word and in his love, not in his substance (whatever that may mean). But it is Whitehead's aesthetic notion of God, who is as much a product of the process as a creator in the process, that we must examine.

It is difficult to translate process metaphysics into story theology because of its monodimensional naturalism. Whitehead's God, Primordial Nature and Consequent Nature, should not be called God. To do so is a kind of idolatry, because they are part of the process, and idolatry mistakes the creature for the creator. It is perfectly proper and philosophically helpful to speak of a primordial and a consequent nature working in the process. But they are nature, not God. The story of God in the Bible never makes this confusion. It is true that one cannot speak of God as author without the story he writes. The author, as author, is for the story and the story is for the author. But an author is a person apart from his or her authorship. God is no less God if he does not create. Yet we may say he is greater God because he creates and still greater because he redeems. It is an absolute necessity that we preserve the integrity of God by not confusing him with the characters and props in his story, even if he enters into the play himself. The infinite qualitative distinction between God and his creatures must be maintained, and this is especially so with regard to those creatures who were made in his image.

Finally we must say a word of criticism about Whitehead's view of time, because it affects his notion both of nature and of God. In spite of his recognition of the reality of time, there is for him only sequential process with its accumulation of value. There is no *ephapax*, which is the unique quality of time in all stories. There is no beginning. There is no ending. There is no kairotic climax. This lack of unique moments, which are once-for-all, means that there is in process philosophy no possibility for the character of Christ to come once into history, and thus to be the redeemer of all who went before and all who come after. This lack means that there is failure in process philosophy to come to terms with the reality of evil as a personal rebellion against the Person of God. As the medieval theologians said to the naturalists of their day, so we must say to the neo-naturalism of process philosophy: You have not yet considered the great weight of sin *(Nondum considerasti quanti ponderis sit peccatum).* And we must say this because Jesus said to his disciples: "If I had not come and spoken to them, they would not be guilty of sin" (John 15:22). The lack of uniqueness in time results in a God who is always only part of the process, and moreover the world then is not fully his creation but is at least partly *causa sui.* In spite of the place for novelty in process there is really no room for the unique surprises of creation and redemption and final judgment.

INTERMISSION ON TIME

It is time in our discussion of ontology to take time for an analysis of time. Stories, which always take place somewhere, begin once upon a time and proceed sequentially to a conclusion. We have seen that in reality space and time are relative to each other. This is so in stories. Stories cannot be told without reference to time, but is time real? Does time have reality in the ultimate scheme of things, or is it only an appearance, a copy, a moving image of a changeless Being, a dancing shadow on the walls of Plato's cave? Augustine said, "What then is time? If nobody asks me, I know . . . but if I try to explain it to one who asks me, I do not know."[30] In one sense time is inexplicable because of its inseparability from our experience, but then that applies to everything from the simplest sense impression to God. We want to say that time is real, however, and not just an appearance or an exercise of memory. Time is not an abstract metronome placed snugly outside the universe. Time is the name we give to the process of reality itself.

Time is both perceived and conceived. Time is perceived psychologically and physically. Time is conceived in ordinary consciousness and in speculative metaphysics.

Psychologically time is perceived and measured subjectively. The lover is oblivious of time, as Shakespeare observes in *As You Like It.* Thomas De Quincey, in *Confessions of an English Opium Eater,* describes the distortions that opium produces in our judgment of time.[31] Time is dull or time is eventful, time is sluggish or time is fleeting, depending on our mood. But physical time is objectively measured against a universally accepted standard. It is true that convention plays an important part in the measurement of time. From perceptual judgment which is submissive to social acquiescence we must proceed to the erection of a standard, and astronomical phenomena prove most useful because they are observable by everyone everywhere. Radiation is another measurement of time. The U.S. Naval Observatory has an atomic clock that keeps time according to virtually unchanging atomic radiation. But as an object approaches the speed of light, radiation slows down and stops altogether at the speed of light. Scientists like to say then that time stops. Temperature also slows radiation. Close to absolute zero, radiation is sluggish and at zero it stops; hence scientists say time stops. But they are talking about the measurement of time, not time itself. When physics talks about relativity and simultaneity in time it is talking about perceived measurement, not about the conception of the nature of time. The spatialization of time into "t" in the formula for measuring distance, with time intervals related to space, is only an abstraction from temporal sequence, and this does not affect our conception of time.

In ordinary consciousness we have a conception of time which may be distinguished from our perception of it. In memory, for example, we conceive of what is past, and know it to be past, but this knowing is at the same time in the present. Henri Bergson observed that we experience the passing of time, *durée,* and we conceptually distinguish between it and time that has passed. He says time is pure duration, flowing. Time may be represented by space "if you are dealing with time flown," but not if you are dealing with time flowing. Freedom is a fact of time flowing.[32]

But when we conceive of time metaphysically we must be careful to avoid confusion. Human imagination is unlimited. We can conceive of infinite regress and infinite progress in time. We can conceive of reversible time, infinitely divisible time, mathematically continuous time, eternal timelessness, infinite transcendence of time. We must distinguish the language that deals with logic and mathematics from the language that deals with fact. Time is alogical. There is something incomprehensible to logic in time. More than motion, with which Aristotle defined time, alogical factors such as contingency, novelty, chance, and change are involved in the passage of time. Infinity, reversibility, and continuousness are mathematical concepts which are useful, but they are tools and not descriptions of reality. Talk about timelessness and transcendence of time drifts into the evanescent mysticism of Meister Eckhart: "I charge you to give thanks unto God while still in time. . . . Once out of time and your chance is gone." My contention is that there is no timelessness, because time is a dimension in the life of God, and therefore it is not a creature like space, although like space it is broken and distorted for us because of sin.

By brokenness I do not refer to the segmented character of time, which is fundamental; rather, I refer to our experience of loss because the segments are disconnected and shattered. The periodicity of time did raise a problem for the ancients, however, who found it to be in conflict with the continuous flow of time. Because mathematics in ancient times could not express continuousness of geometric relations Zeno described the insoluble paradox of Achilles and the tortoise. Achilles could run ten times as fast as the tortoise, but if he gives the tortoise a ten-yard handicap, he can never catch the tortoise because the diminishing distance between them stretches out to infinity. This was paradox for the mathematics of Zeno, but with modern calculus we have a tool that makes use of the limiting function of an infinite convergent series. Alfred North Whitehead mentions in *Process and Reality* a possible solution to Zeno's paradox by means of this limiting function of convergent series.[33] This can be demonstrated by setting up two number series for the respective paths of Achilles and the tortoise. Subtracting Achilles' series from the tortoise's series we get a new series: $S_n = 1 + 1/10 + 1/100 + 1/1000 \ldots 1/10^{n-1}$. By comparing the series member by member with a known convergent series, for example, geometric series $R = 1 + 1/2 + 1/2^2 \ldots 1/2^{n-1}$, we find that all its terms are less than the terms of the geometric series. Therefore the series S_n is an infinite convergent series whose terms approach the limit 0. By ignoring infinitesimal particles the differential equation can bridge the gap. Thus while reality is discrete both in time and space, it is possible to treat it as continuous, both in calculus and practice, by means of a leap. Perhaps, to use unlimited imagination, it may be possible to construct a logic, which is neither the Aristotelian logic of noncontradiction nor the Hegelian logic of identity-difference, but a logic of change which will do for time what calculus does for the discreteness of space.

Not only is time alogical, it is also irreversible, unrepeatable, and unpredictable. Unidirectional time is fundamental. A cycle of events is impossible because each event must of necessity happen at a later date and is therefore a different event. There is a persistence of things in time so that reparability is possible when damage is done, and in our broken time damage is always done, but the "immanence of the past in the present," to use Whitehead's phrase, does not allow repeatability or reversibility. For this reason resurrection, which is not resuscitation, requires a cataclysmic judgment and consumption of the old creation in order that the new creation can begin with its new time. But the time of this consummation is not predictable. Logical and mathematical predictions and forecasts are not temporal. The certainty of logical and mathematical implications cannot survive their application to events. The story is always open to surprises. Everything can always be otherwise. Yet there is an integrity in the story which reveals the end, not in detail but in hope.

Unlike space which may be reversed in direction and mirrored, time is not isotropic. Max Black, in a brilliant essay on time in *Models and Metaphors*, clearly and conclusively establishes the irreversibility of time.[34] In spatial arrangements we have to speak of the order of things on a line with relation to something apart from the line. Thus A is between B and C, and C is between A and D. X and Y are points apart from this line, but is C to the left or right of D? This depends on whether X is speaking or Y. C is left of D for X and right of D for Y:

$$B \ A \ C^Y_X D.$$

In describing this situation, Black says "being to the left of" is an incomplete relation. A theoretical scientist finds this relativity repugnant. He or she will avoid formulations that vary with the choice of an arbitrary body of reference. They search for laws that can be formulated without such arbitrary choices. It is striking that in theoretical physics this demand is everywhere met. Nothing in physics refers to the actual arrangement of bodies in the universe, and consequently nothing will need to be changed in the structure of physics if that arrangement were supposed reversed. Thus arrangement in space is relative and not important, but differences of arrangement can and need to be observed.

Thus if time were isotropic, we would have to say that an order of events (as an order of things in space) could be reversed, and time could flow either way. But Black says, "It seems to me nonsensical to suggest that if A is earlier than B, it might after all still be the case that B is earlier than A. It is part of our use of temporal words that the expression 'A is earlier than B' shall conflict with and be incompatible with 'B is earlier than A'—and not merely in a way in which 'to the left of' conflicts with 'to the right of.'"[35] It is certain that time has only a forward direction.

Although time is sequential and unidirectional, we observe the interesting phenomenon of simultaneity. Because reality is discrete, two or more things can have the same time. And at the same time two sequences can have different paces so that in one instance during a split second almost nothing happens while in another instance simultaneously a multitude of happenings occur. Ambrose Bierce explored this kind of simultaneity in his short story *An Occurrence at Owl Creek Bridge*. A soldier fearfully awaits his execution by hanging. He desperately hopes for escape. Perhaps the rope will break and he will fall into the river below the bridge and be able to swim to safety avoiding the bullets of his captors. He runs through the woods and across the fields. The agonizing chase takes forever, and his mind is crowded with remembrances of his past life and anticipation of his momentary rescue, a moment which never comes. Just when he falls into the arms of his loving wife his neck snaps because the rope did not break. We have experiences in which time appears to stop, but it never really does.

Georges Braque and Pablo Picasso experimented with simultaneity when they developed their cubist style of painting. Picasso's *Les Demoiselles d'Avignon* introduced a vision of many sides of figures which could be viewed at the same time. On a single plane one can see both front and back as well as various sides of a subject. Reality has many sides and they are simultaneous. The artist presents a picture of reality. Again time seems to stop, because in such a presentation one does not have to take time to walk around to see all sides.

Because of the characteristic of simultaneity, reality is replete with paradoxes. One of the grand contributions of the Lutheran Reformation was the recognition of such compelling simultaneities as *Finitum capax infiniti*, *simul justus et peccator*, law and gospel, the two kingdoms. An atemporal logic cannot entertain such paradoxes. If Hegel's logic of identity-difference is introduced, a resolution is found through appeal to a succession in time for the opposing identities. But we experience in reality a simultaneity of opposites, and the category of story is eminently able to embrace them, and to embrace them without falling into a pattern of logical necessity which robs us of our freedom.

A final and extremely important aspect of time for story theology is its kairotic nature. We have seen that time is multiform, and in addition to its perceived and commensurable flow, there is the crucial distinction between *chronos* and *kairos* which Oscar Cullmann described in his biblical study *Christ and Time*.[36] Chronological time has a rhythm that is a regular beat. God created day and night. The rhythm may be simple or complex in varying degrees, but it is always repeated as are the days and the months by the periods of the sun and the moon. We have seasons on the earth and cycles on the sun. Comets return with precise predictability. Chronological time appears to be fixed, but a new theory has challenged this with the suggestion that time itself has evolved with the increasing complexity of natural systems.[37] Precisely what the evolution of time could mean is difficult to envision, but it means that the steady rhythm of mere succession is being questioned with a new concept that attempts to tie the time of physics with the time of the life sciences and the psychological perceptions of human consciousness. Instead of a simple, single, unified time, there are temporal structures that interrelate as layers upon layers.

The distinction between *chronos* and *kairos* is not the same as this theory of evolutionary time, but the notion of time as *kairos* does involve a break in the rhythm and an evolutionary growth toward a climax. Kairotic time refers to seasons of preparation, growing periods, which sometimes are clouded with secrecy and silence and sometimes are filled with joyful expectation. Waiting for birth is kairotic, with the full gamut of fearful and fecund anticipation. Stories are rich with hints and adumbrations and intimations about developments in time which lead to a climax. In spite of the expectation, there is always an element of surprise in the kairotic moment, and the surprise calls for a response, some kind of decision that may result in celebration or grief. The kairotic climax may be a harvest or a judgment or a revelation.

Kairotic time is not simple sequence like beads strung out on a line. It has shape because the end time is already present in the beginning. The first act is pregnant with the eschaton. Milton referred to this in *Paradise Regained* (Book I, line 220) when he said, "The childhood shows the man, as morning shows the day," and Wordsworth echoed it: "The child is father of the man." The New Testament is not only foretold in the Old Testament but it is dynamically present.

I believe it is a misunderstanding of this reality in time which has led to mistaken notions such as realized eschatology and mysticism whereby the real progression of time and the real hope of the future is denied. A good correction of this misunderstanding is to speak of eschatology realizing itself, but to say that the end is present in the beginning does not preclude novelty, nor does it mean that an escape from time is needed because it is assumed that all is already fulfilled.

In the story of reality there seem to be many kairotic moments which break in upon the regular rhythm of chronological time, but the coming of Christ in Jesus of Nazareth is a unique climax which Cullmann calls the midpoint of time. The incarnation is thus the fulfillment of a predestined plan anticipated from before the foundation of the world, and from this climax proceeds the denouement of the story as all things are brought into subjection under Christ until the last day, when they are turned over to the Father (1 Cor. 15:24).

Story time allows for a variety of sequences just as there is a variety of realms in the creature we call space. Stories have times within times. Stories have times in tandem. Stories have various rhythms and occasional climactic breaks in rhythm. Ages come and go, and one age will reach into and across another. The age of God is all-inclusive and cumulative, and the age of this world is partial and broken. God does not lose the past. Each passing event adds to his glory. Human beings lose the past except what remains in memory and relics. Since nothing that God has made is lost to him, however, he can restore through resurrection what we have lost through sin.

Human beings want to measure time with the chronometry of history, but God's time transcends history because it includes in its story chapters that both precede and succeed history as well as chapters that run parallel to history but are not recorded as such. For this reason God's time is described in both Testaments with a quality that cannot be measured: "In God's sight a thousand years are as yesterday" (Ps. 90:4) and "With the Lord a day is like a thousand years, and a thousand years are like a day" (2 Peter 3:8).

A BRIEF WORD ABOUT CAUSALITY

In addition to a discussion of space and time the problem of ontology requires a definitive word about causality. We have seen how Whitehead finds a place for causality in his scheme without presuming the Principle of Sufficient Reason. I would like to affirm Whitehead's treatment of causality because it is congenial to story reality and it does not need to find a place in a metaphysical system. I want to establish the ontology of story but I do not want to erect a rival metaphysical system which might take the place of philosophical systems of the past. My unabashed presumption is that all metaphysical systems say more than we know, and therefore we need to speak of story reality because it will do adequately and indeed eminently well what metaphysics fails to do. I say this in review of the grand systems of the past, including the speculations since the critical analyses of Hume and Kant. Not even language can give us the mirror of reality that metaphysicians seek, because language is arbitrary and pragmatic. As Max Black says, "No roads lead from grammar to metaphysics."[38] It would be especially tempting to speculate from a supposed universal grammar inasmuch as language is the stuff of stories, but this would only distort story into an idea or concept, making it impossible to be the reality that it is.

Story theology cannot allow a universal law of causation. Medieval theology tried to solve the problem of causality by distinguishing primary causality from secondary causes. Somehow in story theology we must describe the function of causality without falling into the trap of determinism either from the First Cause or from secondary causes. Again let me refer to Max Black for a resounding refutation of determinism:

> Any attempt to state a "universal law of causation" must prove futile. To anybody who insists that "nothing happens without a sufficient reason" we are entitled to retort with the question "what do you *mean* by 'Cause'?" It is safe to predict that the only answer forthcoming will contain such scientific words as "event," "law," and "prediction." These too are words capable of indefinite further determination according to circumstances—and are none the worse for that. But universal statements containing schematic words have no place in rational argument. The fatal defect of determinism is its protean capacity to elude refutation—and by the same token, its informative content is negligible. Whatever virtues it may have in encouraging scientists to search for comprehensive laws and theories, there can be no rational dispute about its truth value. Many of the traditional problems of causation disappear when we become sufficiently clear about what we mean by "cause" and remind ourselves once more of what a peculiar, unsystematic, and erratic notion it is.[39]

In story reality the characters encounter one another on the stage of freedom. There are, of course, props placed there by the direction of the author and all the action takes place within the parameters set by them. Unlike the theater of make-believe, however, in which the characters recite lines given to them, real story is a theater of involvement in which the characters are free to make up their own lines, not in any absolute sense but relative to the situation that confronts them. Thus God in his absolute love cares for all things great and small, but in his infinite freedom he meddles in nothing, and he never does for us what we can do for ourselves.[40]

This notion of causality within freedom may help in reifying our ontology. My thoughts are real thoughts, that is, they are not non-thoughts. As thoughts they may have a causal effect upon me and my actions, but they cannot as thoughts *per se* be the cause of anything apart from me unless they are expressed. This means that there is a real world of thoughts but as such it is multifariously discrete. If my thoughts, which include my waking and sleeping dreams as well as my memories and imaginations, are expressed, they become reified and they can impinge upon the consciousness of others. They then can have a causal relationship and this means there is a real world of objectified thoughts. Before such expression occurs, there is only immanental and subjective reality. My dreams have realities that are only immanent; the characters in my dreams do not impinge upon the characters in other people's dreams or upon their waking consciousness. Non-immanental realities which are still merely expressed thoughts, however, impinge upon anyone who comes within their presence. Such encounter calls for response, but the response is not determined.

We can therefore distinguish between three different realms of reality. (1) There is the empirical, historical realm in which we find ourselves as a society of occasions in organic unity among other occasions and societies of occasions. (2) There is the realm of thought which is produced by us through memory, understanding, and imagination. This realm includes hypothesis, potentiality, hope, dream, fantasy, and the like. (3) And there is the realm of revelation which comes to us through faith and includes encounter with God, Christ, Satan, creation as creation, resurrection, heaven, and the like.

Scientific theories arise in the second realm but must be verified by the data given in the first realm. Aesthetic productions of poets and all artists arise in the second realm also but need no empirical verification. The realm of revelation must not be reduced to either the empirical or the imaginary realm. It has its causal impact within the parameter of freedom just as the other two realms. When God expresses his thoughts they come to us in the form of creation and redemption. We do not receive the impact of this reality through our natural senses and categories of understanding, nor do we create this realm out of our imagination. Revelation comes to us through the power of faith given us by the Holy Spirit. In the encounter we have with God as Creator and Redeemer we are given at his election the capacity to enter into the activity of this new world or level of reality. The causality here involved is not causality in the normal sense of the word. Indeed we must say that the metaphor is radically different. We are not caused by God to be his creature; we are called into being by his word. We are not caused to be redeemed; we are called to be baptized and to enter into the life of his body in Christ Jesus. All three realms intersect spatially and have simultaneity of time, yet none is coterminous with the other, since only God's realm embraces them all.

Regin Prenter corroborates this notion of faith as a gift of the Spirit which is never a divine cause:

> It is not possible for Luther to present the relation between the Spirit and faith

as rational and smooth without any logical contradiction because for Luther faith is not a supernatural substance of which the Holy Spirit is the supernatural cause. It is the personal gift of God which is constantly depending on God's renewing and gracious giving. Faith never becomes a possession, and the Spirit never becomes a divine cause. For Luther faith is the life which is brought about by the really present reality of Christ mediated by the Holy Spirit, which is simultaneously an escape from one's own empirical piety.[41]

A narrative ontology will be not only congenial with but reconstructive of the perspectives of Luther, Augustine, and Paul on the multiple structure of the world. The world of sense and the world of mind are members of Luther's kingdom on the left, Augustine's *civitas terrena*, and Paul's *aiōn enestos* or *aiōn houtos*. The world of revelation is the kingdom on the right, the *civitas Dei*, and the *aiōn mellōn*. This world, whether we call it an earthly city or a temporal age, is immediately apprehensible through the senses and the mind as the natural order (with some considerable disorder) of things. Speaking as Christians, by revelation we call the order of nature God's creation. Without the world of revelation the cross is only an execution and the church is another natural order alongside the orders of state, family, economy, school, entertainment, and the arts. With the world of revelation the cross becomes the glory of God through the rising of Jesus as the first fruits of resurrection. The church becomes holy and Christians become saints. God's city is always above and behind Cain's city, both judging and redeeming it.

Luther and Augustine use the stage of kingdom and city as the place for ontic passage. Paul uses the category of time for the passing of scenes, acts, chapters, books of eidetic reality. He speaks of angels and principalities (Rom. 8:38). The author of Ephesians says we wrestle not against flesh and blood but against "the powers of this dark world and against the spiritual forces of evil in the heavenly realms" (Eph. 6:12). Two kingdoms interact, two times intersect. If we call the heavenly realm mythical and the earthly realm historical, we must always speak of the mythical and the historical in real relationship, else we get either a gap or a reduction. We cannot live merely in the mythical, nor can we live merely in the historical. The mythical cannot be reduced to the psychological, nor to the realm of subjective value or meaning. Nor can the historical, the psychological, and the ideational exist by themselves. The ontic and the noetic must never be separated. The mythical and the historical indeed intersect in the water of baptism and the bread and wine of Communion. They met and merged in the virgin birth and in the juxtaposition of empty tomb and resurrection in the story of Jesus. The primordial myth of Adam intersects with each individual's sense of sin in one's personal history.

Construction of a story ontology will reify myth but never do so by developing a metaphysical system. Biblical imagery is eschatological, not metaphysical. It "calls for a redemption of time, and not its end," as Amos

N. Wilder says.[42] Mere historicism drifts into disintegration. To avoid this, there is a natural human tendency to seek escape through gnostic or romantic atemporal myths. The biblical revelation, however, is cosmic in scope, inclusive of the full span of history and extending back to the time of Adam and creation and forward to a new heaven and earth. Infinitely more than an individualistic, historical redemption is revealed in the biblical Word. Again as Wilder says, "The impulse of the early Christian hope could not be satisfied with inwardness or a spiritual salvation. It required a new creation, but one representing the fulfillment of the old."[43]

As we have seen, for Luther and Augustine the ontological metaphor is one of location, the *polis*. For Paul the metaphor is one of time, *ho aiōn*. In story, place and time are constitutive of reality. Temporal events are described as taking place in Eden or Egypt, in the forest of Arden or Narnia. They occur in successive periods, in this present time or in the coming time. Both the spatial location and the temporal era are coupled with and intersected by another realm and time that opens up to us a new world by way of a heuristic revelation. The revealed kingdom and time is not seen or thought but is given to our experience through the compulsion of faith as we are moved by the Holy Spirit. Imagination may also construct (conjure?) mythical realms and times, but these must be distinguished from the revelation that comes from the world of God that is objective to us.

Thus the structure of reality is the structure of a story. It has a plot with characters who play their roles on a stage, but the stage extends into all the world. It might be better to speak of many stages that intersect and some that do not. Being, as we encounter it, has a plurality that includes the world of sensible things (living and inorganic), the world of mind (memory, understanding, imagination), and the world of revelation (those realities that come to us indirectly from God and the angelic and demonic realms). In a story world we are not limited to objects and subjects, because reality must also include events in the unfolding of a plot. The ontology of story is not simply a word about being; it is a story of persons in conflict and community on a stage of props that are changing with the scenes. Reality is relationships, encounters, developments, disintegrations, actions, and passions.

"These are only hints and guesses," and with this incipient experiment the following chapters will attempt to sketch the story shape of basic Christian doctrines.

NOTES

1. David Friedrich Strauss, *The Life of Jesus Critically Examined* (New York: Macmillan Co., 1892), 86.

2. Rudolf Bultmann, *Jesus Christ and Mythology* (New York: Charles Scribner's

Sons, 1958), 35ff.; Rudolf Bultmann, *Essays, Philosophical and Theological* (New York: Macmillan Co., 1955), 23ff.

3. Adolf Jülicher, *Die Gleichnisreden Jesu,* Part 1 (Freiburg: Mohr, 1899), 25–118.

4. Joachim Jeremias, *The Parables of Jesus* (New York: Charles Scribner's Sons, 1963), 20.

5. Mircea Eliade, *Myth and Reality* (New York: Harper & Row, 1963).

6. Paul Ricoeur, "Biblical Hermeneutics," *Semeia,* no. 4 (1974), 100.

7. Amos N. Wilder, *Jesus' Parables and the War of Myths: Essays on Imagination in the Scriptures* (Philadelphia: Fortress Press, 1982), 83.

8. Ibid., 71 and 105.

9. Herschel Baker, *Twelfth Night,* The Signet Classic Shakespeare (New York and Toronto: New American Library), xxv–xxvi.

10. Robert W. Funk, in *Language, Hermeneutic and Word of God* (New York: Harper & Row, 1966), 193ff., says that the parables of Jesus may be analyzed according to a logic of merit or a logic of grace.

11. Cf. John Dominic Crossan, *The Dark Interval: Towards a Theology of Story* (Niles, Ill.: Argus Communications, 1975), 56.

12. Ricoeur, *Semeia,* no. 4 (1974), 122.

13. It is tempting to think of reality as a game, especially since games are a kind of story, but it would be a grave mistake, because in the story of reality conflict is resolved, whereas in games there are only winners and losers. Long before Ludwig Wittgenstein and Hans-Georg Gadamer, Roger W. Holmes in *The Rhyme of Reason* (New York: D. Appleton Century Co., 1939), described the great philosophical systems as games.

14. René Descartes, *The Philosophical Works of Descartes,* trans. E. S. Haldane and G. R. T. Ross, 2 vols. (Cambridge, England, 1931), 1:190f.

15. Cf. Immanuel Kant, *Critique of Pure Reason* (London: Macmillan & Co., 1934), Introduction and Book I, Analytic of Concepts.

16. Henri Bergson makes this observation in *The Introduction to a New Philosophy* (Boston: John W. Luce and Co., 1912), 99: "In short, the whole *Critique of Pure Reason* undertakes to establish the fact that Platonism, which is illegitimate if the Ideas are things, becomes legitimate if the Ideas are relations, and that the completed Idea, after once being returned from heaven to earth, is indeed, as Plato had desired, the common foundation of thought and nature. But the entire *Critique of Pure Reason* rests upon the postulate that our intelligence is incapable of doing anything other than Platonize, that is, of pouring all possible experience into pre-existing moulds."

17. David Hume, *An Enquiry Concerning Human Understanding and A Treatise of Human Nature* (La Salle, Ill.: Open Court Publishing Co., 1938), 214ff.

18. Roderick M. Chisholm, "Brentano on Descriptive Psychology and the Intentional," in *Phenomenology and Existentialism,* ed. Edward L. Lee and Maurice Mandelbaum (Baltimore: Johns Hopkins Press, 1967), 16.

19. The discussion of Whitehead is taken mostly from *Process and Reality* (New York: Macmillan Co., 1941); *Religion in the Making* (New York: Macmillan Co., 1926); *Adventures of Ideas* (New York: Macmillan Co., 1933); *The Function of Reason* (Boston: Beacon Press, 1967); and *Science and the Modern World* (New York: Macmillan Co., 1925).

20. Whitehead, *Adventures of Ideas,* 300.

21. Whitehead, *Process and Reality,* 259.

22. Whitehead, *Adventures of Ideas,* 241.

23. Ibid., 255.
24. Ibid., 266.
25. Whitehead, *Process and Reality,* 427, and *Religion in the Making,* 115.
26. Whitehead, *Religion in the Making,* 80ff.
27. Ibid., 87.
28. Whitehead, *Process and Reality,* 524.
29. It is interesting that the same criticism and the same correction can be applied to Pierre Teilhard de Chardin: *The Phenomenon of Man* (New York: Harper & Row, 1965), and *The Divine Milieu* (New York: Harper & Row, 1965).
30. Augustine, *Confessions,* trans. R. S. Pine-Coffin (Middlesex, England: Penguin Books, 1961), x.
31. Thomas De Quincey, *Confessions of an English Opium Eater* (New York: Heritage Press, 1950), 60.
32. Henri Bergson, *Time and Free Will* (London: George Allen, 1910), 99–110.
33. Whitehead, *Process and Reality,* 107.
34. Max Black, *Models and Metaphors: Studies in Language and Philosophy* (Ithaca and London: Cornell University Press, 1962), 187.
35. Ibid., 192. Black also refers to Percy W. Bridgman, *Reflections of a Physicist* (New York: Philosophical Library, 1950), 162: "Time is unsymmetrical and flows only forward."
36. Oscar Cullmann, *Christ and Time* (Philadelphia: Westminster Press, 1950).
37. J. T. Fraser, *The Genesis and Evolution of Time* (Amherst, Mass.: University of Massachusetts Press, 1982).
38. Black, *Models and Metaphors,* 167. Having said this, Black affirms the function of metaphor in the form of "conceptual archetypes" to bring through imagination a unification of science and the humanities. "Perhaps every science must start with metaphor and end with algebra, and perhaps without the metaphor there would never have been any algebra" (p. 242).
39. Ibid., 169.
40. The ancient Taoist philosopher Chuang Tzǔ said the same thing: "That which acts on all and meddles in none is—Heaven." Cf. Thomas Merton, *The Way of Chuang Tzǔ* (New York: New Directions, 1965), 73.
41. Regin Prenter, *Spiritus Creator* (Philadelphia: Muhlenberg Press, 1953), 87.
42. Wilder, *Jesus' Parables and the War of Myths,* 136.
43. Ibid., 151–52.

4

Reality and the Fantasy Metaphors of Creation

—and God said

The preceding chapters have told us that a narrative hermeneutic and ontology will read the text for what it says in its sequence, conflict, and climax. We will not reduce the text by lopping off everything that is not congruent with historical verifiability, yet we will not separate the text from its historical roots. We will examine the text in its context and also allow the metaphor in the text to lift us to new worlds of reality. With this kind of hermeneutic and ontology of story, what theological construct can be derived from the story of creation?

We would like to know the nature of reality. We cannot bear the loss of that which is fleeting, so we cling to that which we think is abiding. We say the real is eternal and not corroded by the acids of time. Plato, and all the philosophers in the grand manner, found abiding reality in ideas of goodness, truth, and beauty. Aristotle found abiding reality in the immutable perfection of substance. In the Orient, nature and history are thought to be illusion, *Maya;* therefore reality is sought through escape from time into *Nirvana.* Even in modern philosophies which take time seriously reality is fixed in either the necessity of logic, as in Hegel, or the determination of science, as in Samuel Alexander.[1] Hegel's logic of contradiction moves from being through contingency to necessity, and therefore in his concept of reality there is a complete fusion of logic and fact. Alexander's point-event continuum involves a descriptive determinism, which is certainly less dogmatic, but his concept of reality is also restrictive because we are limited to empirical data and the deity thereby becomes just another name for nature. Alfred North Whitehead is unusual among philosophers since Plato in that he has had the courage to restore the Heraclitean flux and declare that reality is not reducible to the static and timeless.[2] For Whitehead, reality is bipolar, having dimensions that are fixed and unchanging on the one hand and also moving and growing with surprising novelty on the other.

What I have to say will be understood better if we are careful to avoid equivocation. Semantics and the analysis of language are essential. Each sphere of experience develops its own vocabulary. One may be translated to another, but only with great precision and with the gift of the Spirit. This is to say that reality has many fields, and each field has its own language. We can move from one field to another with meaningful communication if we can capture the spirit, or be captured by the spirit, of both fields. Christian thinkers, in their attempt to articulate the faith in intellectual terms, translated biblical categories into Platonic or Aristotelian concepts.

Plato said reality is ideal, and therefore timeless, spaceless, non-material, and invisible. This seemed readily adaptable to the biblical concept of an invisible God who is not to be identified with any created thing, and with the Christ who is the same yesterday, today, and forever. "We look not to the things that are seen but to the things that are unseen; for the things that are seen are transient, but the things that are unseen are eternal" (2 Cor. 4:18). The Platonic teaching of the one and the many became the philosophical vehicle for the doctrine of God and his creatures. The Christian doctrine of the image of God became translated into Plato's reflections of reality on the walls of the cave. The Bible speaks of death as the wage of sin. This was translated into the fall of existence with its threat of non-being. The Bible speaks of resurrection as the gift of grace. This was translated as the retention of the soul in immortality with the recovery of the soul through *anamnēsis* ("remembrance"). All of these translations are faulty and misleading, but the last is probably most clearly indicative of the vast difference between the Platonic vision of reality and the Christian revelation.

Aristotle said reality is substantial and relational. This seemed readily adaptable to the Christian concept of the goodness, and therefore the reality, of creation. Also the concept of relational ethics seemed to translate easily into the Christian obligation both to God and to neighbor. Quite obviously the Aristotelian concept of the abiding reality of substance lent itself to the development of the doctrine of transubstantiation. And the concept of static perfection became the basis for Thomas Aquinas' doctrine of God as *actus purus,* the substance that cannot suffer change.

Both Plato's teaching of the one and the many and Aristotle's teaching on substance were used to construct the Christian doctrine of the Trinity. The Godhead is not divided into three substances since perfection must be one, yet under the unified essence of the divine stand three persons who are freely related to each other and to the world.

Because the translations were inadequate they could not sustain the human community for long. Platonism evolved into gnosticism and mysticism with the Christian heresies of docetism in Christology and modalism in the doctrine of the Trinity. Aristotelianism gave support to both rationalism and legalism. These were some of the strands that made up the cultural fabric of the medieval world, these strands of mysticism, rationalism, and legalism, and they were mixed with an animist superstition that found events in nature and history to be controlled by demons and spirits. Rationalism produced the method of science, and its success crowded out the credibility of both mysticism and religious superstition. Legalism survived, however, into the twentieth century first through Puritanism and then through Victorianism and Pietism.

Although these philosophical formulations were noble and intellectually grand, they were not adequate to carry the culture of the Western world. It was the story of the living God of the Jews that gave life and élan to the people as they lived and loved and fought and worked and played. It was not the Unmoved Mover of Plato or the Uncaused Cause of Aristotle that moved the people but the compassionate and angry God of the Israelites. The Jews retained a primitively personal view of reality. It was not abstract reason but concrete story that was for them the vehicle of reality. Hence they lived by the mythical narrative of creation and the garden and by the story they told of their historical adventures in the exodus and the exile.

The significant difference between animism and metaphysical religion on the one hand and Judeo-Christian revelation on the other is the difference between thing and person. Persons produce stories, while things relate either to static ideas or to impersonal processes. Animism may appear at first to be highly personal, but it is really only the contrived personification of impersonal forces. Agni is the personal name given to the force of fire. Poseidon is the power of the sea. Metaphysical religion is the worship of abstract ideals. These are sometimes personified too, as when love is given the name of Lakshmi or Astarte or Aphrodite, or when wisdom is called Athene, and destruction is called Shiva. Such personifications are symbols that point to impersonal forces or ideas, as if the personifications were mere accommodations and basically unreal, while behind them stand the invisible, unchanging realities. *Judeo-Christian revelation, however, does not personify.* It deals with real persons in the form of story. A living God speaks to living creatures. Revelation is possible because there is communication between persons.

The language of philosophy and science is either abstractly rational or empirically descriptive. The language of revelation is the language of story. In the nineteenth century, since reason and scientific method were so successful, reality was sought in their domain, and religion was justified by relegating it to the realm of emotional value. Therefore it became a matter of subjective concern and its reality was only defined in terms of significance and meaning, not in terms of an abiding ontology. The very thing that religion was supposed to provide, eternal truth and destiny, was thus denied. A study of the language of science will show that even in its attention to concrete description the real goal is the abstraction of naming. From Aristotle's physics to the taxonomies of modern statistical analysis scientific knowledge is identification and categorizing, all of which makes possible the process of measurement. Science is counting. But one cannot count until one has reduced the subject under investigation to an identifiable, named thing. This is not reality, this is abstraction from reality for the purpose of a perceived value. Is it any wonder that our culture has become bankrupt when we have given it over to the tinkering of technicians in every field from education to economics?

In contrast, the language of revelation is the concretion of action, not description by naming, but the narration of events in which verbs become the carriers of the story rather than nouns. Here we find truth to be not knowledge but acknowledgment, not cognition but recognition. Truth comes in the surprising event when Oedipus perceives that he is the murderer of his father and the husband of his mother, when Peter confesses that Jesus is the Messiah. The language of science is not false, but it has its own limited function. It makes us comfortable and rich, but it cannot bring us peace and community. Only the language of revelation can speak of love, joy, peace, patience, hope, and faith. And paradoxically, children—and artists—have a closer appreciation of revelational language. It has been observed that children think in terms of action rather than definitions and labels. To a child a nose is to blow; to a sophisticated scientist a nose becomes a proboscis with olfactory nerves. The artist too, in contrast to the scientist, sees the nose in terms of dramatic action, as when Rostand describes Cyrano's nose as a monstrous protuberance, a colossal extension, a veritable peninsula, a flag that waves in the breeze.

In the revelation given to the Hebrews they were like children using words to point to action. This is why they were so hesitant to name God. He cannot be labeled, because he is every action and every passion and he is a mystery beyond all knowing. That is why to the Jew the incarnation is the great blasphemy; to the Christian, however, because of the ironic twist at the end of the story of Jesus, the incarnation is the heart of our faith. It is the supreme paradox. To become flesh and receive a name is human, and, as Nikos Kazantzakis said, "A name is a prison. God is free." We all have names and we are all therefore behind bars. When God became man he took on a name and went to prison. This is the nature of language, for while it communicates it also limits and restricts. God in Jesus limited and restricted himself unto death. But the incarnation is not the end of the story. In the beginning was the Word and the Word became flesh, but the story does not stop here. God broke that prison and Jesus rose from the dead and he rose from the name of Jesus to the unutterable mystery of Christ. Yes, Jesus is a name but Christ is a verb, a mysterious action, and not even a verb but a participle, a verbal adjective, a pointer to a living reality. This is because he is God and God is free. He cannot be contained, he cannot be named, but though he was named in Jesus he is now free from his prison of flesh and death. And Christians repeatedly reenact this liberating wordless drama by eating bread and drinking wine. We take them into the prison of our bodies and make them our sinful human flesh as we receive God in the incarnate Jesus into the form of sinful human flesh, altogether human. But as Jesus rose on the third day so we rise in the mystery of faith and live as liberated new spirits even before the last day.

The ambiguity of the word obtains for creation as well as for redemption, only it is reversed in time. Redemption is a tragicomedy leading from suffering incarceration to liberating resurrection. Creation is a fantasy leading from mysterious freedom to the formed structure of existence, comprehensible though not comprehended. Redemption is the story that moves from the binding necessity of existence to the freedom of a new creation. Creation is the tale that begins with freedom and ends with its loss. The biblical story of creation says that the world began with the voice of God calling out over the void where his Spirit was brooding like a bird in expectant silence. Thus the historical dimension of the Word that came with the conception of the Spirit in Jesus of Nazareth is linked in the beginning with the Word that sang the worlds into being with the moaning of the Spirit. And the act of creation was a passion because as soon as the God who was alone uttered his voice he was no longer the God in the void, silent and alone, but now he becomes the God who is heard. And he suffers himself to be heard so that henceforth he is no longer himself alone but himself and his creature, the articulation of his voice which, paradoxically, because it is *his* echo and image, is not merely an echo or an image but a free spirit.

The Greek philosophers rationalized experience. Seeing a series of events they thought pattern into them and thus fused logic with fact and came up with God as Uncaused Cause. The philosophical category of causality is logical necessity. Logical necessity yields a closed system of sufficient reason which allows for no freedom, no absurdity, no mystery, no conflict, no laughter, no tears, no regret, no hope, no joy. All these are realities of story that cannot be set aside if we are to reckon at all seriously with human experience. The old Greek way of thinking is tempting because it conceives of God as abiding substance in the face of a disintegrating world. C. S. Lewis tells of a woman who said that she thinks of God as substance, but the trouble is he comes out as a nondescript blob, something like tapioca pudding, and unfortunately she does not like tapioca pudding.

Modern people have abandoned the causality of logical necessity for the efficient cause of empirical description. In so doing we have also abandoned God. There is no place for God in a scientific equation. The empirical moderns see causality as simple *a posteriori* antecedence and contiguity. There is no logical necessity in natural behavior, only a practical one. But there is no God, either at the center or on the boundary of existence, either as a first cause or as a final cause.

My contention is that both the philosophical category of logical causality and the modern scientific category of efficient causality are inadequate to provide the abiding reality that humankind seeks. Instead this abiding reality may be found only in the primeval stories that people tell of their origins and paradoxically of their unsuccessful quest for abiding reality. The parallels among the various stories told in cultures around the world are striking. The similarities as well as the differences support the notion that story is basic to reality, that reality is a story that has many chapters, many versions, many characters who may be transmigrations of more basic characters, many genealogies and histories which are simply the way various peoples tell the experience of their part in the story. History is then seen to be less than ultimate in authenticating reality.[3] History is true and real only insofar as it truly and really tells the story of what happened. It should be obvious therefore that there is only one story that embraces all the successive events in time, but there are many tellings of portions of this story and these tellings are not to be despised because of their partiality.

The many parallels in the *Epic of Gilgamesh* with Homer's *Odyssey* have often been noted.[4] The Ninevite version of the *Epic of Gilgamesh* begins with a prologue in praise of Gilgamesh, who was probably the ruler of Uruk in southern Mesopotamia sometime early in the third millennium before Christ. He is listed in the Sumerian genealogy of kings who reigned after the flood. He is represented as part divine and part human, as a warrior and builder of cities with superior knowledge of all things on land and sea. Like Prometheus he seems to be the object of jealousy from the Akkadian god Anu, who sends an adversary in the form of a wild man, Enkidu, to do battle with Gilgamesh and cut him down to size. The struggle is real but Gilgamesh is victorious and Enkidu henceforth becomes a companion and friend. The two men set out on an odyssey in search of immortality. Gilgamesh makes a dangerous journey to find Utnapishtim, the survivor of the Babylonian flood, to learn from him how to escape death. Utnapishtim tells him about the flood and also where to find a plant that will renew his youth. But after Gilgamesh finds the plant, it is seized by a serpent and Gilgamesh returns to Uruk without the immortality he sought. The king must die and only God lives.

The story of Gilgamesh's visit to Siduri on his journey closely resembles Odysseus's visit to Circe and Calypso on their enchanted islands. The divine woman Siduri keeps an inn in a marvelous garden of the sun-god near the shores of the ocean. Like the two Greek goddesses, Siduri tries to dissuade Gilgamesh from his journey in pursuit of immortality by offering him the pleasures of this life. She finally acknowledges her failure when she realizes his determination to have immortality, and she helps him cross over the waters of death. The description of the house of dust and the miserable condition of human beings after their death given by Enkidu remarkably resembles what Achilles learns from his friend Patroclus in the *Iliad*.

The story of a man fighting death by wrestling with temptations for this world's pleasures and powers is told again in the medieval morality play *Everyman*. Everyman is summoned by death and so he goes back to his origins to find someone or something to accompany him as he crosses over. He is refused first by his relatives and friends. Then he seeks to bring with him eternal virtues like beauty and wisdom but he finds they are not his to take. Finally he leaves this earth only with Good Deeds, just the few that he had done in his life, because he could take with him only what he had given away, not anything that he had received.

The story is taken up in the history of Thomas à Becket and then told again in the drama of T. S. Eliot, *Murder in the Cathedral*.[5] Thomas is tempted to cheat death by taking up the pleasures of "fluting in the meadows and viols in the hall," and then later by accepting the secular power of the state and the spiritual power of the church, and finally he is tempted to accept martyrdom and the power it brings to rule from the grave. This is not only the story of Becket; it is also the story of everyman and everywoman because we are all flawed by our human condition and we must decide how we will receive death. The paradox in the story is that we do receive life, but not by escaping death.

While there may be evidence of cultural borrowings among the stories that circulated around the Mediterranean, there seems little evidence of any such conditioning upon the creation stories told by North American Indians. Yet the parallels are equally striking amidst significant differences. One difference, for example, in the Chippewa story of creation is that woman was made first and man was fashioned from her rib. It might be interesting to see what difference this telling of the story may have had on the development of family relationships.

Among the totem pole Indians of Alaska and Siberia, worship was directed to a multiplicity of divine creatures who performed definite creative, re-creative, and managerial functions that were assigned to them by a rather nebulous principal deity who was believed to exist but whose personality and character were unknown.[6] The remarkable resemblance of this notion to Paul's reference to the unknown god of the Greeks in his address on Mars Hill cannot escape notice. Also, both Paul's reference and the totemic myths declare the ambivalence of the hidden God and the revealed God, with the revealed God being the Word that was active in both creation and redemption, and the hidden God being the incomprehensible mystery that is celebrated as the God who reveals himself to us as the God who remains unknown.

The totems of the Northwest Indians were not spirit devices or idolatrous images to be worshiped. They were heraldic symbols of their lineage from supernatural land, air, and sea creatures. The totems were revered as means of recording and displaying a family's genealogy among a people who had no written language. This was their way of telling the story of their heritage and of the events of importance in past generations. The tribes of the

Northwest Coast—Tlingit, Tsimshian, Haida, Kwakiutl, Nootka, Bella Coola, and Quileute—all had genesis stories and flood stories. In one flood story, after a chief's son had seen a vision of carved poles in the ocean depths, sea serpents raised up a tidal wave of salt water during a potlatch, the ritual of raising totem poles. The people were saved from the inundation by changing their skins and bodies into air creatures and flying away from the deluge. It has been argued that there are intimations of Buddhist ideas of the transmigration of souls in different bodies. This would be possible, of course, if there had been traffic with Asia, but if my thesis is valid, such historical borrowing is not needed to authenticate the telling of a real story. As in the Hebrew book of Genesis where a dove figures in the survival after the flood, thunderbirds and seagulls engage in the rescue of Tlingit and Haida Indians. Also another story tells of a chief building a great floating house.

In Siberia, Raven was an agent of the Supreme Being who brought order to a dark world of evil. Raven or Yethl in Alaska was the "Changer" who brought light when darkness covered the face of the earth, when the people had no light. The creator of people was called Nass-shikke-yahl. He put people in an Eden which was identified with the valley of the Nass River on the Northwest Coast. It was a garden but it was dark, so Yethl, like Prometheus, with great perception and compassion, decided to rectify the situation by playing a trick on Nass-shikke-yahl. He changed himself into a hemlock needle and floated on the water of a spring where Nass-shikke-yahl's daughter came to drink. When she swallowed the tiny needle she became pregnant and gave birth to a son, who is therefore the creator god's grandson. As Yethl expected, the grandson was spoiled by the grandfather, who gave him everything he wanted—the moon, the stars, a box containing the light of the sun. One day he went to a riverbank where people were fishing. They were very noisy and rude, so he told them he would let light shine on them and expose them. They did not want to be shown up for what they were, so they taunted him, saying, "You are not the chief who made the world, you do not have light." But he opened the sun box, first a little and then all the way, and let the light shine, and they were terrified.

Raven was at first white, but because of his mischief he was changed to black. This story has the same ambiguity of good and evil lodged in the divine figure that is found in Prometheus. It indicates that in the profoundest stories when the depth of reality is probed there will be found both humor and the conflict of adversaries.

It is interesting to note in these creation stories the realities of place, time, and plot. The stories occur in fantasyland; they are not histories. They have place which is no place; they have time which is no time. They tell of a geography which is named after the valley of the Tigris and Euphrates or the valley of the Nass, but Eden and the land of Nass-shikke-yahl cannot actually be located. The action begins once upon a time but it is not dated.

The fantasyland is not, however, unreal; indeed it is represented in the stories as the ultimate reality and it contrasts with conditions in the historical present which are out of touch with reality, which are twisted because the world is now under a spell. Being separated from our origins and cast out of the garden we have lost touch with the reality that is recalled only through imagination or given by revelation.

J. R. R. Tolkien and C. S. Lewis have given us marvelously imaginative stories that recall primordial reality. In Tolkien's Middle Earth the creatures are not yet completely bewitched as they now are. Tree-forms, for example, have not yet lost the power of speech and they are not yet immobile and rooted to the ground. Their voices are low and their words stretch across the centuries in slow syllables. Pippin in *The Lord of the Rings* tells about one of these ancient treelike species, the Ents: "One felt as if there was an enormous well behind them, filled up with ages of memory and long, slow, steady thinking; but their surface was sparkling with the present: like sun shimmering on the outer leaves of a vast tree, or on the ripples of a very deep lake. I don't know, but it felt as if something that grew in the ground—asleep, you might say, or just feeling itself as something between root-tip and leaf-tip, between deep earth and sky—had suddenly waked up, and was considering you with the same slow care that it had given to its own inside affairs for endless years."[7] Who knows if this is factually true, but certainly it is real, or it opens a window to reality.

Abiding reality is a story, an adventure, a mystery—it moves and turns and grows as it takes us somewhere, sometime.

> The Road goes ever on and on
>   Down from the door where it began.
> Now far ahead the Road has gone,
>   And I must follow, if I can,
> Pursuing it with eager feet,
>   Until it joins some larger way,
> Where many paths and errands meet.
>   And whither then? I cannot say.
>
> Still round the corner there may wait
>   A new road or a secret gate;
> And though I oft have passed them by
>   A day will come at last when I
> Shall take the hidden paths that run
>   West of the Moon, East of the Sun.[8]

C. S. Lewis in *The Great Divorce* describes the situation of contrast between heaven and hell in terms of these categories of reality and unreality.[9] Hell is the place of the dead. They are shadowy figures who live in a gray town that sprawls endlessly like a suburban subdivision. Its houses are mostly empty because people can move away from each other simply by wishing it, and since people in hell cannot abide their neighbors, everybody is constantly moving away. Every Monday there is an excursion bus that leaves for heaven. People can take the trip free, but invariably after visiting heaven they choose to return to hell. The reason for this is that the shadowy ghosts of hell find heaven too real. The grass is so real it cuts their feet, the water is so substantial the ghosts can walk on it. They find themselves to be very uncomfortable in this place where their lies are exposed, their masks are ripped off, and they cannot drift in the evanescent dreams of self-deception. Indeed heaven in the story means the recognition of the great reversal between reality and fantasy. What we normally call fantastic illusion is seen to be reality and what we call hard fact is seen to be delusion. We begin to see that reality is not spaceless, timeless, non-material, invisible. Reality is not the Platonic ideal or the Aristotelian substance. Reality is the story of living beings interacting with each other and with other creatures that have not received the breath of the Spirit. And this story is fantastic, filled with laughter and tears, mystery and excitement, abiding relationships and changing surprises. The search for abiding reality therefore can reach fruition only if you enter into the story, living it, letting it happen to you, and giving yourself to it in the most creative and imaginative way that you can.

NOTES

1. Cf. G. W. F. Hegel, *The Logic of Hegel*, trans. William Wallace (London: Oxford University Press, 1950); Samuel Alexander, *Space, Time, and Deity* (London: Macmillan & Co., 1920).

2. Alfred North Whitehead, *Process and Reality* (New York: Macmillan Co., 1941), 317ff.; see also Alfred North Whitehead, *Science and the Modern World* (New York: Macmillan Co., 1925), 165ff.

3. Cf. Northrop Frye, *Spiritus Mundi* (Bloomington and London: Indiana University Press, 1976), 179ff.

4. Cf. Joseph Campbell, *Hero with a Thousand Faces* (New York: Pantheon Books, 1949).

5. T. S. Eliot, *Murder in the Cathedral* (New York: Harcourt, Brace and Co., 1935).

6. Cf. Joseph H. Wherry, *The Totem Pole Indians* (New York: Thomas Y. Crowell, 1974), 52ff.

7. J. R. R. Tolkien, *The Lord of the Rings*, Part Two: *The Two Towers* (New York: Houghton Mifflin Co., 1965), 66.

8. Tolkien, *The Lord of the Rings*, Part One: *The Fellowship of the Ring*, 82–83 and Part Three: *The Return of the King*, 308. In his essay "On Fairy-Stories" in *Tree and Leaf* (Boston: Houghton Mifflin Co., 1965), 68, Tolkien speaks of the journey "West of the Moon, East of the Sun" as the consolation of a happy ending. Fairy stories have a comic return that brings the plot to an end in which the characters live happily ever after. He calls this *eucatastrophe*. "It does not deny the existence of *dyscatastrophe*, of sorrow and failure: the possibility of these is necessary to the joy of deliverance; it denies (in the face of much evidence, if you will) universal final defeat and in so far is *evangelium*, giving a fleeting glimpse of Joy, Joy beyond the walls of the world, poignant as grief."

9. C. S. Lewis, *The Great Divorce* (New York: Macmillan Co., 1946).

5

A Beginning Scientific Prescript on Understanding Life's Origins

—a flashback

In the age of great philosophies sophisticated people took for granted a Parmenidean unity in the structure of reality. They then had to explain the multifarious diversity which we encounter in human experience.[1] Today in the age of science the intellectual world assumes reality to be in Heraclitean flux and the problem for explanation is to find a meaningful pattern that comprehends the variety in our experience. In physics, both molecular physics and astrophysics, these explanations are expressed in terms of mathematical equations which are neat shorthand résumés of a wide range of observations. In biology, explanation is sought in terms of genetic descriptions of changing forms.

Whereas in former times the biblical revelation of creation was translated into philosophical categories, today attempts are made to articulate our faith in terms of scientific models. Creation was intellectually understood for centuries as the process of secondary causes behind which stood a single Primary Cause. The transcendence of the Primary Cause could be conceived as a movement from above attracting all things like a magnet (Aristotle) or as a movement from below providing the ground of Being (Plato). In either case it was easy to identify the transcendent Cause with the Divine Creator. But when such transcendence is abandoned, when all metaphysics is rejected because there is no empirical evidence for it, then we are left with the process of efficient causality, and all "explanations" are limited to empirical descriptions of verifiable changes. The description of genetic change is called the theory of evolution. This kind of explanation has no more need for transcendent Cause than the physicist has need for God in the equation $e = mc^2$.

Here we must be very precise in our use of language. The theory of evolution speaks about the origin of life but says nothing about God as the creator of life. This does not deny God, nor does it substitute for God an all-sufficient process. It simply describes, on the basis of the data we know, how genetic changes take place. It is a serious mistake to confuse language by saying that evolution is an alternative to creation. The biblical story of creation uses narrative language to tell *who* made the world. It does not offer precise scientific measurements about *how* the world changes.

Evolution is a word that comes from Latin, and it means "to turn out." In science it refers to a theory that tries to explain how we "turned out" to be what we are. Evolution is gradual change upward. Its scientific statement is the law of biogenesis: ontogeny recapitulates phylogeny. In lay terms this means that each species in the animal and plant kingdoms goes through stages in its own life history that correspond to stages in the general groupings of species.

The simplest animals are grouped into the category of protozoans, one-celled animals such as amoeba and paramecium. Human beings at one time in their development are one-celled animals. The fertilized ovum divides and grows. In the late nineteenth century Ernst Haeckel noticed that the human fetus grows in a fluid-filled sac like forms of life that live in water. At one point human beings even have gill slits like those in fish, and then they disappear. The unborn human passes through all the levels of the eleven phyla or groupings that Darwin knew in the classification of the animal kingdom. Finally it reaches the vertebrate stage. Here it resembles in remarkable ways the primates: chimpanzees, baboons, monkeys, and apes who walk upright and have ten digits. Because of this resemblance it was possible to use monkeys in laboratory research to develop an effective polio vaccine for human beings. It does not mean that human beings evolved from monkeys.

Besides biological evidence of evolution, there is in the human species evidence of gradual social change upward—from cave dwellers who simply gathered food, to hunters to farmers to city dwellers who manufacture things. Anthropologists have discovered human remains in Africa dating back millions of years. From these early beginnings changing levels of social structure have been described. Fairly accurate dating of paleolithic artifacts is possible through chemical analysis which takes advantage of the measurable breakdown of radioactive carbons, and more recently with potassium and argon.

Along with evidence of evolutionary development in nature and society there are evidences of "devolution." Biological species and social orders become extinct. Two explanations were given by Darwin for this double process: (1) Like begets like, but in the process mutations or alterations occur, and (2) according to a success-failure ethic, some mutations aid survival and others do not. Only the fit survive. Some bacteria, for example, adapt through genetic changes to resist penicillin, thus surviving in a new environment. Likewise dinosaurs died out, but mammals survived when the earth cooled and dried. Today all life is threatened by environmental pollution and the possible human abuse of nuclear power. Evolution gives us sardonic hope, because even the worst atomic blast cannot destroy all life, only life as we know it. There is still the possibility that new life will emerge and rise again through the long and arduous process of evolution, just as society replenished the earth after the flood. But what a terrible gap between bacteria and Bartok![2]

Today the desire is to articulate the Christian faith in language that is congruent with scientific thought patterns rather than philosophical concepts. Philosophy uses root metaphors such as idea or substance or monad or impression or process.[3] Science uses models such as atoms and molecules and waves and cells.[4] Notice that the various philosophical metaphors are disjunctive and irreducibly elemental but the scientific models are conjunctive and structured. In this respect the category of story is closer to scientific models than to philosophical categories because it is structured. In our attempt to satisfy the need to express our faith in the context of a scientific age we must be careful to avoid a double danger. Either we will mistranslate because we find something coming from science that appears to give a nod to God, or we will be intimidated by the successful independence of science and therefore we will attack science as the enemy of God. In so doing, as we often do in the political realm, we unnecessarily create an adversary out of an innocent partner in the human enterprise.

An example of the first danger is the misuse of Werner Heisenberg's uncertainty principle. This principle states that the position of a subatomic particle is intrinsically imprecise in the measure that its momentum is precise, that is, it is impossible to determine simultaneously both the location and the velocity of a particle with accuracy.[5] This principle does not apply to ordinary objects such as sailboats, for instance, which can easily be both located and measured for velocity at the same time. Electrons, however, will be knocked about in an unpredictable way whenever their speed is measured, and this has nothing to do with inadequacies in the measuring instruments or the technique of the observer. It is due to the structure of particles and waves in the subatomic realm. This observation by Heisenberg, when elevated to a theory about the nature of atomic matter, calls into question the assumption of universal efficient causality. Since nature has built into its structure some uncertainty, it is argued that there is room for human freedom of will, and from here we can easily move on to the possibility of miracles.

It may well be that nature, or what Christians call creation, has some uncertainty. Indeed the biblical story of creation demands this. Along with the meaningful, structured work of the Word there is the spontaneous creativity of the Spirit. The truth value in this scientific observation is that it dispels a closed-system determinism and allows us to think of the universe as open-ended, in process, perhaps still being created. There is no reason to deny that God made the world with its particles to fall or jump freely where they may, under certain circumstances and within certain limits. Such uncertainty makes for a world in which the future is never fixed. We will always be excited by its surprises and challenged by unexpected situations.

But it would be a mistake to confuse this natural uncertainty with a responsible freedom of the will, even if both derive from the Creator Spirit. When we speak of human freedom we are not talking about the indeterminate way we fall or jump in natural circumstances. We are bigger than atoms and our location and speed can be measured together. When we speak of human freedom we are talking about our capacity for self-determination, our action and reaction with responsible decision. Human beings are not simply the product of conditioned responses. They freely and creatively contribute to their own development and the production of ever-changing cultures. The debate between behavioristic determinists like B. F. Skinner and generative grammarians like Noam Chomsky may continue forever, but it cannot be denied that language freely grows and culture changes. This would not guarantee God, however, any more than Heisenberg's uncertainty principle guarantees human freedom. The apology for God, if he needs one, comes from the recognition that the story we live in has an author. We are given the stage on which we play and we are called forth to speak our lines. Yet we are free to stumble and stutter and even to create our own words.

The other pitfall in an age of scientific success is the fear that God as creator is no longer needed. One result of this fear is the attempt by some people to construct a so-called science of creationism from biblical evidence which supposedly will compete with and defeat the science of evolution. This kind of literalistic theologizing would not be worthy of consideration except for the fact that an overwhelming number of conservative Christians are swayed by it. For my purpose, however, it provides an interesting example of faulty translation and fuzzy reasoning. Among the many arguments marshaled against evolution by the proponents of "scientific creationism" is the contention that evolution is impossible since the universe is said to be running down according to the law of entropy, or the second law of thermodynamics.[6] Entropy is a function of energy and mechanical work in a closed system. It is the quantity of energy rendered unavailable by the work that is done. Entropy therefore increases during an irreversible process, such as the change of a solid to a liquid to a gas when the system is working. When this happens, the orderly pattern of constituent atoms decreases, and so an increase in entropy can be equated with an increase in disorder. Since all spontaneous processes are irreversible, it has been said that the entropy of the universe is increasing. More and more energy is thus wasted, rendered unavailable for doing work.

This scientific model is taken to be the secular translation of the biblical revelation that the world is under a curse because of Adam's fall and is therefore doomed to final destruction. It may be true, in the scientific model, that the universe is cooling down, but the law of entropy must not be confused with the biblical revelation of Adam's fall. In the first place the law of entropy does not preclude the possibility of several systems which balance each other. Thus the entropy of one system may decrease and compensate for the increase elsewhere. Evolution among living beings may involve a decrease of entropy, but this will balance out in the entire system of the universe. And in the second place, apart from the faulty use of scientific law, the theological meaning of the story of the fall does not require, and can never have, empirical verification. The meaning of the fall is a broken relationship between God and his creatures. It is not concerned with the slowing down of molecules, which indeed could be part of God's original design.

Let us shift gears radically. If science says nothing about God as creator, what does the Bible say? The Bible is not a textbook of science or even of history. It is a collection of many different kinds of writings. Although all of them were written by human hands, we believe them to be "inspired." Through them God has revealed himself, his nature, his will, and his relationship to human beings and all he has made.

Thus creation is a *story*, not a theory of origins. Indeed there are many stories of creation. Even the Bible has two different stories of creation in Genesis, and there are similar stories in every culture around the world. Details differ but all have common characteristics:

1. A single, supreme being exists alone prior to creation. There is no being or thing prior to his existence.
2. The creator is all-wise and all-powerful.
3. He creates with purpose, consciously, deliberately, and with a definite plan.
4. The creation is an expression of his freedom. He does what he wants.
5. After creation he rests, sleeps, or removes himself from his world.
6. He is a sky god who creates from nothing or an earth god who dives into the deep and brings up a particle from which earth grows or who dismembers a primordial being or who hatches a cosmogonic egg.
7. Either during creation or immediately after there is a rupture of the primordial harmony and perfection of creation.
8. From the beginning there is redemptive activity by the creator to set things right. This involves some kind of sacrifice.

There are all kinds of variations on these themes. Sometimes the creator deities are described with sex. Then the world is the progeny of a primordial mother and father. In myths of this kind the parents arise out of a prior substance of chaos. The biblical Creator is neither a sky god nor an earth god, however. Genesis 1 says the human being is made in God's image from nothing. Sexuality is not in the image of God. Animals, not in God's image, have sex. Genesis 2:7, on the other hand, says the earth creature (Adam) is made from the dust of the earth, and God breathes life into his body so that he becomes the chief of all creatures. Other creatures are made as companions for the human, but none are satisfactory, and therefore God makes woman (the female) from the rib of Adam.[7] She can be his partner because she is made from him, his equal, identical with his substance.

My purpose is not to expatiate on cosmogonic myths.[8] I wish only to call attention to the fact that the Bible uses story language to tell about origins, not the language of science. Then what is the problem between evolution and creation? There is no problem, because we are comparing two categories that should not be mixed. It is like comparing apples and oranges and faulting an orange because it does not make a good apple. Evolution is scientific theory. Creation is theological story.

The creation story is neither empirical science nor recorded history. It is a tale of religious consciousness that reaches beyond sensory experience and logic. It deals with deep truth and reality. We have collective experiences that go beyond the empirical and the rational into deep disclosures and feelings of awe in the presence of the transcendent. We have what we call revelation through the word of God in nature, history, Scripture, and the church. This must be distinguished from psychotic hallucination and wishful subjective piety. Two marks of distinction are the collective sharing in the community of believers and the objectivity of the content of the experience. It is never the subjectivity of my faith that defines the spiritual experience. It is always the objectivity of the Word, whether this comes to us through the given historicity of the cross or the account of Scripture or the proclamation of the gospel or the grace of the sacraments. True spirituality is always shaped by the object of worship, not by the subjective experiences of it. And only the language of story with its metaphoric and metonymic structure can express such a reality.

Science, on the other hand, deals with facts of sensory experience that are brought into meaningful relationships through the use of logic.[9] It deals with actuality but not with the deep reality described by story. When the Bible speaks of creation it does not isolate causes and consequences as the scientist does with the view to manipulate and control nature. The story of creation does not tell us that God is the first in a series of causes, as we might identify the finger that triggers a gun and sends a bullet to its target. Theologically speaking, God did not *cause* the world. He created the world out of nothing by what he *said:* "Let there be light." This is not a literal account reported to bystanders as in a scientific description or as a journalist might report news with action camera. This is the deepest poetry of the human spirit as God speaks in us and to us about the wonder of creation.

Creation and evolution do not contradict each other. Both are useful for separate purposes. The scientific account tells how things happened according to its working models of molecules and light-years, and according to its ethic of survival. These are not unchangeable absolutes. They are only tools that we discard when better ones are made. Science describes and then abstracts in order to put to use what we experience according to what we value. Science does not deal with deep reality. It is our invention, and today's science is tomorrow's superstition. Evolution is the best theory we have about the development of life but not the last.

The biblical account of creation tells a story with dramatic action and passion. It must never be taken as scientific record. The language of poetry is not literal but analogical. It is closer to truth than the literalness of science because it relates not *what* happened, but *who* made it happen. It says something about the mystery of why it happened and about the cost of its happening. God made it happen so that he might have someone like himself to love, and so that we might freely enter into his glory.

God spoke. He sang the worlds into being. Sterile loneliness lifted into tragic communion. God suffered himself to be heard. Ancient ages ache for answer because the creature's babble has stilled God's word. The celebration of creation is without constraint, but throughout there is subtle, profound recognition of the devastation done by the demonic, the shameful awareness of the pain that comes from defiance. But into this condition of rebellion and victimization comes renewal. The God who suffered to create suffers more deeply to redeem. In the midst of ambiguity there is the mystifying certainty and the holy arrogance of grace. This is the tale that is told.

A final word should be said about the character that comes into being from God's creative imagination. Adam is made in the image of God. The image that is the product of God's imagination cannot really be like God and merely be a mirror image or an echo of God's voice. Because God is a unique, intelligent, and free person we who are in his image are also unique, intelligent, and free persons.

It is paradox indeed to say that we are unique because God is unique. God is one in that there are no other gods like him. We have our personal identity because each of us as his creature is different from every other creature, and also different from God. Our distinctive character of uniqueness in the image of God the Father gives us a creative capacity. We cannot create from nothing, but, given the props and characters on our stage, we can arrange the setting in original patterns of infinite variety with creative advance. The possibility of creative configuration of inorganic and organic creatures gives rise to the orders of the arts, the sciences, the economy, the state, the family, and religions.

Our intelligence is in the image of God who speaks his Word and begets the Son. In speaking out, there is purposive, meaningful communication. We speak to one another and to God because he speaks to the Son and to us. Communication is response-ability and it brings responsibility. As creatures spoken to, we are given the responsible care of the earth. This is not an imperial domination but a communicating service in which all things are brought into accountability. As earthlings from the dust of the earth we find ourselves in a familial relationship with sun and moon, mountains and lakes, fish and fowl, and all the creatures in this garden of our exile, spoiled as it is by the spell of our sin yet beautiful beyond our wildest imagination. We are one with animals and plants, rocks and water, but because of our unique intelligence we may and must speak to them with loving care.

As the Spirit is free and blows like the wind where and when it wills, so we are free spirits who can use our uniqueness and intelligence as we choose, even to the extent of denying them. If we act like clones and clods, it is not because we are so but because we choose to be so. Because we are in the image of the Spirit, we are persons hidden and revealed, full of surprise, mystery, humor, pathos, power, gentleness, and decision. As unique persons of health and holiness we couple the disciplined logic of our intelligence with the spontaneous creativity of our spirits, but when we separate understanding from imagination we shatter our personalities and play a tragic role.

We are one with all God's creatures in our creatureliness but alone among God's creatures in our uniqueness, intelligence, and freedom. If we speak of an infinite diversity in nature, a cunning in animals, an indeterminacy in quantum mechanics, and identify these qualities with human nature, we are equivocating. Ironically it is our bondage to sin that tells us of our special relationship to God as creatures in his image. Only human beings are guilty of sin, because only human beings seek to be other than what they are. In this quest through failure it becomes manifest to us under the judgment of God's law that we have lost our original goodness and potentiality to be maturing children of God. When we believed the serpent's lie we tried to be as God, and we set ourselves apart from him. We lost the clothing of his glory and found ourselves naked. When we see ourselves as sinners we get a glimpse again of the image God imagines us to be.

The comic return and redemption from this bondage to sin is the subject of the next chapter.

NOTES

1. Cf. Zachary Hayes, O.F.M., *What Are They Saying About Creation?* (New York: Paulist Press, 1980).

2. It is interesting to note that Charles Darwin had an optimistic view of the triumph of virtue as a result of natural selection. He said in *The Descent of Man* (Norwalk, Conn.: Easton Press, 1979): "Looking to future generations, there is no cause to fear that social instincts will grow weaker, and we may expect that virtuous habits will grow stronger, becoming perhaps fixed by inheritance. In this case the struggle between our higher and lower impulses will be less severe, and virtue will be triumphant" (p. 108). Even belief in God enters into his purview of evolutionary

natural selection: "With the more civilized races the conviction of the existence of an all-seeing Deity has had a potent influence on the advance of morality" (p. 320).

3. Cf. Stephen Pepper, *World Hypotheses* (Berkeley and Los Angeles: University of California Press, 1962), 222ff.

4. Cf. Max Black, *Models and Metaphors: Studies in Language and Philosophy* (Ithaca and London: Cornell University Press, 1962), 222ff.

5. Cf. Victor Guillemin, *The Story of Quantum Mechanics* (New York: Charles Scribner's Sons, 1968).

6. Cf. George N. Hatsopoulos and Joseph H. Keenan, *Principles of General Thermodynamics* (John Wiley and Sons, 1965).

7. *Ha adam,* the earth creature, is not sexed in the beginning of the story. Only after God, as anesthetist and surgeon, takes a rib from the earth creature and makes woman does the earth creature emerge as male. And the Hebrew words now used are *ish* for male and *ishah* for woman. Cf. Phyllis Trible, *God and the Rhetoric of Sexuality* (Philadelphia: Fortress Press, 1978), 98.

8. For this, see Alexander Eliot, *Myths* (New York: McGraw-Hill Book Co., 1976).

9. Cf. Karl Pearson, *The Grammar of Science* (London: J. M. Dent, 1937).

6

Reality and the Tragicomic Metaphors of Redemption

—the cosmic *eucatastrophe*

In the human search for abiding reality, besides the yearning for recovery of the past and its consequent journey back to the fantasy of origins, there is also in the human breast a hope for a turn in the future that will bring redemption. We will need to look at tragedy first and then at comedy before we dig deeper into the tragicomedy literature of redemption, but we should always remember that throughout there is an ambiguity of the comic in the tragic and the tragic in the comic—even in the extreme forms of satire on the one side and burlesque on the other.

Before following this outline we must clarify the distinction between the fantasy metaphors of creation and the historical metaphors of redemption. Fantasy stories are not historical. They have geography and history, they have place and time, but their places and times cannot be located or dated. They speak of fantastic realms that may be called illusory from the standpoint of empirical history, but they are not a delusion, and far from being unreal the presumption is that their primordial reality is as yet unspoiled by a fall or a spell. These stories are of such nature that no amount of archaeological research will uncover their mystery and give them historical verification.

Some redemption stories, and all Christian redemption stories, on the other hand, although they also have a nonempirical dimension apprehensible only to faith, are rooted in some evidence of locus and occasion. There may have been many floods or there may have been only one, but the stories of the flood all tell about deliverance from a disaster that took place somewhere, sometime. The historical dimension of the disaster and the deliverance is coupled with an appreciation of the ambiguity that both the disaster and the deliverance are sent by God. Redemption stories, no less than creation stories, with all their ties to history are nonetheless controlled by the fragile presence of the transcendent.

An understanding of the nature of time is required. Not all redemption stories told around the world have a historical dimension. The mystery stories of the Magna Mater or of Isis and Serapis tell of the yearning for recovery of life over death, and they celebrate the experience of this victory in the cycle of nature. There is a cyclical progression which nullifies time through the wheel of the eternal return, and since everything repeats itself, there is nothing new under the sun. There is therefore no real future, no novelty, no surprise, and no tragedy since nothing can be otherwise than it is. Time in such a view is unreal, and reality can be found only in a mystic escape from its broken succession. The story nature of reality is supported nevertheless even by these mystery cult myths, because within the myths time is real and the plots move through a climax to a denouement. It should be understood that the story nature of reality presupposes that time is real, that a timeless eternity is not a real fantasy but is a delusion.

One reason for the appropriation of the Father metaphor in the Judeo-Christian revelation, rather than feminine imagery, is the aggressive surprise of time as against the repetition of nature. Creation does not arise out of a matrix; redemption does not naturally emerge from a womb. Grace is given and the creature is receptive to the action of the giver. The amazing thing about grace is that it comes from above, not from within, and that it therefore brings freedom from fate.[1]

The time that we now know, however, while not an illusion, is broken and therefore must be distinguished from the time of God and the time of the creation stories. The time we experience is a shattered succession of occasions or periods or eras, and between the events are gaps, so that as we pass from one moment to another we lose the past moment except through the dim recovery of memory and the residual objects that remain in space. In contrast to our experience of time, God's time is cumulative and nothing is lost.

What is said about time applies also to space because in our fallen world space is twisted even as time is broken. Redemption stories all tell of our yearning for release from this brokenness and contortion. Some people think we can achieve this by escape from time and space, but, with its tie to the historical, Judeo-Christian revelation tells us that reality is temporal and spatial. It is the fragmentation of time and the twistedness of space that are corrected in redemption, not the succession of events or the extension of space. Succession and extension are real and good and do not need redemption. Redemption then means resurrection of the past with a thrust into an ever-growing, free, novel, surpriseful future. Resurrection is not simple recovery or resuscitation, however; it involves purgation and new creation.

Tragedy tells of the pain of dislocation and the anguish of lost time. It tells of separation, death, and the rending of relationships, so that people can no longer speak to each other and express their love. But the truly tragic vision sees reality to be a movement of free relationships which are destroyed by the hero pushing himself to his extremities and getting inexorably caught in his own trap. In his demise we are purged of the evil and we learn knowledge of the good. The interplay of fate and freedom, the ambiguity of good and evil, thus deepen the sense of the tragic. In some ways tragedy is to comedy in storytelling what law is to gospel in the formulation of doctrine. Tragedy brings us low so that we can be purged of our defiant rebelliousness and cleansed.

Tragedy developed out of the ritual celebration of the festivals of Dionysus.[2] The word comes from the Greek *tragōidia,* or goat-song, and probably derives from the ritual chanting over the sacrifice of the sacred goat in the worship of Dionysus. There was an interesting parallel in the historical development of tragedy in Christendom out of the celebration of festivals in the church year. The mystery plays and morality plays then gave rise to Marlowe and Shakespeare much as the Dionysian tragedies gave rise to Aeschylus, Sophocles, and Euripides. The parallel extends to the deeper sense of ambiguity expressed by the later writers of both cultures. Aeschylus said that suffering need not be embittering but can be a source of knowledge. Marlowe's Faustus is caught by his yearning for power over space and time, yet being a Christian, that is, a liberated modern man, he must take the risk of losing his soul. He *might* have avoided his fate but he *could* not avoid it. Fate is inexorable but only after inner inadequacies have pushed the tragic hero to his extremities. I think extremity is a better translation for *hybris* than pride, because it is the overweening and defiant obtuseness, the arrogant insolence, of the hero that brings him down, as, for example, King Lear's temper and Macbeth's ambition, or Oedipus's stubborn pursuit of truth about himself. Inner evils combine with external pressures and follow their course to inevitable doom, *moira* or fate. Lear's temper mixed with his daughter's thanklessness produces madness; Macbeth's ambition plus Lady Macbeth's importunity produces murder. Like Prometheus, Oedipus, and Medea, Shakespeare's tragic heroes are at the extremities of their natures. Hamlet and Macbeth are at the edge of their sanity and Lear is thrust beyond; Othello too, only momentarily. The stories of Jephthah and Samson also exhibit the tragedy of lapsed sanity born of *hybris.*

Tragedies begin with free options, but they move to a binding trap; thus they reflect the movement from the tree in the Garden of Eden to the tree near the Garden of Gethsemane. Tragic stories are always told against a backdrop of freedom, justice, and rationality. The events of the story might always have been otherwise, but they cannot be otherwise because of the defiance in the extreme of our characters. But through the tragedy, knowledge of the good is found and the evil is purged. The hero may die, but in his tragedy he has given us life.

The characteristics of the tragic vision are paradoxical. There is a mixture of good and evil which avoids both the sentimental and the cynical. There are terrifying divisions in nature which reflect and coincide with division in our humanity. Tragic stories tell of love that both creates and destroys. Their characters are at once pitiable and fierce. Destructive actions are willed, yet they are also seemingly destined. We feel the force of providence as well as predestination in their lives, yet predestination does not mean predeterminism. As in the biblical revelation, the predestination of tragic characters is a calling to a task which may be freely done or refused, but the inner defiance in the hero's character fatefully controls his destiny. Yet the sequence of events is also controlled by an imagination that learns as it goes and so there is a purgation of evil in the telling of the tale. Saul the chosen king freely chooses a course that inevitably brings madness.

Examples to illustrate these characteristics may be found readily in the new form of the novel developed by writers such as Emily Brontë, Joseph Conrad, Fyodor Dostoevsky, and Herman Melville. Dostoevsky's heroes—Raskolnikov and the three brothers Karamazov: Ivan, Dmitri, and Alyosha—plunge into the "heart of darkness," but each wrings out a kind of victory too, albeit morally qualified and partial. Melville's Captain Ahab is an Oedipus, Job, and Lear all rolled into one.

The inexorable doom into which these tragic heroes plunge must not be thought to be a violation of freedom. In the course of their story they change from rebels to victims, and thus we both judge them and pity them, but always the action occurs in the arena of free and responsible choice. As Shakespeare's Cassius says, "The fault, dear Brutus, is not in our stars, but in ourselves." This means that throughout the portrayal of the tragedy there is the declaration of the human capacity to learn. The tragic end of the hero is not the end. In his Nobel address William Faulkner said, "I decline to accept the end of man." The subject of art, he said, is the human heart in conflict with itself. Guilt is the evidence of our fate, but the possibility of expiation is the assertion of our freedom.

A coherent and affirmative view of humanity, society, and the cosmos is vital to tragedy. But unresolved questions remain at the end of every tragedy. There is always an irrational factor that exists alongside the coherency, a mystery that is disturbing and foreboding, and not to be resolved by the sufficient reasons of philosophy, the dogmas of religion, or the successes of science. And this is because the nature of reality includes an ultimate mystery that cannot be solved. But if it is not resisted and if it is celebrated instead, it becomes a source of joy and elevation. To be sure, there is an irretrievable loss in tragedy, usually the death of the hero, but through the loss comes purgation, redemption, and hope for renewal. Always there is struggle between real freedom and real fate. The fate may be manifest in the will of the gods or in chance or in the power of the past or in psychological, personal forces or in sociological, racial forces or in institutions of society; but always these pressures play themselves out against the backdrop of freedom in a concrete world of place and time.

In contrast to all that has been said about Western drama, Oriental drama to a degree lacks the tragic sense because it lacks a sense of the reality of place and time.[3] It is Platonic, not Homeric. Its tone is set by the Hindu and Buddhist denial of reality to the world and assertion of reality to thought. An example is the Japanese Noh drama *The Hoka Priests* by Zenchiku Ujinobu. This is the Oresteian theme of Hamlet, a son who is called to avenge the death of his father. He is indecisive, and so he gets the help of his brother, who is a priest. He disguises himself as a priest and the two of them go to the murderer and pretend to talk to him about religion, about Buddhist mysticism. Finally they cry out, "Enough, why hide our plot?" Then, instead of carrying out the plot and killing the murderer, the murderer ceremoniously departs from the stage leaving his hat behind, and the two priests ritualistically kill the hat. Thus Noh plays do not involve the audience in the direct action of the play, much as the later Platonic criticism took violent action off the stage and thereby made it "obscene." On-stage action only hints at a spiritual struggle in the heart of the hero, and resolution of the struggle is always portrayed didactically in favor of traditional teaching. The same simplistic propagandizing may be found in Chinese Maoist ideological drama. The tragic vision is lost because the ambiguity of reality with its ultimate transcendent mystery coupled with the concrete immediacy of places and times is missing.[4]

We have seen that there are two world views that militate against the thesis that story is the nature of reality, the world views of scientism and mysticism. Nietzsche understood well the danger that science poses when its method is blown up into a world view. He insisted that we have art so that we may not perish through truth. Only when science, and by science he meant Socrates' panacea of knowledge, has run out its course can there be a rebirth of tragedy.[5]

Camus saw clearly the rebellion against this world that ends in mysticism.[6] He said only two possible worlds can exist for the human mind, the sacred (or, to speak in Christian terms, the world of grace) and the world of rebellion. The disappearance of one is equivalent to the appearance of the other. And today we live in an unsacrosanct moment in history. Therefore rebellion is one of the essential dimensions of humanity. It is our historic reality. Camus was aware of the bankruptcy of scientific technology pretending to be the touchstone of reality. He was aware also that the contemporary loss of the Christian sense of the sacred has set the stage for a new religiosity which he would have deplored. The irony of recent history since Camus is that he has been proven right in the current rebellion against the unsacrosanct, but it has been a rebellion of new radicalism in religion, the fatuous grasping after the gaseous in the charismatics, the faith healers, the exorcists, and the devotees of the occult. The rebellion has manifested itself also in a recrudescent gnosticism that seeks escape from time and history because of weariness in this world but yet finds no joy in any other world.

As Herman Melville says in Moby Dick, "Though in many of its aspects this visible world seems formed in love, the invisible spheres were formed in fright."[7] We can see it in the painters from the legalistic gnosticism of Piet Mondrian, who abstracts with geometrical precision to show his distaste for the ambiguities of nature, to the antinomian gnosticism of Wassily Kandinsky, whose chaotic swishes and swirls express a similar rebellion against the reality of space and time. It is true that when we look to the center of our culture we find it broken, and instead of a solid core we find an abyss beneath a gossamer deceit of empirical and historical reality.

When things get bad enough, and when our loss of the tragic vision plunges us into depths of pessimistic despair, there comes a time of redemptive reversal in which we look about ourselves and begin to laugh through our tears. The comic return as a dimension of reality can be more profound than the tragic turn.[8]

The parable of Valentin the clown, which I told in the Prologue, is appropriate for our time because in our current mood we search only in the light where it is easy to see. Today science, industry, and the military are a powerful triumvirate. They bring us riches and comfort and power, but they look only where it is easy, where the light is bright, where we can measure facts and count profits. They have not brought us peace and freedom from fear. For these we must look in the dark, where we must be more agile and precise and humble and wise than the scientist ever dreamed, because in the dark are hidden mysteries, powers that we cannot control but that control us. And there we must be wary too lest we fall into the hands of the evil one rather than the hidden mystery of God.[9]

Here the comic is seen to be the incongruity that releases us from the delusion of too serious attachment to ourselves. Søren Kierkegaard said salvation is laughter, seriousness is sin. He tells about the sin of extraversion, the sensate attachment to the superficialities of the moment, release from which is possible through humor. Forgiveness comes through laughing at oneself. A peasant had lived all his life in the country and he longed to see the sights of the big city. He saved his money and bought himself a pair of patent leather shoes and silk stockings. He went to Copenhagen, where he wandered wide-eyed like a bull before a new barn door. He was a simple bumpkin, a country clod. At the end of the day he went to a pub and spent the rest of his money drinking strong beer. He stumbled out of the pub and fell in a drunken stupor on the cobblestone street with his head in the gutter. Along came a carriage and the driver shouted, "Hey there, you drunken peasant, get your legs out of the road or I will drive over them." The peasant rose from the gutter and looked at his legs, but he did not recognize the shiny shoes and silk stockings, so he said, "Drive on, they are not my legs." So the driver drove on and cut off the peasant's legs.[10]

Henri Bergson wrote of the corrective purpose of laughter. He said laughter brings the comic character back into conformity with society when he slackens in the attention due to society. Its purpose is to hold up a mirror to society to reflect its follies and vices in the hope of bringing about amendment.[11] While this may sound moralistic, it must be granted that there is therapy in laughter. Aristotle said tragedy is the catharsis that comes through the sense of pity and fear which makes it possible for us to become effective in a rational world. It has been said that Aristotle might have defined comedy as the catharsis that comes through the sense of the ridiculous so that again we can become effective in a rational world. Aristotle said tragedy deals with persons of high estate. The tragic hero is larger than life, better than the average person. Comedy, he says, deals with lowly types; comic heroes are worse than the average person. Moreover, tragedy deals with matters of public import, while comedy deals with private affairs of mundane life. Tragic figures are historical and true; comic characters are feigned. Styles differ too, with tragedies being heavy and comedies being light. Tragedies end in defeat or death, while comedies end in happiness and victory. And when tragedy and comedy are mixed in style the result is a burlesque in which a ponderous tragic manner is applied to something trivial or a serious subject is given vulgar treatment.

These observations by Bergson and Aristotle seem true enough, but they miss the center of the target and leave unsaid much that must be said. Nathan Scott says tragic man is not better and comic man worse than the average man, as Aristotle would have it, but tragic man is an extremist who brings himself and others down by his *hybris*, trying to be an angel when he is only a man; and comic man is "an example of the contingent, imperfect, earth-bound creatures that in truth we all really are, and it is also his function to awaken in us a lively recognition of what in fact our true status is."[12] He is saying that comedy does not merely show the ludicrous; it tells the whole truth about human beings in society. Comedy evokes more than laughter; it lifts us to our dreams and its poignancy gives rest to our hearts. Kierkegaard said, "Wherever there is life there is contradiction, and wherever there is contradiction the comical is present."[13] The tragic and the comic are both based on contradiction, but tragic contradiction is suffering contradiction and comic contradiction is painless because there is a way out. It is this way out that makes comedy the vehicle for redemption. William Hazlitt said, "Man is the only animal that laughs and weeps; for he is the only animal that is struck with the difference between what things are, and what they ought to be."

Perhaps we may venture to say that tragedy is the picture of an insane person in a sane world and comedy is the picture of a sane person in an insane world. Tragedy shows the judgment on *hybris* for an individual—and the havoc he or she wreaks on others who are innocent. Comedy shows redemption which comes to humility and faith and acceptance—and the salvation it brings to others who are guilty. But these definitions cannot be ascribed universally. Ahab surely was insane, but was Billy Budd? And Charlie Chaplin in *City Lights* gives redemptive grace to insane technocracy, but Tartuffe is hardly a model of sanity. Yet the definitions may apply to the stories, if not directly to the heroes.

It should be clear that we can no more separate tragedy from comedy than we can separate law from gospel, judgment from mercy, in the story of reality. This mixture has always been found in the great character portrayals, as, for example, in the tragic aspects of Shakespeare's Falstaff and the redeeming qualities of Shylock; but it is particularly evident in the medieval mystery plays of England and in the tragicomedy of the twentieth century.

In the Pinners and Painters Play of York the guilds' actors amuse the audience with horseplay beneath the cross in spite of the grim seriousness of the action. And there is justification for this from the brief accounts of the Gospels in the mocking of the mob and the dicing of the soldiers. Also Herod, the slayer of innocents, is the prize clown of the show, and Satan and his devils contribute to the fun when sinners are thrown into hell. The play has the tragicomic effect of the paintings of Hieronymus Bosch with his depiction of monstrous cloacal absurdities in the final judgment. Also the Chester portrayal of the flood gives Mrs. Noah a shrewish character and finally she has to be led into the ark by her nose. The Second Shepherd's Play from Wakefield parodies the birth of Jesus most profoundly with the jolly coarseness of Mak, the *extra* shepherd who turns out to be a sheep thief, and with the raucous groaning of Gyll, who hides the stolen sheep in the cradle where she is supposed to lay her baby which she never had. After Mak's crime is discovered and he is tossed in a blanket, an angel sings the Gloria in Excelsis. These instances, says J. L. Styan, indicate that it is natural and human for an unfettered audience to feel jokes about what is revered.[14] The humor of heaven is reflected here with its power to redeem us from seriousness.

In modern times tragicomedy may have begun with Henrik Ibsen's *The Wild Duck,* a bitter play about a young man blissfully ignorant of his own and his family's lies until an outsider, committed to an ideal of absolute truth, exposes them. Or we may cite *The Cherry Orchard* by Anton Chekhov, or *The Dance of Death* by August Strindberg, subtle pictures of humorous situations that are ridiculously painful. Sharper focus comes with contemporary writers like Samuel Beckett, Eugène Ionesco, Harold Pinter and Edward Albee. The rollicking hilarity in Albee's *Who's Afraid of Virginia Woolf* is wonderfully matched by the searing tragedy of a relationship shattered by lies and rubbed raw by the cruel games people play with each other. The logic of mere comedy is that illusions exist to be dispelled, and once dispelled, everyone is supposed to be better off; but the logic of tragicomedy is that illusions make life bearable, and to destroy them is to destroy our basis for happiness.

The humor in much of modern tragicomedy, however, is sharp as the sword of the law, and its function is more a schoolmaster leading to Christ than the redemptive love of Christ himself. The laughter of *redemptive* tragicomedy, on the other hand, has in it the paradox of love which is both an active passion and a passionate action. Every child knows this paradox. Look at the clown. Clowns are close to children, they speak the language of children without words. They have a grin like a crescent moon; it stretches from ear to ear and they are all joy. But they always have large tears dropping from their cheeks. Their hearts are full of pain, as every child knows. I spoke of Cyrano, who had a nose that stuck out on his face like a Bartlett pear, but Cyrano had the soul of a poet, the heart of a lover, and his spirit had the beauty of holiness. He loved, and you can imagine how he suffered. He was both hilariously funny and pathetically sad.

To be a fool for Christ is to rejoice in our suffering. The First Letter of Peter speaks of the many blessings of suffering for Christ and then concludes by saying, "Dear friends, do not be surprised at the painful trial you are suffering, as though something strange were happening to you. But rejoice that you participate in the sufferings of Christ, so that you may be overjoyed when his glory is revealed" (1 Peter 4:12–13). Those of us who live by the Christian story bear our pain because we know that our ultimate concern is Christ, who will release us in the end. But often when we become concerned, ultimately concerned, we forget joy, we lose laughter, our chins drop to our knees, and we mope as if God were dead. A story is told about Katherine, the wife of Martin Luther. One day she dressed all in black, with a black veil over her head and face. Luther said to her, "What is the matter? Why are you dressed in black?" "I am in mourning," she said. "Mourning?" said Luther. "Who is dead?" "God is dead," said Katherine. "God is dead! What do you mean?" "Well," said Katherine, "you have been so gloomy for the past week, nothing will make you laugh. If it is as bad as that, God himself must be dead." This did make Luther laugh and he remembered that Paul had said, "Rejoice in the Lord always, and again I say, Rejoice."

Of course there are many kinds of laughter. There is the silly laughter of the fool, the boisterous laughter of carelessness, there is ribald laughter over dirty jokes, there is the hollow laughter of cynicism and cruel laughter at the expense of another, and there is the hysterical laughter of fear. The laughter of derision has the ring of judgment in it, but redemptive laughter has the heavenly mirth of angels who sing and laugh with joy over a single sinner that has been saved. The Christian life of love, filled with the holy humor of God, is a quiet joy that makes us smile in our sorrow and sing in our sadness.[15]

Redemptive laughter is not without earthiness, however, as for example when Lot's daughters got him drunk or when Abraham bargained with God like a hawker in a bazaar for the salvation of Sodom and Gomorrah.

Will you spare the city for fifty good souls? Then he began to count on his fingers and said: For forty? For ten? Or the story of Jonah, the runaway prophet who sulked over his own success.

An interesting paradoxical twist in the redemptive story may be seen when the stories of Sodom and Jonah are placed alongside the story of Paul's shipwreck off the island of Malta. The pagan story seeks resolution by casting out evil to save the good. Jonah's ship is in distress and his shipmates, with typical pagan outlook, cast him overboard because he has done wrong. In the story of Sodom, however, there is the intimation that the good people may be the occasion for the salvation of the guilty. And on Paul's ship the one who was elected to bring goodness to the Gentiles did indeed become the reason why the rest were spared. Because one is evil in the pagan story all are condemned, but because one is good in the Christian story all shall be saved. In the cosmic sense this is the tragicomic metaphor of the great *eucatastrophe* in which Christ, the Elect One, died for the world so that none should perish but all who believe will have everlasting life. For the sake of this one good man, the Lamb of God, the whole world is raised again.

Not only is there a twist and a significant change from the pagan story to the Judeo-Christian story but also there is a significant shift of revelation from the Old Testament to the New. The flood stories tell of the salvation of some so that everyone and everything is not lost. In the biblical version of the flood story God repents of this method of salvation and henceforth the story of Israel is the tale of God's faithfulness to preserve his people. "You prepare a table before me in the presence of my enemies." Not only does God desire Israel's endurance but he wants Israel to be a light to the Gentiles so that they too can endure. The story of the flood says that some are saved so that all is not lost; but the story of Israel is that some have been saved in order to preserve the rest. God has promised to preserve Abraham's seed to be a blessing to the nations. Jacob may wrestle with God and be oppressed by his enemies, but he will endure in the face of all adversity if the covenant is kept, because God's word is sure. Salvation therefore comes in spite of suffering. Job says, "Though he slay me, yet will I hope in him; I will surely defend my ways to his face" (Job 13:15).

In the New Testament the story shifts to a tale of redemption, not in spite of suffering but through suffering. Because he slays me, I have been saved, I am being saved, and I will be saved. In the New Testament story the Elect One does not endure. He dies.

This radical turn in the story is such a shock that it is both an obscene scandal and a holy hilarity. The incongruity that God should become man, that the Holy One should become a sinner and then die as a blasphemer, is matched only by the supreme mystery of the resurrection and the promise of the messianic banquet.

The story model for reality means that creation is a growing complexity which, unlike a machine, is free, mysterious, surprising, meaningful. Machines can have purpose but not personality, and the purpose they have is only what is given them by their makers and users. The story model means that creation is God's story. God is the author. He is not the story, but he is in the story with all he creates. What he creates has the meaning and purpose he gives it, but, again unlike the analogy of the machine, the creatures have the freedom to develop their own personalities.

A story-shaped creation makes possible free interaction between creator and creature. God can encounter his creatures without violating his own image in them. The Bible speaks of such encounters in the stories of the flood, the covenant with Abraham, the exodus from Egypt, the giving of the law, the establishment of the Kingdom of Israel, the prophetic warning and hope at the time of the exile, and finally the atoning work of Jesus Christ with all the signs and wonders that accompany these events. This is difficult because God never encounters his creatures directly. The "acts of God" can be perceived only by faith, not by sight. No one has seen God at any time. He is no respecter of persons. He does not intervene in such a way as to show favoritism. Indeed the nature of God's intervention, both for providential and for redemptive purposes, is extremely problematic. As we have seen, in our scientific era the natural course of events cannot be perceived as being interrupted. Furthermore, we do not wish to fall into hallucinations prompted by pious imagination. Nevertheless we need not deny the reality of maieutic activity on the part of a divine or transcendent being whose encounter with his creatures, albeit unseen, results in actual changes on the stage of history.

A story view of reality makes possible the recognition of God's special redemptive acts, without arbitrariness and obscurantism, because no reported activity can be allowed to violate the integrity of the story. Miracles as signs *(sēmeia)* or as wonders *(thaumata)* may or may not be taken literally, but in faith we see some incidents as pointers to a grand and concluding purpose. A story reality thus makes possible apocalyptic imagery for the eschaton. Stories come to an end. Machines rust or blow up or are smashed, but stories end with a denouement after a climax when the last word is said. The story ends when the author reveals all he or she had in mind from the beginning. This resolves all the problems and conflicts latent in the plots and subplots. The "miracles" are the glimmerings, intimations, and adumbrations which break through from time to time and reveal the otherwise hidden mystery. Thus the end influences every part of the story leading up to it.

And finally, if "all the world's a stage, and all the men and women merely players," then a redemptive climax will occur in the story of reality. There will be a sudden turn in which change comes to all the characters, even, and perhaps especially, to God. And if the Bible is read as a story, it will not be divided into two testaments, as if to separate a Jewish book from a

Christian book, but the coming of Jesus will be seen as the climax that fulfills all that went before.

It might help to read the Bible the way we read a play. Let us take, for example, Shakespeare's *The Tempest*. Literary critics have debated for centuries whether this play is Shakespeare's farewell to the theater or more profoundly a symbol of the struggle between nature and art.[16] To me *The Tempest* is a story taken from the story reality of the storm of rebellion that is conquered not by vengeful force or magic might but by redemptive forgiveness. Prospero is, of course, the rightful Duke of Milan in the play, but metaphorically he acts like God. He commands the wind and the waves. He controls the lives of all who enter his realm. His early utterances sound like the imprecatory psalms or the scathing, unrelenting judgment of Amos: "For three sins of Israel, even for four, I will not turn back my wrath" (Amos 2:6). He appears at first to be crassly manipulative, but suddenly in the last act he changes, giving freedom to Caliban and Ariel, and forgiveness to Antonio, Alonso, and Sebastian, and blessing to Miranda and Ferdinand. And it seems that the change comes by the prompting of Ariel. The shipwrecked lords of Italy have become imprisoned by Prospero's spell and their own guilt. In remorse they are now ready for repentance. Ariel describes their sorry condition and suggests to Prospero that his feeling for them would become tender if he beheld their wretchedness. Prospero says, "Dost thou think so, spirit?" And Ariel responds, "Mine would, sir, were I human" (Act 5, sc. 1).

This is the climax. Prospero chooses this moment to break his wand, to set free his captives, to forgive his enemies, to liberate Caliban and Ariel. No more will he use magic, miracle, and might to manipulate others. No more will he meddle because "the rarer action is in virtue than in vengeance" (Act 5, sc. 1). Certainly this is the climax, because all the characters are changed radically at this point, even and especially Prospero. It is not clear whether he completely reverses himself or just appears to do so. There are indications from the beginning that he will free Ariel and that his vengeance might be more disciplinary than punitive. But Prospero too is liberated at this moment. His kingdom is restored to him, but more profoundly he concludes this drama by entering into a new liberty for himself and all the others which paradoxically brings a new bondage. By giving freedom and abjuring manipulation, he is now dependent upon the thankful response of love. And so at the end of the play, when all have gone off to their newly given freedom, Prospero turns to the audience and says:

> Now my charms are all o'erthrown,
> And what strength I have's mine own,
> Which is most faint. Now 'tis true
> I must be here confined by you,
> Or sent to Naples. Let me not,
> Since I have my dukedom got

> And pardoned the deceiver, dwell
> In this bare island by your spell;
> But release me from my bands
> With the help of your good hands.
> Gentle breath of yours my sails
> Must fill, or else my project fails,
> Which was to please. Now I want
> Spirits to enforce, art to enchant;
> And my ending is despair
> Unless I be relieved by prayer,
> Which pierces so that it assaults
> Mercy itself and frees all faults.
> As you from crimes would pardoned be,
> Let your indulgence set me free.
> (Act 5, sc. 1)

By entering into our humanity, by taking upon himself our humanness, God knows what it means to be human, and his "affections ... become tender." Instead of visiting his wrath upon us, he delivers us up to our own sin. Instead of intervening with miracles, he lets the world come of age, in Bonhoeffer's phrase. But this grace is costly, costly for all but especially for God. There is no forgiveness without the thankful response of *worship*. God's grand design to free us will not work unless the heavens ring with the doxology of prayer.

There is multiple meaning here. On one level the actor is asking for the applause of the audience. On another level the playwright pleads for acclaim for his craft as he bids farewell. And above all, God calls for praise from his creatures in their prayers.[17]

NOTES

1. Cf. Robert Hammerton-Kelly, *God the Father* (Philadelphia: Fortress Press, 1979).

2. Cf. H. D. F. Kitto, *Greek Tragedy: A Literary Study* (New York: Doubleday & Co., 1955). It is believed that the origin of the drama in China similarly arose from the exorcism of evil spirits. Three times a year officials dressed in bearskins, and armed with spear and shield went from house to house for ritual cleansing. They were followed by an excited populace, and the result was a progressive drama with characters and audience. Cf. Herbert A. Giles, *A History of Chinese Literature* (London: Heinemann, 1901), 257.

3. Daiji Maruoka and Tatsuo Yoshikoshi, *Noh*, trans. Don Kenny (Osaka, Japan: Hoikusha Publishing Co., 1974).

4. This is not to say the Orient is without stories, nor that Oriental stories are lacking in reality. It is to say rather that mystic vision and didactic moralism tend to blunt the paradoxical reality of transcendence and actuality. Chinese opera and Japanese Kabuki, Bunraku, and Noh magnificently reflect reality in all its dimensions in spite of Buddhist transcendentalism.

5. Cf. Friedrich Nietzsche, *The Birth of Tragedy* (New York: Random House, Modern Library, 1967), 268ff.

6. Cf. Albert Camus, *The Rebel* (London: Hamilton, 1953).

7. Herman Melville, *Moby Dick* (Norwalk, Conn.: Easton Press, 1977).

8. Northrop Frye, in his *Anatomy of Criticism* (Princeton: Princeton University Press, 1963), says it is altogether characteristic of anything explicitly Christian that the tragic should be a prelude to comedy (p. 215).

9. Dan O. Via, Jr., shows how parables have two basic plot movements: comic, in which the protagonist moves toward well-being and inclusion in society; and tragic, in which the protagonist falls and is isolated from society. Some parables are comic, some tragic, and some have the form of the gospel itself which moves to victory through tragedy, as in the classic Christian parable of the prodigal son. Cf. Dan O. Via, Jr., *The Parables, Their Literary and Existential Dimension* (Philadelphia: Fortress Press, 1967), 145.

10. Søren Kierkegaard, *Sickness Unto Death* (Princeton: Princeton University Press, 1941), 85.

11. Cf. Henri Bergson, *Le Rire. Essai sur la signification du comique* (Paris, 1910).

12. Nathan Scott, "The Bias of Comedy and the Narrow Escape Into Faith," *The Christian Scholar,* Spring, 1961, 19.

13. Søren Kierkegaard, *Concluding Unscientific Postscript* (Princeton: Princeton Univesity Press, 1951), 459.

14. J. L. Styan, *The Dark Comedy* (Cambridge: Cambridge University Press, 1968), 10–11.

15. Søren Kierkegaard, *Christian Discourses* (London: Oxford University Press, 1939), 101ff. Kierkegaard speaks of "Joyful Notes in the Strife of Suffering."

16. Cf. Robert Langbaum, *The Tempest,* The Signet Classic Shakespeare (New York and Toronto: New American Library, 1964).

17. Ibid., xxxiv: "In spite of its fantastic elements, *The Tempest,* as F. R. Leavis has pointed out, never confuses but rather clarifies our sense of reality." My point is that stories, including the Bible, illustrate reality precisely because reality is story.

7

The Tale of the Dragon and the Lamb

—the meaning of atonement metaphors

Because theology deals with subjects that are free, it must use explanations that are categorically different from the explanations used by the sciences. Theology in the Middle Ages was called the queen of the sciences because she had regal respect. Following the example of our Lord, theology might better be called the servant of the sciences. In any case, theology should not pretend to be a science, nor should it imitate the methods and goals of the sciences. It is true that theology is an intellectually ordered discipline which bears scrutiny and is therefore distinguished from enterprises such as astrology or the occult. In this broad sense the Germans call it *Wissenschaftslehre,* but in America the word "science" is used for descriptive disciplines that use mathematical constructs. Theology deals with non-empirical subjects and therefore needs another kind of explanation. Science cannot deal with either God or freedom, because it chooses to find causes. Probability and indeterminacy in science are only waiting for operations to be devised to eliminate them.[1] Any talk of God and freedom in nature or history will necessitate metaphorical use of language. The literalism that science requires is precisely what theology denies. The language of story provides metaphors that make it possible for us to speak of God and devil.[2] In this chapter we shall look briefly at some of the metaphors the Bible uses to tell the story of Jesus, and then we shall examine the motifs of victory and sacrifice in the tale of the dragon and the lamb.

Paul speaks in 1 Cor. 5:7 of the Lord Jesus as our Passover lamb, sacrificed for us. Here is a metaphor of sacrifice. It is a metaphor because in it Jesus and his cross are compared to the ritual sacrifice that the priest performs in the Feast of Passover. The cross was not literally a ritual sacrifice, but it really did what ritual sacrifice was supposed to do. It was certainly a killing, but the ritual atonement cannot be appreciated except by faith.

Another such metaphor is ritual cleansing. Besides rituals of sacrifice, both pagan and Jewish religious practice included ritual ablutions. Paul speaks of the atonement between human beings and God as a washing away of sin. "But you were washed, you were sanctified, you were justified in the name of the Lord Jesus Christ and by the Spirit of our God" (1 Cor. 6:11).

In Rom. 8:14–15, Paul describes atonement as an adoption of sons: "Those who are led by the Spirit of God are sons of God. For you did not receive a spirit that makes you a slave again to fear, but you received the Spirit of sonship." A metaphor takes something from common experience and relates it to a special experience under question. The thing under question is the atonement between God and his sinful creatures. Adoption is common to all experience. Atonement is like adoption, but again, as in the case of sacrifice and washing, the real fact that is related to the metaphor cannot be apprehended except by the power of the Spirit through faith. Thus in the passage Paul says the Spirit bears witness with our spirit.

In Romans 6, Paul speaks of atonement in terms of raising us from the dead, as dying and rising with Christ. Renewal, rebirth, rising from the death that controls us in this world seem to be aspects of the faith-fact of atonement. It should be evident that other metaphors, such as justification, redemption, and reconciliation, fall into place alongside each other to amplify meaning, without any one taken to be adequate by itself. Justification is a metaphor taken from the law court, redemption comes from the slave market, and reconciliation from the battlefield. Paul is able to jump from one to another with perfect ease. His custom of mixing metaphors and compounding several in a single sentence should eliminate reductionist theories either of juridical objective type or moralistic subjective type.

Two of these metaphors are especially interesting, however, because they provide compelling motifs for the Christian story. These are the motifs of victory and sacrifice. The mysteries of sin, death, law, and wrath involve a conflict between God and his adversaries which is resolved in a triumph through suffering.[3] And the chief of God's adversaries, in true story fashion, must necessarily have nothing less than Draconian dimensions.

Of all the clever wiles in the devil's bag of tricks the cleverest is the deception that he does not exist. By this delusion he snares the sophisticates who by their superior knowledge are the rulers of this world. How is it possible for sophisticated people to be ignorant of the devil? Can it be that they are right and that the devil is only a symbol for the mass of subjective evil? This would be a contradiction indeed were it not for the fact that Christian knowledge is hidden from the wise and revealed to babes. This concerns our knowledge of the devil as much as it does our knowledge of God. Both are unseen spirits, and both are known only indirectly by what they have said and done. Only when we hear and see with the understanding of the Spirit can God or devil have meaning. But what meaning can we ascribe to the devil in a world in which truth must be captured and calculated in a mathematical equation or processed through a mechanical brain?

It is more than interesting that there has been a lively *literary* concern with the devil from the Middle Ages through Marlowe and Goethe to Charles Williams. Of course there are vast differences between Dante's Satan and Goethe's Mephistopheles and Williams's Hell. These differences represent the climate of opinion in various ages in which these stories were written. Dante's devil is a demon of fury and punishment who finds his place in a rigid system of moral retribution. Milton in *Paradise Lost* is primarily concerned with the Christian vision of reality. Bunyan in *The Pilgrim's Progress* seeks for the distinctive life of the Christian.[4] Goethe's theme in *Faust* represents the wishful optimism of the Enlightenment in which the devil exacts his price on the human soul only when one seeks to rest and fails to progress: "Verweile doch, du bist so schön." Williams, however, with greater simplicity and depth in *The House by the Stable* represents the devil as a guest who throws dice with man for his soul and tries to win by cheating; but he is thwarted only at the last moment by the interrupting cry of a woman giving birth to a child, the Child that saves the world. Williams is closer to Scripture than any of his literary predecessors. He does not depict the devil as the ruler of hell, or the goad of progress, but rather as the sly father of lies, the cheat who wants to win the human soul. He is not the lord of the dead but the tyrant of the living. He rules not by his just right to punish but by his usurped power as a tempter.[5]

The fact that the devil motif is of perennial concern in the literature of the Western world indicates that it must be more than a superstitious hallucination. Indeed our call for serious consideration of the story of the devil does not invoke a return to falsifying myths of the demonic. Our reaction against scientific literalism must not result in poetic primitivism. If we reject the oversimplified demythologizing of the devil, we cannot return to a world of the occult with shamans and exorcisms.[6] In modern times Broadway has appropriated the theme in both the light musical comedy *Damn Yankees* and the searching morality play of Archibald MacLeish, *J.B.* Ironically the satire of *Damn Yankees* with its humorous defeat of the devil is more in harmony with the biblical revelation than MacLeish's treatment of the story of Job. MacLeish wrestles with the question: If God is good, he can't be God; if God is God, he can't be good. His play *J.B.* is an attempt to answer the devil's accusation that people worship God only because God is the giver of many gifts. To prove that people will remain loyal without the gifts, God strips J.B. of everything he has but his life. And J.B. answers like Job, "Though he slay me, yet will I hope in him." Thus it is demonstrated that human beings need God for everything and God needs human beings for one thing. God needs human beings to worship him as God.

All of this is simply dramatic foil for a philosophical question that is meaningless because it is falsely put. The biblical drama of Job is not the philosophical question of *J.B.* The Bible is not concerned to reconcile the *concept* of evil with the *concept* of a good God. The Bible declares the action of God as he redeems his creatures through suffering love. The suffering of Job is the faithful participation in this divine sacrifice. This is no poetic presentation of a profound system of thought. It is, rather, the dramatic telling of the story of salvation in the experience of one sinner who was saved through suffering. It is not that God needs human faithfulness to prove to the devil that he is God, but rather that God being good meets evil with suffering love. Peter has the best commentary on Job: "Beloved, do not be surprised at the fiery ordeal which comes upon you to prove you, as though something strange were happening to you. But rejoice insofar as you share Christ's sufferings" (1 Peter 4:12–14).

The literary history of the devil theme, however, demonstrates that reality is not some static truth that can be mythically represented as we might illustrate an abstract law of physics, as we might say that the behavior of gases is like the explosive antics of children when let out of school. Reality is the story itself, the action of the children moving in all directions at once. This is extremely important to recognize inasmuch as the modern world is prone to engage in what is called in sophisticated circles the demythologization of the Bible. The story of the devil is then relegated to an outworn myth which can no longer be used to express what is conceived as the fundamental truth about good and evil. But the contention of faith is that, although the language of the story is necessarily metaphorical and must not be taken with wooden literalness, nevertheless the dramatic action portrayed describes what really happens in a way in which philosophical or theological categories are found not only inadequate but dangerously deceptive. We are not looking for stories to illustrate "truth" as if truth were some kind of idea or moral or message behind the story. Rather, we are looking for true stories that participate in the story of reality. Thus faith declares from the witness of both experience and Scripture that the devil comes as a person and speaks in our hearts and minds in precisely the same way that God does—except that he speaks lies. This speaking is the story of sin and death just as God's speaking is the story of faith and life.

The story of the devil that is told in the Bible, from the serpent in the garden to the great dragon that was thrown down to earth from heaven in John's Revelation, must not be confused with Oriental or Hellenistic myths of the demonic. The stories of Satan in Zoroastrian folklore and of Pluto in Greek mythology think of the devil as ruling in hell as if he were the king of the dead or the eternal opposite of God. The biblical story tells us that Satan is an angelic creature of God who usurped God's power and through deception has become the ruler of this world. He has therefore been cast out of God's heavenly presence and he dwells on the earth, where he reigns in darkness over the souls of human beings who fall into the trap of his lies. Far from being an eternal absolute in a cosmic dualism, the spirit of evil functions sometimes as the direct agent of God, as in the case of the "evil spirit from the Lord" that troubled Saul (1 Sam. 16:14).

The Bible gives the devil many names. He is called *Belial*, the reckless, lawless one, in the Old Testament and in the Qumran literature. Jesus calls him *Satan*, the hateful accuser, and *Beelzebul*, the lord of dung. Other names are *father of lies, prince of the power of the air, ruler of darkness, prince of this world*. Just as God sends his Messiah to save, so the devil sends his antichrist, his son of perdition, his man of lawlessness, to deceive. Besides his simple role as accuser in Job the devil functions as the great tempter and seducer (Matt. 4:10; 16:23; Luke 22:3, 31; 1 Thess. 3:5; Acts 5:3), the provoker of all pain and illness and death (Luke 13:16; 2 Cor. 12:7; Matt. 12:24; Heb. 2:14), the arch deceiver (John 8:44), the ruler of this world (Eph. 2:2; 6:12; Matt. 12:26; Luke 4:5–6; Rev. 20:7), the adversary of God (1 Peter 5:8; Rev. 20:2), and the hinderer who can change himself into an angel of light (1 Thess. 2:18; 2 Cor. 11:14).

Satan was the serpent who tempted Adam and Eve; Satan was the tempter who quoted Scripture as he offered his usurped kingdom to Jesus; Satan was the devil who entered Peter when he was offended at Jesus' teaching that the Son of man must suffer many things; Satan entered the heart of Judas and provoked him to betray Jesus; Satan was the accuser who desired to have Simon. In his deceit the devil is also the provoker of all pain and illness. A woman, whom Jesus healed on a Sabbath, Satan held with a spirit of infirmity for eighteen years. He was a messenger of pain to Paul, buffeting him in the flesh beyond human endurance. He possesses with his demonic spirits the deaf and the dumb and the insane. He visits the earth with hurtful disturbances as he rules the elemental spirits and holds the world in bondage to decay (Gal. 4:3; Rom 8:21). In all these temptations and spiteful visitations Satan speaks lies to lead people away from God. He lied to Eve when he said she could eat the forbidden fruit without dying. He lied to Jesus when he offered Jesus a kingdom that was not his to give. Yet he rules over this world, keeping it under a cloud of darkness far from the light of its Creator. He has enthralled Adam, who was given the dominion of this world, and the result is that everything under Adam and everything after him has come under the sway of Satan. As such he is the adversary of God, the archenemy, who while seeking to destroy human beings was destroyed by a human being in the person of Jesus the Christ.

Seen in all these roles throughout the story of salvation, the devil is the lofty creature who rose in prideful and hateful rebellion against God, usurping the kingdom of this world until he was defeated by the suffering death of God's Messiah. Thus the man of truth came and exposed the man of lies, and henceforth his lies are of no effect. So long as Satan's lies are believed, his power is effective, but once he is exposed by the truth and this truth is accepted in faith, then the strength of sin and the sting of death are removed. Satan's power is never genuine, yet it is not unreal. Once the truth is known, however, only an irredeemably perverse person would accept his lies.

It should be abundantly clear that the reality and effectiveness of the devil in no way discounts the responsibility that human beings have for evil. We are tempted by Satan, not coerced. The devil's existence does not rob us of freedom; he only exercises it, and if we lose it, we have ourselves to blame.

Natural disasters in a story view are not acts of God but the mysterious result of a world out of joint because of the rebellion of creatures both on earth and in heavenly places. The sickness unto death provoked by sin and the adversary has distorted all natural processes, so that in the midst of the good they produce there is tragedy and pain.

Moreover, the existence of the devil is no contradiction of the omnipotence of God. Actually the reverse is true. God's omnipotence is magnified by the fact that he creates beings whom he gives independence. Only omnipotence can give without holding on, can give completely and yet retain power.[7] All finite power is perverse in that when it gives it seeks to gain control over the recipient, but God gives in order to enhance the freedom of the recipient. This is quite different from the rationalist explanation that while God works good, he only permits evil. The gift of freedom also creates the possibility of evil, but this risk is taken with the foreknowledge of the cross. Thus if it appears that God is sending evil, it is only because he is also suffering it. God elected his Son to suffer for our sakes from before the foundation of the world, choosing to make us free even at the great cost of redeeming grace.

Far from outworn myth invented to explain evil, to which liberal and existential philosophy would consign the devil, he is a living, acting, tempting, lying, fearful deceiver whom yet we need not fear, because he has fallen like lightning from heaven (Luke 10:18). In truth we cannot claim that the devil explains evil, for evil remains an unfathomable mystery second only to the higher mystery of God. What we can say about the devil is the experienced fact of his nefarious maliciousness. His virulence is of the deepest personal nature. He operates, as does God himself, on this most profound level in the hiddenness of spirit. No one has seen the devil at any time, and if we are asked what he looks like, we must answer that he does not look like *anything* at all. Yet in all his mystery the devil is as real as birth and death, sin and faith. Certainly we cannot describe his nature in philosophical categories or measure his dimensions with scientific calculations. He can be represented, however, in story as the vicious antagonist of God who seeks to entice us into his treacherous trap.

Likewise the work of God in Christ cannot be explained in intellectual categories, but it can be told in the story of Jesus, for this is the way God chose to do it. Jesus is not just the illustration or symbolic pointer to this hidden work of God; he is the work itself, he is God working to win victory over the evil one through suffering sacrifice and service. He is God taking away his own power to give the greater glory of redemptive passion.[8]

In Jesus the servant figure that is prophesied in the Old Testament is humiliated through sacrifice but exalted in victory over the power of evil. The Son of man passages tell us that Jesus fulfilled a life of suffering service, and the reason for this suffering is best indicated when he says, "The Son of Man did not come to be served, but to serve, and to give his life as a ransom for many" (Mark 10:45). If we continue through the rest of the New Testament tracking down passages that concern the subject of the sacrifice of the Son of man, Christ, or Lord, we will find an amazing number of interesting ones. The key word is the preposition *hyper*. Does this word mean "instead of," "on behalf of," or both? Was Christ sacrificed instead of us or just on our behalf? It involves the atonement—is it vicarious or merely an influence? It involves the meaning of sacrifice—is it a work pleasing to God or is it an expiation psychologically effective for human beings?

Perhaps the key passage which surrounds this key word is Eph. 5:2: "Christ loved us and gave himself up for us as a fragrant offering and sacrifice to God." This verse alludes to the ordination of the sacrifice of the ram in Exod. 29:17–18: "Cut the ram into pieces and wash the inner parts and the legs, putting them with the head and the other pieces. Then burn the entire ram on the altar. It is a burnt offering to the Lord, a pleasing aroma, an offering made to the Lord by fire." Paul is now saying that Jesus, in offering his life's blood on Calvary, is the lamb of sacrifice offered to God, an offering that is pleasing to him.

Here the whole concept of sacrifice is brought into play. Jesus is the lamb which takes away the sin of the world, the paschal lamb, the lamb that was slain that sits on the throne. He is the Son who is well pleasing to the Father, the Son whose sacrifice is offered to God for a sweet-smelling savor. He is the mercy seat of the Holy of Holies, where the blood of sacrifice is sprinkled, the same blood that is sprinkled on the people. This is the sacrifice which now replaces the lamb given to Abraham *instead of* and *on behalf of* his son Isaac.

This concept is difficult for modern people who, in their sophistication, conceive of God in rational terms as an abstract idea of justice and mercy. The idea of God being pleased by a sacrificial fire of burnt animal flesh with its acrid odor is utterly revolting, and to substitute for the animal an innocent man is so horrifying a scandal as to become ludicrous. Even to regard it "only" as a metaphor is an unutterable offense and at best bad taste. How can the death of a man centuries ago be any help to me in my problems? Is there some hidden pyschological value, a religious therapy, in this vicarious offering? To kill an innocent victim—how can this rid me of my guilt? As George Bernard Shaw said, who wants forgiveness? A man will pay his own debts. But at least this modern man in all his shallow cleverness recognized the need to pay the debt, and with it the actuality of the debt of sin! Everyone owes God a death. How shall this be paid?

This is precisely the crux of the atonement problem. Guilt is present and blood must be shed for this guilt. A payment must be made for restitution. Yet my blood cannot be shed without killing me. While restitution may then be made, reconciliation is impossible since I am dead, the victim of my sacrifice. Hence a substitute must be found that is acceptable, some sacrament or token remembrance. But this token remembrance is always unsatisfactory. It must be repeated many times with utmost fastidiousness of performance for fear that it will not satisfy.

This is why the sacrifice of Jesus is so completely satisfying religiously and theologically. It is a perfect gift and it is the gift of a true human being. The author of the Letter to the Hebrews declares that the prerequisites of an acceptable sacrifice are that the gift must be spotless and it must be offered by one from the people of God. The priest must represent the people and the victim must be pleasing. Jesus does both. But the whole nature of sacrifice is changed by Jesus. In his suffering gift we see that our most religious efforts to make amends for our sin are stained with guilt. All killing of consecrated victims, from whole burnt offerings of bullocks in ancient Israel to the self-immolation of the flesh in Protestant piety, is unacceptable sacrifice.

But the acceptable sacrifice of Jesus was not his death. It was his life of obedient service, "obedient unto death, even death on a cross." Death is not a thing to be bargained with. Death has no shape that can be called meritorious or pleasing to God. Certainly death is not offered to appease an angry deity in satisfaction of justice. That story has been told, but it is not the Christian story. Nor is death offered as a sop to Satan, according to the ancient metaphor of the deception of the human flesh on the barb of Christ's deity. God does not deceive even Satan, and Scripture is clear in its teaching that the demons perceived who Jesus was (Matt. 8:29).

Death is, rather, separation from God. As such, sin is the agent of death (death is the wage of sin) because sin separates us from God. Death is a condition into which persons enter. In this sense we cannot speak of a vicarious atonement. We are already in the condition of death, and Christ's entrance into death is no substitute for our death. It is a sharing of our separation from God.

But Christ's work of sacrifice was vicarious in another sense. Christ does not offer his death to God, but he does give his life. The gift of blood is the seal of his life. This he can do inasmuch as he rose from death and lives eternally. Hence he can continually intercede for us, offering his life both on our own behalf and in our stead. Also Christ's work of sacrifice was vicarious in that he defeated Satan both on our behalf and in our stead. We are powerless to battle Satan, but Christ suffers this for us.

When we say we owe God a death we cannot mean we owe him some *thing*, such as a payment of a penalty. This would make God the agent of punishment. God's wrath is not to be understood as punishment from an angry deity who can be appeased by the right shape of death. God's wrath is his very nature as I confront him in the separation of my sin. When I confront him in forgiveness this same God is all compassion.[9] This is due not to vacillation in God but to a change in me wrought by a suffering change in God. It can be said that the death I owe to God is paid only if by payment we mean that I am obliged by my sin to die to myself. This dying to self is separation from the old Adam who rebelled against God. This I can do only by suffering the gift of grace and sharing Christ's death, that is, entering into his life of God-pleasing obedience.

The humiliating vicarious sacrifice reveals how restitution has been made for sin, and the glorifying victory of Christ over death in his resurrection exhibits how reconciliation is made between newborn sinners with the living God. The question is, how can the death of Jesus save me? The story of cosmic conflict clearly shows how Satan is disarmed with love. But what does this mean for me? I still have my own sin to contend with.

Perhaps the best answer is given in the Gospel of John: "Now is the time for judgment on this world; now the prince of this world will be driven out. But I, when I am lifted up from the earth, will draw all men to myself" (John 12:31–32). This is clearly an ironic adumbration of Jesus' exaltation through the humiliation of being lifted on a cross. God is glorified through victory over Satan and by our being drawn to Christ in thankful *worship*. This atonement is appropriated by us personally as we meet and receive Christ in Word and Sacrament. The ritual story brings about a revealed consciousness of the hidden story of reality. The brute reality is that as sinners we all have murdered the innocent Son of God, a sin far more heinous than the sin of Adam. And the hiddenness of God in the incarnation is far more difficult to perceive than the hiddenness of God in creation. Therefore only by a story theology in ritual confession, proclamation, and sacrament can we come to grips with the dragon and the lamb. No theory of satisfaction or moral example can tell such a fantastic tale.[10]

NOTES

1. What was excluded by the indeterminacy principle, as Max Planck, Albert Einstein, and Bertrand Russell pointed out, was not causality but only the precise

knowledge of it in subatomic particles. Cf. the article "Rationalism" in *Encyclopaedia Britannica*, 14th ed.

2. Cf. Sallie McFague, *Metaphorical Theology* (Philadelphia: Fortress Press, 1982), 106. In science there is a dispute over whether models are merely heuristic and illustrative or ontological and essential, but in theology, since there are no tests of verifiability or falsifiability, models cannot be dispensed with at all, and the more models the better.

3. Cf. Anders Nygren, *Commentary on Romans* (Philadelphia: Muhlenberg Press, 1949).

4. Cf. Roland M. Frye, *God, Man, and Satan* (Port Washington, N.Y., and London: Kennikat Press, 1972).

5. Cf. Charles Williams, *Seed of Adam and Other Plays* (London: Oxford University Press, 1948).

6. Robert W. Funk, *Parables and Presence* (Philadelphia: Fortress Press, 1982), 133ff., offers a helpful caveat against this temptation to reverse time.

7. For a discussion of the power of love as unmotivated giving see Anders Nygren, *Agape and Eros*, 3 vols. (New York: Macmillan Co., 1936–39).

8. The best and most enduring treatment of atonement is Gustav Aulén, *Christus Victor* (New York: Macmillan Co., 1931).

9. Nygren, *Commentary on Romans*, 97ff.

10. Gerhard O. Forde, in a short essay, "Caught in the Act: Reflections on the Work of Christ," *Word and World* III, no. 1 (1983): 22–31, has trenchantly commented on atonement theory in story language.

8

Christ and the Trinity

—obscene action
in the flies and the wings

What will story theology mean for the doctrines of Christ and the Trinity? What will happen to the shape of our teaching, and the communication of it, concerning the One who saves and his place in the Godhead?

CHRIST

The story of the virgin birth was told before the doctrines of the two natures of Christ and the three persons of the Trinity were constructed. Earlier than the virgin birth stories was the kenotic hymn which Paul quotes in Phil. 2:6–11. It tells a story of God emptying himself of divine glory and assuming human sinful mortality. And certainly the first interpretation of the story of Jesus is given by Peter when he addressed the crowd in Jerusalem on the Day of Pentecost, telling them in story form that "God has made this Jesus, whom you crucified, both Lord and Christ" (Acts 2:36).

The first question posed by the historical events of Jesus, coupled with the heraldic claim of his salvific power, was whether he came down from above and assumed human nature or rose up from below and was adopted into divine nature. Was he the God who became human or the human who became divine? Out of this question all kinds of controversies arose. Was Jesus one in being with God or merely like God (Arianism)? Was God in Jesus really human or merely so in appearance (Docetism)? Did Jesus have two natures, divine and human, or merely one divine nature (Monophysitism)? Did Jesus have a free and independent will or was it always and only God's will (Monothelitism)? Invariably these controversies arose and were settled in terms of philosophical presuppositions that happened to be the climate of opinion.

The reality of the ideal, in Platonism, as over against the unreality of mere appearance, was used to support the divinity of Christ and the hypostatic unity of the Trinity. Logical consistency need not be broken by historical fact in discussing the Trinity, but when it is said that the second Person becomes the Messiah in Jesus of Nazareth, we enter a new universe of discourse. Now we must deal with empirical events, and we cannot simply discount them as mere appearance. Platonism will no longer work. As Melanchthon says in his Apology to the Augsburg Confession, the kingdom of God is not the ideal utopia of Plato's Republic.[1] This shift from the reality of the ideal to the reality of the actual is made explicit in the Solid Declaration of *The Book of Concord:*

> Although the Son of God is a separate, distinct, and complete divine person and therefore has been from all eternity true, essential, and perfect God with the Father and the Spirit, yet, when the *time* had fully come, he took the human nature into the unity of his person, not so that there are two persons or two Christs, but in such a way that Christ Jesus is *henceforth* in one person *simultaneously* true eternal God and also a true man. (Italics mine)[2]

Notice how the categories of substance and essence are useful in speaking of the relation of Christ as Son of God in the Trinity, where the divine person is true, essential, and perfect God; but when the Son is spoken of in his humanity the category of time must come in. There is a henceforth in the person of God. There was a time when he was not what he is now and henceforth will be. And there is a simultaneous aspect which means there are at times sequences running beside each other. This makes it necessary to speak of God not in substantial terms but in dynamic, living terms. The language of philosophy must give way to the language of story. Only acts and events can be simultaneous. God is not an essence with qualities now; he is a living being who acts on the stage of history in a way he did not act before. He acts henceforth both as God acts and as a man acts.

But the old philosophy does not die easily, and when sixteenth-century Lutherans tried to account for the story reality of temporal change in the single person of Jesus Christ, they defended their truth with a logic that is overblown, tortuous, and prolix. On the two natures of Christ the Solid Declaration says:

> We believe, teach and confess that henceforth in this single individual person there are two distinct natures: the divine, which is from all eternity, and the human which was assumed in time into the unity of the Person of the Son of God. These two natures in the person of Christ will henceforth never be separated, blended with each other, or the one changed into the other, but in the person of Christ each remains in its nature and essence through all eternity.[3]

As soon as the Lutherans had said this, it became necessary for them to invent the doctrine of the *communicatio idiomatum* in order to avoid Zwingli's *alleosis* doctrine. Zwingli contended that when we say Christ died we mean only that the man Jesus died, since Christ is God and God cannot die. The problem goes back to the ancient church when Gregory of Nyssa disputed Apollinaris. If the cross is Christ's saving work, said Apollinaris, then God must have been present on it. Gregory contended, however, with the consistency of the Greek philosophical tradition that God is impassible and therefore he could not have died according to the divinity of Christ but only according to his humanity. Eusebius tried to resolve the dispute by distinguishing between the being of Christ and the work of Christ, *kat' ousia* and *kat' oikonomia*. According to his being, Christ did not die but according to his work he did.[4] Zwingli picked up Gregory's argument, but then it appeared that the one person Christ Jesus is divided. Thus the Lutherans contended that the one person Christ Jesus really died, and really rose, and is really present in the sacrament. This one person is both true God and true human because the whole fullness of deity dwelled in Christ Jesus bodily (Col. 2:9). The Lutherans wanted to say that God was in Christ reconciling the world unto himself by way of the cross (2 Cor. 5:19).

The full development of the Lutheran doctrine was achieved by Martin Chemnitz, who said there are three kinds of exchange of properties among the two natures and one person of Christ. The *communicatio idiomatum* has three *genera*. (1) The *genus idiomaticum* is the kind of exchange that ascribes properties of both natures to the whole person. Aristotelian logic says that deity cannot suffer and die, and while this is true according to a logic of noncontradiction, nevertheless since there is only one person, all that happens to the humanity happens also to the deity. Hence you must say that the person of Christ dies, the Son of God suffers. "Although, so to speak, the one part (namely, the deity) does not suffer, nevertheless the person who is true God suffers in the other part (namely, in the humanity)."[5] The Son of God, this person who is God, is truly crucified for us according to the humanity. (2) The *genus majestaticum* is the kind of exchange that ascribes divine majesty to the human Christ. Christ was majestically divine at his conception in the womb and Mary was truly the mother of God. He did not receive majesty after resurrection; he received resurrection because of God's majestic work on the humiliating cross. It is not meant that this majesty is manifest in miracles performed by Jesus. The Gospels report the miracles as the work of the Spirit and they could be done by others whom the Spirit chooses, such as Elijah or Peter. The majesty of God in Jesus was rather that he who is God was born and died. What happens to all sinful human beings happens also to God in Jesus. (3) The *genus apotelesmaticum* refers to the kind of exchange in which Christ used the properties of either nature or of both natures according as they were appropriate to the act in question. Thus the Solid Declaration says that all the properties of human creatureliness are communicated to the divine nature so that the one person Christ Jesus may be said to have all authority in heaven and earth according to his human nature. Christ did not receive just a measure of the Spirit's gifts as did the saints. The entire fullness of the Spirit is his. Again as the author of the Letter to the Colossians said, the whole fullness of deity dwells in him bodily.

In spite of the labored logic, we cannot help admiring the correctness and the precision of this Lutheran doctrine. Everything was said in order to avoid dividing Christ into two persons, but it was said within the framework of Aristotelian logic which began with the premise that God cannot suffer or be acted upon, because he is by definition *actus purus*. If, however, the Lutherans had been free to discard their medieval *Weltbild* and Aristotelian system of logic, they could have said what needed to be said without getting into this artificial doctrine. Simply begin with the living God of the Bible, the Father of our Lord Jesus, and you can affirm that God was in Christ reconciling the world unto himself and winning this victory through suffering. God and Jesus come to us then as characters in a story, a story that is real. God's glory is not sullied but magnified by such a story proclamation. Indeed it is precisely the glory of God in the story that he suffers in the Son. *He* suffers, not just the Son suffering as humanity but God suffering as God. This is what Luther knew as he is quoted in the Solid Declaration: "If it is not true that God died for us, but only a man died, we are lost."[6]

The important thing to see is what sixteenth-century Lutherans were fighting against. This was the Zwinglian notion that only a man died on the cross and that only God is present in the sacraments. The Lutherans maintained that one person, the God-man, is present both on the cross and in the sacrament. The reason for the quarrel and the reason for the prolix logic is the first premise about the impassibility of God. Also of equal importance in this debate is the false notion that death is passing from being into nothingness. If it is granted in the first place that God in his being is living, and therefore capable of changing, growing, suffering, passing from glory to glory, then there is no problem in his coming in sinful human form and suffering what human sinners do: dying and going to the place of the dead. And second, if this dying does not mean passing from being to nothing—extinction, annihilation, or obliteration—but rather a passing from communion with God to separation from God, then it is entirely possible to speak of God dying both as God and as humanity. Death means separation from God. When God's creatures are separated from him, he is also separated from them. The creatures suffer the consequences of this separation, the pain, the fear, the defeat of living away from God's immediacy. In our death, God is hidden and distant. By the same token, God suffers the consequences of this separation. He is lonely and hurt by our rebellion, as David was hurt by Absalom. And when God sees what this separating death does to us his creatures, he, like David, would rather die in our place. Hence the one person Christ Jesus dies both as God and as humanity. God in Christ Jesus suffers and is glorified as God; God in Jesus Christ suffers and is glorified as humanity; humanity in Christ Jesus suffers and is glorified as God; humanity in Jesus Christ suffers and is glorified as humanity. The logic is complete.

No matter how complete the logic may seem, however, it was not complete enough for Paul Tillich, who rejected the whole construct because he found the incarnation itself a contradiction.[7] Tillich made the distinction between paradox and contradiction. Paradox is a situation that seems to be other than what it really is. Contradiction is a locution against itself. The cross is the paradox that seems to be the execution and defeat of a good man but really is the disclosure of God's mercy. The incarnation is a contradiction in which words are used nonsensically because they deny each other: God is God and human beings are human beings, and the principle of noncontradiction in logic forbids the identification of the two. Hence Jesus is not the Christ, but he may be the broken symbol that discloses to us the Christ, Tillich argues.

The complicated construct of orthodox confessionalism and the cutting critique of Tillich, however, can be replaced by the simplicity, the lucidity, and the adequacy of the story model. The logic of orthodoxy is too cumbersome and it needlessly proceeds from the false premise that God is impassible and that death is nothingness. Tillich's critique of the incarnation, in spite of his penchant for casting his theology in the dress of Hegelian triads, reveals that he is a Platonist using the logic of noncontradiction.

Before we construct the doctrine of the incarnation on the story model, I think it will be helpful to examine Hegel's logic of contradiction because it is an honest attempt to grapple with contingency and change in reality. It provides opportunity for an intellectual grasp of the notion that in a moment of time a change can occur in which God can become human. In the course of our examination, however, we shall also see how Hegel himself spoiled his own system by trying to embrace the whole of reality with a reduction to rationalism.

A Philosophical Excursus on the Logic of Hegel

Hegel's Critique of Metaphysics,
Empiricism, and Intuitionism.

The old metaphysics before Kant and Hume had the unquestioning belief that reflection is the only means of ascertaining truth. Socrates had set the stage when he said that truth is not the object of the senses but the object of thought. The objects of metaphysics were then taken from popular conception without any critical analysis of the process by which they were thought. The result of such metaphysics could not help being dogmatism, consisting of arbitrary definitions and logical formalism. Cobwebs of syllogistic reasoning were spun with the industry of the arachnids, but these could never reconcile the contingent facts of nature. Multifarious differences in phenomena were therefore considered by the old metaphysics and Scholasticism as spurious and passing. Appearances were seen as mere reflections of a Platonic realm of ideas. Matter was perceived as the superficiality behind which the real enjoys a permanent and pure being.[8]

Hegel quite correctly attacked the formal emptiness of such theory because it leaves the concrete inadequately accounted for. When the old theory had to face a cold fact, it either contorted its syllogism and became inconsistent or denied the fact and left a form without content. But such formal abstractions are indeterminate, and consequently of not specific value to us. We must take into consideration the contingent because its actuality is real. This was the clamant cry of Søren Kierkegaard, repeatedly on behalf of the individual but especially for the *ephapax* or once-for-all event of the incarnation.[9] While it is true that the contingent is transitory, nevertheless that is the nature of the world in which we live—changing and developing. The permanence which runs through the flux is what Hegel sought to identify.

This need for concrete subject matter gave rise to empiricism. Truth is now sought in experience because its data are considered legitimate objects; but simple sensations cannot be left as they are unless we as observers remain at the animal level. Empiricists labor under a delusion if they think their analysis of objects leaves sensations as they are. Analysis is a process from sensation to thought. Indeed, says Hegel, to oppose actuality and thought is absurd.[10] Hume's postulate of habit as the means by which we insinuate intelligibility into facts is, to my mind, untenable since, according to it, any type of induction is as good as any other type. We know to the contrary, however, that the relative criterion involved in the process of sampling produces better results than other criteria. Taxonomies are therefore useful in the sciences. On the other hand, I agree with Hume against Hegel that reason cannot be identified with fact. In short, Hegel quite rightly criticizes the empiricist assumption that facts can be left unblemished through reasonable analysis, but he wrongly identifies fact with reason. This is important to our understanding the incarnation, because the incarnation cannot be received simply as a sense fact (flesh and blood have not revealed this to us), nor can it be reduced to an object of thought.

The critical philosophers (Kant, Fichte, and Schelling) looked for truth in experience. They correctly included universality and necessity as functional parts of this experience. Hegel objected to these philosophers, however, particularly treating Kant, because they denied knowledge of the *thing itself.* Hegel thought that anything which is not concrete is not complete; and since the things in themselves which Kant spoke of were in an abstract realm, they were empty and indeterminate. Similarly Kant's consideration of the will as practical reason leaves the Good without content. To say "Do your duty for duty's sake" is to say very little of concrete value. The concretion of the incarnation as a movement from the Absolute into particularity is obviously significant.

Finally, having criticized the rational metaphysicians and the empiricists, both the pure empiricism of Hume and the critical philosophy of Kant, Hegel examined the intuitionist school of thought, particularly Descartes and Jacobi. The intuitionists put their faith in the truth of immediate consciousness. This school more recently may be recognized in philosophers such as Schleiermacher and Husserl. Hegel found intuition to be as abstract and arbitrary as Kant's moral idealism. The only criterion in such philosophy is *consensus gentium,* a dubitable one indeed. We too shall have to distinguish between intuition and faith.

Hegel's System of Logic

Hegel's system of logic progresses through the stages of Being, Essence, and Notion. These three abstractions have identical determinate forms in nature. Reason and fact are one. This form of logic then gives the thesis for a new triad in the realm of nature. The thesis of the abstract triad has its antithesis in the determinate triad of Being, Essence, and Notion. Nature is the antithesis of logic, and the two synthesize to the philosophy of Mind.

Hegel developed a noble and imposing system. His conception of Being as empty abstraction which needs determinacy is a valuable contribution. Being in itself is empty and stinted. Likewise Hegel's emphasis on Essence as ostensible otherness is a penetrating observation. The many contradictions in nature which are outlined by Hegel add considerably to the description of the world. His goal was to bridge the gaps between reason, fact, and value and bring them into a unified whole of panlogism. We may illustrate his problem and solution in the following way.

It is well known that the inductive argument can be given deductive form.

1. Whatever is true of A, B, C, D is true of all red-haired people.
2. Ill tempers characterize A, B, C, D.
3. Therefore ill tempers characterize all red-haired people.

The conclusion is valid since it necessarily follows from the premises and is inherently contained in them. The question immediately arises concerning the truth of the premises. The second premise can be directly observed and verified; but the first premise is a universal proposition which cannot be held unless all samples of the class have been investigated. The logic is valid but the content cannot be said to be true. This is precisely the objection Hume gave to the ascription of logical necessity to facts. Hume maintained that the first premise is experientially untenable. There is an irreconcilable distinction between logical necessity and matters of fact which we discover in the causal sequence of nature.

It is this gap which Hegel tried to bridge. Since all the samples of many universal propositions cannot be investigated, because of their nature, the passing of time, and the limitation of our perceptive powers, some method must be devised that can bring unity back to nature. In the realm of science we find causal sequences which Hume claimed to have no logical necessity, and in the realm of society we find value judgments which likewise have no necessary connection but are relative to custom alone.[11] The fields of science and value tend in opposite directions and both are distinct from reason. Hegel's problem was to unify reason, fact, and value by setting forth a new intellectual method, the logic of dialectic.

As a mere description of the dissolution of conflicting tendencies in the course of history, there is no reason to object to Hegel's analysis; but Hegel regarded his system as logical law, not as mere description. Hegel wanted the law of noncontradiction to be superseded by the law of identity-difference, a law of fruitful opposition. For example, ancient Greek fatalism said that because a thing is as it is, so it ought to be; but Hegel pointed out that in fact things are not always as they ought to be. There is a conflict between a thing's Being and its Actuality. Moreover, in Christianity we find a resolution of the conflict in personal aims and ultimate destiny. Thus the logic works itself out through the conflict of Being and Actuality to Necessity. In this logic of Hegel's that which ends in Necessity comes to be truth through the opposition of its own Freedom and Actuality. There is in Christianity a true subjectivism which unites the two, making the subjective immanent in the fact. Thus there is an absolute consolation for the Necessity which is in Actuality.[12]

The three elements in the process of Necessity are the Condition, the Fact, and the Actuality. The necessary is the result of a condition which is translated into a fact; but immediately this abrogates itself by its immediacy and is lifted up into actuality. Thus Necessity is the unity of Possibility and Actuality. The process is so directed that the rigid externality which it first had is given up and members are seen to be linked, not as foreign elements but as elements of the whole, each freely conjoined and determined. Thus a good man is aware that his conduct is obligatory and yet he is free. And the punishment for a crime is not a foreign constraint but the necessary manifestation of the very act provoking punishment.[13]

The Notion is then the principle of Freedom which expresses necessity in its complete determinateness. The Notion is the Absolute, as was Being and Essence, but now it is concrete. We characterize Notion as development, but by this we do not mean that the inherent elements in the first stage are the same as those in the last stage in actual existence. To illustrate this compare the seed and the plant. Jesus was talking about this when he said we must become like a seed that goes into the ground and dies. Furthermore Christianity says that God created the world as an other, but at the same time he has begotten a Son with whom he is himself at home.

Hegel's description of development through contraries is helpful in understanding history. It has a story quality which Sholem Asch, for example, used in his novels *The Nazarene* and *The Apostle*. In *The Nazarene*, Jesus and Judas provide opposing forces for the synthesis of the risen Christ, and in *The Apostle*, Paul and Peter find resolution in the author of the Letter to the Hebrews. The contrived artificiality is evident, however. Hegel's real purpose is not to acknowledge the reality of the contingent. He really wants to bring the contingent into Necessity. He said Necessity is the unity of Possibility and Actuality. Kierkegaard said this triad could just as well be turned around, and if it is to describe reality, it should say that Actuality is the unity of Possibility and Necessity.[14] Hegel's mistake is his confusion of the contradictory with the contrary.[15] He wanted to replace the law of noncontradiction with a law of identity-difference, but he treated the differences as if they were contradictory, when they were often only contrary. A political situation, for example, may have forces that make for peace and forces that make for war, but these forces are not contradictory to each other. They need no logical resolution, but they do need historical resolution. To ascribe necessary connection between contraries is bad enough, but to ascribe it to contradictories is worse. The proof of this arbitrariness came when Marx turned the idealism and nationalism of Hegel's use of his logic into materialism and internationalism.

Hegel's system revolves on a double-bitted axis: The real is rational and the rational is real. The metaphysical assumption is more than I am willing to grant. I would rather say that human beings have the gift of reason, and the real is open to the use of that gift as a tool for understanding and using its riches. Human beings can insinuate reason into matters of fact, but we do so only as a foil, as a tool to help us control nature. Logic and mathematics are such tools, but the relativity of both cannot be denied. When a brief résumé of uniform behavior is formulated we have a scientific "law" of great service, but such a "law" does not have logical necessity in it, neither the logic of noncontradiction nor the logic of identity-difference.

Neither the logic of Aristotle nor the logic of Hegel is bound to the structure of reality. Both are useful as tools in perceiving and organizing reality. Reality is often perceived as ordered, and we can helpfully say that a thing is itself and not its opposite or anything in between. God is God and not his creature or any chimeric *tertium quid*. But reality is also often perceived as contradictory, and we can helpfully say that a thing is both itself and its opposite or any number of things other than itself. Christ is God and Christ is human. Christ is wholly God in the hidden reality of the Trinity; Christ is wholly human in the revealed reality of Jesus of Nazareth. And the logic of contradiction not only embraces opposites but it also advances to include development in time, a development which at the same time moves and changes temporally and retains within itself that which had been changed. Thus we can say God became human and yet at the same time, while affirming this radical change, we do not say he is no longer God. In Jesus the Holy One becomes a sinner without losing his original sinlessness. Also the Christian is a person who has become justified but yet remains in sin, thus doing both saintly and sinful things. Syllogistic logic cannot contain this contradiction, but it is a narrative description of reality.

RETURN TO THE STORY OF INCARNATION

Let us return to the story of incarnation. If it is true that the two logics, the logic of noncontradiction and the logic of contradiction, are tools and not structures of reality, then we may use either of them when we find them useful. Reality is not bound to the simple identities of Aristotle's system, nor is it bound to the contradictory triads of Hegel's. In theology we can use Aristotle to affirm the distinction between God and his creatures, between holiness and sin, between circles and squares. And we can use Hegel's triad to describe how God can become human without ceasing to be God, how a seed will die to itself to become what it is in its flower, how a sinful child will die with Christ to be born into newness of life.

But stories can use both logics or neither. In stories, without a tortuous twist of logic, it is entirely possible to have one person of the drama play two different characters. Shakespeare's *Measure for Measure* provides a good example. It is the story of the Duke of Vienna, who finds his realm in moral decay. He decides to leave his role as kingly ruler and go among his people in the guise of a friar, thus to perform a lowly servant role. He is no less the Duke when he becomes the friar, but he has emptied himself of his ducal power. It is the Duke in him that prompts him to do what he does as friar, but as friar he is seen by his people not as Duke but as servant. All that he is as friar he certainly is as Duke, since he is not another person but the same person. What the Duke necessarily is as Duke and possibly is as friar he actually becomes in the course of the play. The dialectic dramatically fulfills itself.

And what is it that the Duke tries to do as friar? He had ruled with law, but now he tries to do with repentance and forgiveness what the law in its strict observance failed to do. The law is fulfilled by love; justice is tempered with mercy. The principle he puts into action is, "Forgive, and you will be forgiven. Give, and it will be given to you.... For with the measure you use, it will be measured to you" (Luke 6:37–38). The reference is to the kind of measure, not just the quantity. So in his place when he goes incognito the Duke installs Angelo, a harsh legalist and hypocrite, who brings down the law with a vengeance, closing all the brothels and imprisoning the whores and their pimps and their tricks, and especially Claudio, who has gotten his girlfriend Juliet pregnant. Now the Duke as friar wants to set things right and satisfy the needs of everyone. But in godly and artful detachment he finds that existence is full of surprises. If he is the God-Christ figure, he cannot simply coerce human events. Freedom brings strange twists of both perversion and goodness. The deputy Angelo is aroused to ungovernable lust by Isabella, the sister of Claudio. Angelo offers to free Claudio if Isabella will yield her body to him. When Claudio hears of this he pleads with Isabella to yield, since it is his neck against her honor. The friar must clean up this mess with indirection, and he succeeds in the end with all parties repenting and forgiving, and himself hinting strongly a proposal of marriage to Isabella, an intimation of the relationship between the Lord and the Bride of Christ.

I do not know whether Shakespeare intended this allegory. Some critics have suggested it. Older critics like Coleridge found *Measure for Measure* a "hateful work" with an outrageous breach of justice, but contemporary critics see in it a triumph of Christian grace in which Angelo is blessed and given "measure for measure," not as an "eye for an eye" but as a tragicomic advance on justice.[16] My purpose in relating it is simply to show how one person on stage can play the roles without a contradiction. In the story of reality God can become a man, always remaining God in the man he becomes, yet also really being the man whose role he plays. When God comes to us in the form of man he is seen to be the man he is but not the God he is. This God is really in the condition of human mortality.

If the New Testament is clear about anything at all, it is clear that Jesus of Nazareth was truly human, flesh of our flesh, and moreover he was a male, born of a woman, under the law, according to the flesh descended from David. Jesus was an offense to his own people because he so obviously had human origins and yet made messianic pretensions. The people of Nazareth wondered, "Isn't this Joseph's son?" (Luke 4:22). At Capernaum they said, "Why does this fellow talk like that? He's blaspheming! Who can forgive sins but God alone?" (Mark 2:7). In Jerusalem they murmured at the temple, "Is this not Jesus, the son of Joseph, whose father and mother we know? How can he now say, 'I came down from heaven'?" (John 6:42).

Yet in spite of the fact that Jesus was known to be a man, an early heresy was the docetic belief that denied that he was truly incarnate. Basilides taught that the Word did not really become flesh; it only dwelt among us in the appearance of Jesus' flesh, and when Jesus came to die on the cross Simon of Cyrene was somehow substituted for Jesus, while the true Christ mingled in the crowd and smilingly looked on. This heresy was prompted by offense in incarnation. It was unthinkable that God who is Spirit could be contaminated by material flesh.

Oriental and Platonic axiological dualism was not shared by the Hebrews and early Christians. For them the things of this world were considered good because God made them. After he made whatever he made God said, "Behold! It is good." But in another sense to the Hebrew and the early Christian, God was indeed removed from his creation. Although this is a good creation, because of the sin of Adam everything in it is under a curse.

The whole world groans as in travail. While before his fall Adam enjoyed equal companionship with God, living peacefully in the garden, after the fall there was broken communion, crammed with enmity, anxiety, and despair. There was enmity because Adam tried to be as God and thus do without him. There was anxiety because Adam tried to worship God as an idol bending God's will to his own. And there was despair because both attempts always ended in failure.

Failure meant that God was henceforth hidden. As John says: "No one has ever seen God" (John 1:18). This sense of the remoteness of God is rooted in the tradition of the Old Testament. Moses cannot see God face to face, only his hinder parts, the things God has done after he has passed by. The Ark of the Covenant is so filled with the holiness of God that death will come to anyone who touches it. This is what Rudolf Otto calls the *mysterium tremendum*, the awesome, repelling and fascinating presence of the holy. The glory of God is blinding to the naked eye.[17]

Indeed it is our nakedness that characterizes our sin and separation from God. Before the fall in Adam we did not know ourselves to be independent of God, and hence we were clothed in the glory of God. After the fall into the bondage of sin we find ourselves to be naked, and we are ashamed to have lost the cloak of God's glory. So henceforth we have made every attempt to clothe and protect ourselves, from the original fig leaf to the latest Paris fashion, from the rags of Pharisaic righteousness to the "garbage" of the monk, from the armor of Goliath to the radar screens on the Alaskan DEW line. We stand naked before God like the emperor in the fairy tale, and in our nakedness we cannot see him. The drama of his glory is too powerful for us. It must be played out in the flies and the wings. The action is obscene.

Therefore if God is to be seen at all, he must be seen not as he really is but indirectly in a form that we can see. And the only form we can see is our own form of sinful human flesh. So he came in Jesus, and so he comes repeatedly in bread and wine. God comes to us not in God form to be seen by the naked eye but in creature form to be seen as revelation through faith. He is indirectly communicated to us the way an audience grasps reality through the make-believe of the stage. Tennessee Williams introduces *The Glass Menagerie* by having Tom Wingfield tell us that the deception of the play-acting is more true than our perception of reality. Kierkegaard says God gives himself to us, betrays himself to us, in a maieutic method because the Holy Spirit can never be grasped directly. Direct immediacy is the characteristic mark of an idol.[18] Luther often spoke of the *larva Dei*, the mask of God, in which the *Deus absconditus* comes to us as *Deus revelatus*, the hidden God comes to us as the revealed God, the glorious God comes to us humiliated. There is no docetic unreality about this mask or veil; indeed it is so real and so much a part of our creatureliness that it becomes a scandal and an offense. But flesh alone cannot reveal God. The Spirit must give us power to see God behind the mask, as Jesus said to Peter on the way to Caesarea Philippi. As the audience sees reality through the deception on the stage by losing itself under the power of imagination, so God may be seen by the power of the Spirit through Word and Sacrament.

The mask of flesh thus becomes both the means of revelation and the stumbling block, to the Jews an offense and to the Greeks foolishness. This is the profoundest humor of God, the divine irony. "God chose the foolish things of the world to shame the wise," foolish things like a criminal on a cross and a baby born in a cold and dirty manger (1 Cor. 1:27).

So the Word of God became flesh and lived for a while among us. Two stories in Scripture say that the Word became flesh by way of a virgin birth, the stories of Matthew and Luke. Perhaps a narrative hermeneutic based on the reality of story will shed new light on the doctrine of the virgin birth. John, Paul, and Mark say nothing about it, nor is there mention of it anywhere else in the New Testament. Some passages speak of Jesus being born of a woman (Gal. 4:4) or of the seed of David according to the flesh (Rom. 1:3), but the early kenotic hymn of Phil. 2:6–11 ignores it and Paul says nothing about it in other references to incarnation (Rom. 8:3; 2 Cor. 5:21; Gal. 3:13). But the early church quickly included the teaching in its credal confessions. Later pious legends said that Matthew and Luke got the story directly from Mary, but there is no evidence for this. It seems more likely that this is a narrative way of explaining a mysterious action of God.

The story of Jesus' miraculous birth is unique. There are many stories in past cultures about gods and heroes being born of virgins, but these were always tales about gods or angels coming in human or animal form to have intercourse with mortal women. Usually the stories were mythical, not legendary, with the purpose of explaining the origin of some tradition or institution that arose out of the distant past. In Matthew and Luke the historical role of Mary is unique. Not only are the virgin birth stories of the New Testament lacking in any pagan parallelism but there is also no Old Testament background for the stories. Instead of other similar stories, we find prophecies in the Old Testament that were interpreted in the New Testament as being fulfilled by the birth of Jesus. God is described as doing what he had promised through his covenant. One example is where Isa. 7:14 says a child will be born to a young woman and the child will save the world. Whether Isaiah had in mind a virgin birth the way Matthew did is not known. Discussion of the meaning of the words *almah* or *bethulah* and *parthenos,* whether they mean virgin or young woman, seems to be fruitless. It may not have occurred to Isaiah that this would be a "virgin" birth. The method of birth is not the issue. What did occur to Isaiah was that God had spoken and promised to act to deliver Israel through a child whom he would send. This is a miracle in the true sense: divine power acting in a personal way on the stage of freedom. And the early Christians saw Jesus as the fulfillment of that promise.

Why then did they say the birth was virgin? Because they saw in Jesus the holy God come to them in the form of a baby. They did not read the story as Schleiermacher did. He understood Jesus to be unique in that he only among all human beings fulfilled a perfect God-consciousness which is inherent in all of us. Jesus was the elevation of one human being from natural humanity to divinity because he accomplished what is inherent in all of us.[19] This is a story too. One might even tell it without Pelagian implications by saying that it was God who raised Jesus to this holiness. But it is not the story told in the New Testament. Rather, I think joining the Isaiah prophecy with the virgin birth story requires us to say that Jesus is unique because God, the Holy One, emptied himself of his holiness and came into the realm of sin, becoming sin with us, Immanuel. The virgin birth story is told to reveal that what was holy came into sinful flesh, the womb of Mary, not that God raised up something sinful and made it divine but that God took what was divine and made it human, and not only creaturely human but also sinfully human (Rom. 8:3; 2 Cor. 5:21; Gal. 3:13). Thus for Irenaeus the virgin birth was testimony of Jesus' humanity in being the second Adam: true humanity.[20] Luther has the same idea in his catechism when he says Jesus Christ is true God, begotten of the Father from all eternity, and also true man, born of the Virgin Mary. It is theological error, therefore, to say that Jesus is divine because he was born of a virgin. The truth is the other way around. It is theological error to say that Mary was immaculate. The point of this virgin birth story is that the holy God entered the sinful flesh of Mary.

What then does account for Jesus' divinity in the story of his birth?[21] The power of the Holy Spirit. The virgin birth is told in terms of the activity of the Holy Spirit bringing the new creation at the end time, just as the Creator Spirit was active in the beginning. The virgin birth is comprehensible to us only as a mystery comparable in cosmic dimensions with the original creation. The coming of Christ is the new creature, and the new creature comes from God, as did the first creature. As the first creature came from the dust of the earth with the Holy Spirit breathing life into Adam, so the new Adam comes from the flesh of Mary and the Holy Spirit breathes life into Jesus.

What about the activity of Joseph in this story? As the story is told, Joseph is angry when he finds that Mary is pregnant. He was not the father of her child. But on the other hand the story does not tell us that the Holy Spirit is the biological father of the child. We have said that the point of the story is not that a biological miracle guarantees the divinity of Christ. Instead of biological sequences described in the story we have narrative metaphor and the language of mystery. It says in Luke 1:35 that the power of the Most High will overshadow Mary, *episkiasei,* the same verb used in the transfiguration story for the cloud that overshadows the transfigured Christ and the disciples. Luke also says the Holy Spirit will come upon Mary, *epeleusetai,* and he uses the same verb in Acts 1:8 when the risen Lord promises the power of the Holy Spirit. The activity of God here is the mysterious presence of the Holy Spirit making all things new.

What can we make of the fact that Joseph is rejected as father and Mary is affirmed as mother? Males at first will pout like Joseph and females will rejoice, but both would be wrong, for Joseph realized that this child was of God and Mary's heart was pierced with a sword. Joseph need not lament, because his rejection was not a rejection of human fatherhood or his male sexuality. His rejection in the story is representative of God's repudiation of human sin. It indicates the death of humankind in the process of salvation. And Mary's affirmation does not elevate virginity above marriage, as in Roman Catholic piety, but it indicates the acceptance of the creature as the object of God's love. This is not an affirmation of human motherhood or of Mary's female sexuality as such. The virgin birth tells a different story, not a story about biology and sexuality but a story about a new creation. The rejection of Joseph is the judgment on our sinfulness; the election of Mary is the affirmation of our creatureliness.

As part of the whole Christian story, the virgin birth story has had a remarkable role in shaping a new society, in creating a culture in which both patriarchal and matriarchal structures are replaced by the church as our mother and God as our Father. This narrative explanation may be seen when we compare the virgin birth story with the classical drama of Orestes. Ancient cultures vacillated between matriarchal and patriarchal social structures. The Orestes story tells about the search for justice by affirming a shift from a matriarchal to a patriarchal system. It is quite realistic in telling how the sins of the fathers and mothers are visited upon the children. Orestes kills his mother, Clytemnestra, because she has killed his father, her husband, Agamemnon. Clytemnestra and her lover Aegisthus usurped the throne of Thebes from Agamemnon because he had sacrificed their daughter Iphigenia in order to get favorable winds from the gods. Now Orestes is on trial for killing his mother. The Furies are the prosecuting attorneys. They charge that matricide is the worst crime because it is a blood crime, worse than Clytemnestra's crime because she only killed her husband, not a blood relative. Apollo is the defense attorney. He argues that matricide is not as serious as regicide, since the king is given his scepter by Zeus, the father of the gods. But moreover and chiefly, Orestes is not guilty of a blood crime because a mother is really no parent, only a workshop for the father's seed. Early religion was matriarchal and conception was thought to be by the wind. No father was needed. Later when the father was understood to be causal in conception, the phallus became a religious fetish and patriarchy the social structure. Some critics therefore see the judgment of the goddess Athena in favor of Orestes to be the narrative explanation for the advance in societal structure from matriarchy to patriarchy, and the conflict between the old law and the new law is seen to be resolved as the Erinyes become the "Kindly Ones."[22]

In contrast the virgin birth story in Christianity may be seen as a repudiation of both matriarchal and patriarchal societies and the affirmation of a new human relationship produced by the creative power of the Holy Spirit. This story in its fullness creates a culture free from the abuses of sexual fetishes of either gender and the tyrannies of both sexes. History has shown, however, that we have fallen far short of this in practice. Mary's song of praise still prods us to redress the wrongs perpetrated by the strong and the rich because God showered his favor on a poor and weak woman.

Stories exhibit the ambivalence that humanity entertains in our attempt through myth to explain the cosmic forces which both control us and are at our disposal. Throughout history there have been shifting inversions of the role of women. In the Sumerian myth of Inanna and Enki, Inanna, the goddess of Erech, gains by seduction the *mes* of civilization which are the rules of religious, social, and cosmic realities. A goddess thus becomes the patron of civilization. Enkidu in this Sumerian myth is also "civilized" by a temple prostitute, a representative of Ishtar (Inanna). Through intercourse with a woman, man is tamed.

The same idea is prevalent with Pallas Athena, the goddess of Athens who grew in myth out of a combination of the Minoan goddess of the city and the house (domestic wisdom) and the Dorian goddess of battle. Perhaps it was this martial quality in her genetic constitution that accounted for her "wisdom" in the Oresteian decision which favored patriarchal society.

In Christianity, Mary overcomes Eve. Eve also is associated with wisdom. In her seduction by the serpent Eve chooses to be wise rather than innocent, but in the biblical story this is a fall! Also in the Greek myth of Pandora, unlike that of Athena, woman becomes a curse. The early church fathers pondered the inversion of the role of woman in salvation. For Irenaeus, not only does Mary counter Eve's disobedience but she becomes the "cause of salvation" (*Haer.* III, 22). Tertullian says, "What by that sex had gone into perdition by that same sex might be brought back to salvation. Eve had believed the serpent; Mary believed Gabriel; the fault which the one committed by believing, the other by believing has blotted out" (*De Carn. Christ.* 17).

Wisdom was feminine in Hebrew (*hokmah*) and was associated with Spirit (*ruach*). This has led to speculation among some Christians about the plurality of personality in God, even the possibility of constructing a Trinity with a female member. However, it explicitly says in both Prov. 8:22 and Sirach 24:9 that God created wisdom. It was this notion of a created wisdom that led Arius to insist that Christ as *logos* must also be created.

Logically Arius was right, but his premise wrongly identified the original Word with created wisdom. It is interesting to see how in human mythmaking a christological exegesis was transferred to a Mariological exegesis as Mary became more and more exalted as the throne of God, holding Christ on her lap. As the mother of God, Mary is immaculately conceived and bodily assumed, the co-redemptrix who is near to being worshiped as divine.

But along with this exaltation of Mary, from the end of the Middle Ages to the seventeenth century, the Western world was obsessed by another female image: the witch. J. Edgar Bruns says this was because it was a time of drastic change and upheaval, and therefore a scapegoat was sought.[23] The witch had secret knowledge because she was Satan's familiar. As Satan's whore she was the opposite of the virgin mother. When the Enlightenment brought confidence and stability again, the female image became the goddess of reason.

Today we are once more in ferment. Male chauvinism, the Protestant work ethic with its exploitative imperialism, and technical wisdom are under attack. We have women's liberation calling for soft values such as peace, nurturing, and sharing. Bruns offers an analysis of the parabolic play, *Tiny Alice,* by Edward Albee, in which God is presented to us as a woman. Five protagonists (six when understood) are in a transaction involving the transfer of a large amount of money between Miss Alice and the emissaries of the Catholic Church (a cardinal and his youngish secretary, brother Julian). One of Miss Alice's requirements is that Julian take up residence in her home. In it is a model of the mansion. Everything that happens in the mansion happens in the model. It is a space within a space, a time within a time, a story within a story. The mansion and its occupants appear to belong to the realm of reality, not to the realm of make-believe, which the model-doll's house represents. But do they? We learn that these people really have no meaning apart from the model and its invisible inhabitant Tiny Alice. "Albee seems to be saying that God (Tiny Alice) is real because he (she) is make-believe, and *our* 'reality,' removed from make-believe, is shabby, pitiful and even absurd. Further, if the only reality with meaning is make-believe, and the only meaningful world a veritable doll's house, then God must be a woman, for a doll's house is the plaything of a girl."[24] This goddess, thinks Bruns, is the antithesis of the goddess of reason because her world is a childish feminine whim. He expects that one hundred years hence male dominance will return and then we will have another male deity because the dominance of one sex over another will always be reflected in popular religion.

The analysis of Bruns is brilliant and correct, but as Christians we should ride out the storms of both male and female dominance and avoid the idolatry of both male and female deities. Story theology understands how myths are made but subjects them to scrutiny under the light of the story of revelation.

THE TRINITY

In stories we deal with *dramatis personae,* persons of the drama. It is not difficult to think of God the Father as a person, nor is it difficult to think of God the Son as a person, but God the Spirit raises special problems. We have been talking about the activity of the Spirit in conjunction with the Word in creation and again in conjunction with the birth of Jesus Christ in the new creation. How can a story view help us see the Spirit as a person in a trinitarian Godhead?

Christian theology has regarded the Holy Spirit as the source and giver of life, the communicator of revealed truth, and the comforting helper and guide to loving conduct. It has been the work of the Spirit to participate with the Word not only in creation but also in redemption. In this dual function the Spirit reveals both the nature of God and the destiny of humankind. God acts as a free, purposive person. We know ourselves as persons only because through the Spirit we see ourselves in the image of the divine Person. Contemporary theology has sometimes lost this biblical understanding either by seeking to know God on the model of impersonal process or by constructing God on the image of subjective human experience. A recovery of the full scriptural dimension in the theology of the Spirit will alert us to the presence of that Person in the Godhead whose work is radical and sustaining, spontaneous and comforting, mysterious and revealing.

References to the Spirit in the Old Testament indicate a host of contradictions. The Spirit does the spontaneous, once-for-all work of creation, yet throughout the history of the covenant people we recognize the abiding presence of God in his Spirit. Israel is a people in whom the Spirit dwells. Although the Spirit occasionally acts in a wonderful way upon certain individuals, as when he came to David under the anointing of Samuel (1 Sam. 16:13), nevertheless he is present at all times undergirding and strengthening the corporate life of Israel. Even their craftsmanship is acknowledged to be a gift of the Spirit (Exod. 31:1–5; 35:31). But in spite of this presence of the Spirit in things great and small we find stormy prophets reminding the people that the Spirit has left them. The Spirit is the *presence* by which Israel lives currently; yet because of the *absence* of the Spirit, prophets and seers guide the people to look to the future when in the day of the Messiah there will be a comforting outpouring of the Holy Spirit (Isa. 42:1; 61:1).

All these apparent contradictions can be understood only if we grant that the Holy Spirit is purposive, acting toward his creatures always in a personal way. He speaks, guides, gives gifts, abides as a comforting presence, withdraws for discipline, returns as a future solace. None of these activities can be ascribed to an impersonal force or process. Their very contradictoriness is the mark of the mystery of the Person. A person comes and goes and cannot be mechanically controlled. A person's behavior is unpredictable, yet can be seen to pursue a purposive goal. The Spirit of the Lord is such a Person working mysteriously and purposively in the drama of salvation.

In the New Testament we see the activity of the Spirit in the birth of Jesus. After centuries of a seeming dearth of the Spirit, suddenly at the birth of Jesus there is an abundant outpouring of his gifts and power. The stories of Zechariah, Elizabeth, Simeon, and John the baptizer contain the Spirit as the character who turns the tale. Especially wonderful is the presence of the Spirit in the story of Jesus at every point along the way. The presence of the Spirit at the baptism of Jesus confirms what we have said about the work of the Spirit at his birth, because here in the beginning of Jesus' ministry the Spirit descends along with the unleashing of the prophetic voice, and the creation of the new kingdom is begun. And after the baptism Jesus is led by the Spirit to be tempted in the wilderness. Furthermore, Jesus vanquished the power of evil by the power of the Spirit: "But if I drive out demons by the Spirit of God, then the kingdom of God has come upon you" (Matt. 12:28). Strangely, when the demons recognize Jesus as Messiah he charges them to secrecy, as he does also with his disciples. This is because as a pneumatic person Jesus ran the danger of being put in the category of a charismatic healer along with others who were perceived to perform similar miracles. Once his ministry was acknowledged to be messianic the exorcisms take on great significance because they indicate that Jesus brings spiritual power to subdue the empire of the adversary. The work of the Spirit thus heightens the ambiguity of the plot. It was not simply a means of revealing Jesus' Messiahship; it was rather at the same time a concealment. We find at this point a characteristic mark of the Spirit which has major significance: He is a mystery who works to reveal through concealment. In the exorcisms some saw merely the magic of a thaumaturge and they were either hardened against Jesus or attracted to his "magic." Others who were moved by the mystery of the Spirit could understand and celebrate the true messianic significance of Jesus, but flesh and blood did not reveal it to them.

Just as the miracles were ambiguous signs, so likewise the prophetic teaching of Jesus was a revelation in mystery. This again is due to the nature of the Spirit as a person in the drama who is both hidden and revealed. Sometimes Jesus is moved by human suffering compassionately to perform miracles as signs of the power of the Spirit which rests upon him. At other times he sharply refuses to give signs. Sometimes his words are a saving comfort and at other times people fall away because his sayings are too hard. What he says and does shows forth a power (*dynamis*) which is available to all who see and hear, but the authority (*exousia*) for what he says and does is not openly manifest and is acknowledged only in the presence of the Spirit. The power is thus the anticipated power of the Spirit but not the naked Spirit unimpeded by the veil of human and worldly relativity. Jesus was the Messiah, but he was not in any obvious sense identifiable with the end of the world as the Messiah was expected to be. Hence the paradox: the authority was there but always concealed. As Messiah, Jesus was the bearer of the Spirit, but he kept his Messiahship secret because it was to be a Messiahship of suffering and death which only the Spirit could reveal to be a glorification of God. Openly he was a scandal, but secretly in the Spirit he was the glory of God. The real action was going on in the flies and the wings, but those who had eyes to see and ears to hear understood and rejoiced.

The work of the Spirit in the church we shall discuss in the next chapter. For now, it is enough to say that the Spirit is the Person who, in the language of Luther, calls, gathers, enlightens, and sanctifies all who build up the church. Again the Spirit is not the impersonal force that drives a cultural institution, nor is the Spirit the subjective sentiment that brings people together voluntaristically as mutual God-lovers. The Spirit is the objective Person who creates us anew, the Subject who stands over against us convicting us of our sin, condemning the prince of this world, and creating a new heaven and a new earth (John 16:8–11).

All the things we have been saying about the Spirit support the conviction that he is the Creator-Redeemer Person who belongs with the Father and the Son in the Godhead. Now it remains to be seen how the story model can help us construct a doctrine of the Trinity.

Within the grand tradition of those who uphold the Trinity there has been a quarrel between those who follow the Cappadocian Fathers (Basil and the two Gregorys) and those who follow Athanasius. The Cappadocians said God is a Trinity and the mystery is that he is also one. They emphasized the distinctions between the Persons to such a degree that their modern adherents can even speak of a "social Trinity." There is no question of the Spirit being personal, but the unity of the three hypostases is an abstract impersonal essence. For Athanasius, on the other hand, God is a unity and his mystery is in the threeness. The Persons of the Trinity are three modes of being in the one God, and therefore distinctions between the modes blur. Thus there is biblical support for all three Persons being active in both creation and redemption.

Immediately we must ask in our historical review if today we mean the same thing by the word "Person" as did the ancient church fathers. Heretofore we have been using the word "Person" to designate the Holy Spirit, but now we must sharpen our language to avoid equivocation. Arnold Come says quite bluntly, "It is absolutely misleading to refer in the contemporary scene to the three 'Persons' of the Godhead. For us today, 'person' unqualifiedly designates the unique, discrete, self-determining *subject*. The early church meant no such thing."[25] When the ancient church formulated the doctrine of the Trinity both the Greek word (*prosōpon*) and the Latin *persona* meant face or mask. Usage of masks in the theater indicates that the word designated a character or a function, not a subject or person in the modern sense.

If the credal meaning intended to convey this operational and functional designation for the Persons of the Trinity, we must next determine whether such a meaning is supported by biblical revelation. Certainly the monotheism of both Testaments would require beginning with the unity of God and then proceeding to explain his threefoldness. Yet the threefoldness cannot be regarded as three divine attributes or as departments in the divine essence. This would destroy the personal relationship in which God comes to us, whether as Father, Son, or Holy Spirit. Perhaps here is the hint of a solution to our modern semantic problem. God in his unity is Person in the modern sense of discrete subject, yet in his various functions he does not operate in a mechanical way but comes to us on all three levels of relationship as Personal Agent, wholly Personal in Father, Son, and Holy Spirit. This may point the way to a satisfaction of the Cappadocian concern for the personal quality of the three functions of the Godhead while at the same time retaining the Athanasian concern for the Person of the God who is a wonderfully multifarious unity.

Probably the greatest advance in the history of the trinitarian doctrine has been made by Karl Barth. His contribution to its career derives from the Word as revelatory communication. It therefore supplies great support to a story construct of the Trinity. Barth says there is no possibility of knowing God truly in ourselves before he comes to us, but when the Word speaks to us in Christ the grace is given us to know. He therefore shifts all theology from the *analogia entis* to the *analogia relationis*.[26] Instead of deriving a doctrine of the Holy Spirit by examining the human spirit, he seeks to listen to Christ and learn from this hearing in faith who is the Spirit. The Spirit becomes known through the relation of his revelation to us. It is the nature of revelation itself that gives Barth his doctrine of the Trinity. If there is a *revelation* of God's Word in Christ, then there must be *one who reveals* and *one who is revealed*. If there is a Son who is the Word, there must be also a Father who speaks this Word and a Spirit that is the Son's and the Father's revealedness.

The Spirit clearly in such an analysis remains over against us in the transcendent Godhead, and both a mechanistic process and a subjective sentimentality are avoided. Barth furthermore, following his *analogia relationis*, declares that human beings are related to God through an I-Thou encounter which is derived from the self-encounter that takes place in God himself between Father, Son, and Holy Spirit. Much of Barth's language smacks of the old modalism that was rejected by the ancient church, but if we distinguish between Person as discrete subject for the Unity of God and Personal Agent as the free-willing character that God presents to us in relationship, we can avoid that difficulty.

It might be argued that the analogy of relations is not so free of human experience apart from revelation as Barth would have it. All communication involves a trinitarian relationship. Every word spoken must have a father in the thought that conceives it. When that word becomes flesh and is uttered in audible or visible form it remains hidden in meaning until there is a common spirit of communication. If I think the word *Bagunara*, even though I give that word flesh by speaking it aloud, I cannot communicate my meaning unless there is a common spirit of language between myself and the one I address. (*Bagunara* is a word of greeting in the Telugu language.) It seems that Barth's analogy of relation has itself an analogy in the general being of communication. I believe this is true, however, only because communicability is possible precisely because of the prior address of God to humanity in a story-shaped world.

Like Barth, Karl Rahner has also constructed a doctrine of the Trinity on the model of communication. Rahner says that when God steps outside himself in self-communication "it is and must be the Son who appears historically in the flesh as man and it is and must be the Spirit who brings about the acceptance by the world (as creation) in faith, hope, and love of this self-communication."[27] Rahner thus distinguishes God's communication in his creative act from his communication in the redemptive act. In creation God posits realities other than himself and in so doing he reveals himself as over against them. But such revelation does not disclose his full reality as Trinity. This fuller disclosure comes only when he incarnates himself as a creature so that other creatures may come to see him as he is in himself. And this coming to see him as he is in himself occurs through the power of the Spirit. It is not a self-evident communication, nor does it bring us knowledge of God's aseity. We see by faith not merely the flesh of Jesus but the mystery of his divinity as the Spirit gives us faith. But although we see more than the creature Jesus, we do not see all that God is.

This means that the Trinity is not merely a collection of three hypostases which have three functions that may be exchanged at will. Only the Son can become incarnate and only the Spirit can reveal and inspire and call to faith. It should be obvious that this communication theory is strongly supportive of a story construct of the Trinity. The story construct requires this particularity and progressions of persons because in the story the incarnation precedes the descent of the Spirit. It cannot be the other way around. Hence only the Son can assume the character of a man, and only the Spirit can come down to guide us to believe this man to be God. Furthermore, this view is consonant with Luther's emphasis on the paradox of *Deus revelatus/Deus absconditus*. The God who communicates *himself* reveals that he is the *hidden* One.[28]

Also in truly becoming a man, God in the story does not remain a mode of God. The character of humanity that God assumes is really human, that is, not-God. Modalism would be the different story of God coming incognito, but the real story that is told in the Bible and Christian history is the story of God assuming (not adopting) human character and agency and personhood.[29] Moreover, if God is to communicate himself—he who is Person—he must create persons to receive him. The communication construct of the Trinity tells us something about ourselves as persons. "The self-communication of the free personal God who gives himself as a person (in the modern sense of the word!) presupposes a personal recipient. . . . If God wishes to step freely outside of himself, he must create man."[30]

The story view of the Trinity affirms that God communicates himself in two modalities (apart from his communication in the creation), the modality of history in the flesh of Jesus who is received by us as truth, and the modality of the Spirit who moves us to love.[31] "Modality" is Rahner's term. He also proposes as a substitute for the word "persons" the phrase "manners of subsistence." Like Arnold Come, he notes that in modern semantics "persons" means discrete, individual spiritual centers of independent activity, and this meaning is inappropriate to the Trinity. In spite of the precision in the term "subsistence" (*hypostatis*), I think this return to ancient Greek vocabulary is both clumsy and opaque to modern people. The function of self-communication provides us with an "economic" Trinity which tells us who God is in himself as the "immanent" Trinity. The communication—the storytelling of God—is about himself, not just about an effect of his communication upon us. To speak of an "immanent" Trinity in this story way requires thinking of the Persons in relationship with each other and with creaturely persons to whom the communication is given. The persons are not static essences then but living characters who freely act and are acted upon.

Jürgen Moltmann is critical of both Barth and Rahner, even though they depart from the substance theology he rejects and even though they affirm an event theology that is harmonious with his own emphasis on the reality of history.[32] He labels Barth's construction monarchic modalism and Rahner's idealistic modalism. He says Rahner's Trinity ends in the mystic solitariness of God. Moltmann charges Rahner with failure to understand Martin Buber's view of personhood as an I-Thou relationship. Persons are not discrete individuals. We become persons only in the limiting and liberating relationship we have with others. And when we apply this notion to God we see that his unity does not begin with a discrete individual being but with the "perichoresis of the divine persons."[33] The error in Rahner and Barth derives from the psychological theory of the Trinity that was first developed by Augustine and revived in modern times by

Richard Rothe, who took Augustine's metaphysical construction and made God an "absolute personality." This reduces to a modalism which leads to the modern bourgeois world's cultivation of the individual: every individual must be able to develop himself or herself into a many-sided personality. It is true that we know God to be personal insofar as we know ourselves to be personal, but the analogy of personality does not say anything about God's triunity. The analogy leads me to discover something about my personhood. It does not tell me anything about how the Father and the Son and the Spirit are related to each other.[34]

Moltmann wants a doctrine of Trinity that is socially liberating. Hence he opposes Rahner because he thinks Rahner is too preoccupied with God's "*self*-communication." Moltmann wants to see the Trinity as the "trinitarian history of God."[35] Salvation history reveals not the unified substance of God or the absolute personality. It reveals, rather, a suffering God whose struggle frees us and builds us into a community. "The perichoretic at-oneness of the triune God corresponds to the experience of the community of Christ, the community which the Spirit unites through respect, affection and love."[36]

Robert W. Jenson adds his voice to those in current trinitarian discussion who have substituted the metaphor of God as event for the traditional metaphor of God as substance. If God is not to be seen as a timeless being but as an actor on the stage of history, then God in the Old Testament story is the one who got Israel out of Egypt, and God in the New Testament story is the one who raised Jesus from the dead.[37] This event theology clearly sees God and his creatures on a time line with a real future. Jenson says, "To be God is to anticipate a future self by an inexhaustible interpretative relation to an other that God himself is; to be a creature is to anticipate a future self, by a finite interpretive relation to an other that the creature is not; being is interpretive relatedness across time."[38] This understanding of God and time has led Jenson to offer a scathing repudiation of the process theology which also claims an event metaphysics but which in fact does not specify God's being as event. "God is in this analysis," says Jenson, "not an event but an in itself timelessly given structure of relations between all events."[39] This is indeed an accurate description of Whitehead's notion of the Primordial Nature of God, and furthermore the Consequent Nature of God cannot be related to any identifiable reality other than the concrete process of the world itself.[40] "In any event" process theology will not allow a trinitarian construct.

I have referred to Barth, Rahner, Moltmann, and Jenson because, in spite of their sparring with each other, they all present a construction of trinitarian theology that supports story theology because they substitute God as event for God as substance. To say that God is event is at least minimally required if we are to move on to a claim that God is the person who is the author of all events. And the events that God authors have their own genuine time: past, present, and future. They do not simply revolve in circles around God as the eternal event in the center. God creates them as free beings who have growing, changing relationships. And into these relationships he himself comes as another creature disclosing himself as the God who creates and the God who redeems, who has done this specifically in the events of nature and history. But the specificity which came in Jesus has revealed that God is trinitarian because God comes to us only as Son in Jesus, not as Father or Spirit. And God comes to us only as Spirit in the gifts of faith, hope, love, joy, patience, and so forth.

It is communicability that shapes the doctrine of the Trinity in a story theology. Communications are events. The events of Jesus and Pentecost make the difference. Jesus and Pentecost bring together Word and Spirit so that the trinitarian God is revealed. Jesus is a fact of history. The details of his life and death are open for inspection to everybody. He has the uniqueness, unrepeatability, particularity, and contingency of every historical event. Pentecost as a corporate event in the lives of Jesus' disciples has the same historical qualities. But when the Pentecostal experience is brought together with the event of Jesus, a universal and absolute significance is given to this combination of historical events. This has traditionally been called guidance of the Holy Spirit through faith. The Spirit speaks to the one who has been chosen and brings him or her into conversation with the Father. Through this conversation the chosen one can in faith acknowledge Jesus to be Lord and also say *Abba*, Father. Without this work of the Spirit we can know neither the Son nor the Father. Lack of the Spirit makes it impossible to recognize the Son when the Father sends him. We do not begin with the Father and come then to the Son and finally to the Spirit. We begin with Jesus and his heritage in Israel, and we come then to see him to be Messiah-Lord-Son of Man-Son of God-Savior. And this we come to see by faith through the gift of the Spirit. This is the way to the Father: by way of the historical Jesus and his Israelite heritage (which means for us in these later times by way of Word and Sacrament in the church) through the Spirit to the Father. We must not get the acts in the play out of order.

God is seen to be three Characters in one Godhead because of the once-for-all events of Jesus and Pentecost. God is not rationalistically understood to be three Characters in that he shows us three masks or faces of his single substance. This would result either in a modalism which takes away the mystery of his threeness or a Godhead that is metaphysical substance and not personal. Also God is not three in the modern sense of three functions of a common agent. Of this lean functionalism we might ask: Why just three functions? Why not reduce the functions to two and have a binity of Creator and Redeemer, or why not more than three and have a multiplinity of Creator, Judge, Redeemer, Sustainer, Sanctifier, and so forth? Here we must insist on using the word "Person" for the unity of God, and find new words from story language, words such as "character" or "personality," to designate the roles that God plays when he enters into relationship with us through Jesus and Pentecost.

On the basis of what has happened in the story of salvation we can say that two events in a common action combine to reveal the nature and work of God in such way that we have the disclosure of two actors leading us in meaningful conversation to a third. The Spirit through the Son leads us to the Father. The Father, Son, and Holy Spirit are agents, or characters, or personalities, not persons in the modern sense of independent, discrete individuals, but purposive agents who speak as responsive subjects to responsible subjects. The Father sends the Son. The Son prays to the Father. The Spirit intercedes with the Father for sinners. The Son as Word is all God but not all that God is. The Word is intelligent and intelligible, but there is room in God for the surprise, the novelty, even the humor and whimsy of the Spirit. The Trinity is not a universal idea of God. The developing triad does not end in Necessity. It ends in Actuality which is included in a Reality that transcends both reason and the senses without denying either. Finally God's self-communication discloses the hiddenness of God as the One whose awesome majesty is invisible, intangible, silent, and inscrutable. Yet, as Jenson says, "God is not hidden from us by mere metaphysical distance, so that if we do get a little toward him he will be less hidden; God is hidden precisely by his ineluctable nearness to us."[41] Glory be to God: Father, Son, and Holy Spirit!

Better than all these poor pedestrian words, even with their careful precision, the poet Gerard Manley Hopkins sings a sonnet that searches and satisfies:

> The world is charged with the grandeur of God.
>   It will flame out, like shining from shook foil;
>   It gathers to a greatness, like the ooze of oil
> Crushed. Why do men then now not reck his rod?
> Generations have trod, have trod, have trod;
>   And all is seared with trade; bleared, smeared with toil;
>   And wears man's smudge and shares man's smell; the soil
> Is bare now, nor can foot feel, being shod.
>
> And for all this, nature is never spent;
>   There lives the dearest freshness deep down things;
> And though the last lights off the black West went
>   Oh, morning, at the brown bring eastward, springs—
> Because the Holy Ghost over the bent
>   World broods with warm breast and with ah! bright wings.[42]

NOTES

1. Theodore G. Tappert, ed., *The Book of Concord* (Philadelphia: Fortress Press, 1959), 171.

2. Ibid., 592.
3. Ibid.
4. For an interesting discussion of this historical dispute, see the essay on Gregory of Nyssa by Jaroslav Pelikan in *The Scope of Grace* (Philadelphia: Fortress Press, 1963), 77.
5. Tappert, *The Book of Concord*, 599.
6. Ibid.
7. Paul Tillich, *Systematic Theology*, 3 vols. (Chicago: University of Chicago Press, 1951–63), 2:94.
8. Cf. Arthur O. Lovejoy, *The Great Chain of Being* (Cambridge: Harvard University Press, 1942).
9. Søren Kierkegaard, *Philosophical Fragments* (Princeton: Princeton University Press, 1936), 17ff.
10. G. W. F. Hegel, *The Logic of Hegel*, trans. William Wallace (London: Clarendon Press, 1892), 142.
11. David Hume, *An Enquiry Concerning Human Understanding and a Treatise of Human Nature* (La Salle, Ill.: Open Court Publishing Co., 1938), 61ff.
12. Hegel, *The Logic of Hegel*, 147.
13. Ibid., 157.
14. Søren Kierkegaard, *Sickness Unto Death* (Princeton: Princeton University Press, 1941), 55: "For it is not true, as the Philosophers explain, that necessity is a unity of possibility and actuality; no, actuality is a unity of possibility and necessity."
15. Cf. David Hume's discussion of matters of fact in *An Enquiry Concerning Human Understanding*, 23.
16. Cf. S. Nagarajan in the introduction to Shakespeare's *Measure for Measure*, The Signet Classic Shakespeare (New York: New American Library, 1964), xxx.
17. Cf. Rudolf Otto, *The Idea of the Holy* (London: Oxford University Press, 1923), 12–41.
18. Søren Kierkegaard, *Training in Christianity* (Princeton: Princeton University Press, 1944), 78–144.
19. Friedrich Schleiermacher, *The Christian Faith* (Edinburgh: T. & T. Clark, 1928), 64.
20. Cf. Gustaf Wingren, *Man and the Incarnation: A Study in the Biblical Theology of Irenaeus* (Philadelphia: Muhlenberg Press, 1959), 96.
21. Cf. C. K. Barrett, *The Holy Spirit and the Gospel Tradition* (London: S.P.C.K., 1954), 5ff.
22. Cf. Aeschylus, *The Oresteia* (Norwalk, Conn.: Easton Press, 1979), introduction by Rex Warner, xvii.
23. J. Edgar Bruns, *God as Woman, Woman as God* (New York: Paulist Press, 1973).
24. Ibid., 87–88.
25. Arnold Come, *Human Spirit and Holy Spirit* (Philadelphia: Westminster Press, 1959), 144.
26. Karl Barth, *Church Dogmatics* (New York: Charles Scribner's Sons, 1936), I/1, 353ff.
27. Karl Rahner, *The Trinity* (New York: Herder & Herder, 1970), 86.
28. Martin Luther, *WA*, 18:597; 43:435–59.
29. Rahner, *The Trinity*, 89.
30. Ibid., 88–89.
31. Ibid., 99ff.

32. Jürgen Moltmann, *The Trinity and the Kingdom* (New York: Harper & Row, 1981).
33. Ibid., 145.
34. Robert W. Jenson, *The Triune Identity* (Philadelphia: Fortress Press, 1982), 179. Jenson makes the same point: "There indeed obtain the analogies which Augustine discovered.... But what the analogies discover is my *personhood*, not triunity; they do not, as Augustine thought, reveal God's triunity or give meaning to trinitarian language about him."
35. Moltmann, *The Trinity and the Kingdom,* 157.
36. Ibid., 157–58.
37. Jenson, *The Triune Identity*, 7–8.
38. Ibid., 182.
39. Ibid.
40. Alfred North Whitehead, *Process and Reality* (New York: Macmillan Co., 1941), 524.
41. Jenson, *The Triune Identity,* 27.
42. G. Woods, H. Watt, and G. Anderson, *The Literature of England,* (Chicago: Scott, Foresman & Co., 1941), 2:941.

9

Baptism and the Church

—going back to the beginning again

Stories have stories within stories. Baptism is a personal story of individuals within the grand story of the church. Historically (and history itself has the structure of story) the church began at Pentecost, but the story of the church begins with God "in the beginning." Likewise the history of our personal salvation begins at baptism, but the story of it begins before the foundation of the world when we were called by name for a destiny with Christ and when God prepared our good works that we should walk in them (Eph. 1:4; 2:10).

The story within a story sheds light on the greater story. The play in *Hamlet* revealed to the characters in the greater play the portentous events that had been going on in the court of the king. Baptism and the history of the church will tell us something of what God is doing in the story of salvation. And in the unfolding of this plot we will see what story theology means for the great paradoxes of the Christian revelation, the paradoxes of God being *absconditus* and *revelatus,* of God being in Christ and in the neighbor, of Christ being with the Father and in the bread and wine of Eucharist, of baptized Christians being *simul justus et peccator,* of Christians being predestined and responsible, of time bringing the future into the present.

BAPTISM

We need to take a new look at baptism. From the beginning of Christianity the overwhelming majority of Christians have always practiced infant baptism with the understanding that baptism is a sacramental means of grace.

The sacramental view of baptism says that baptism is God's act in which he gives us a new creation through water, the laying on of hands, and incorporation into the church. Baptism is God's gift to his sinful creatures in the form of a token or pledge or promise which has outward signs for inward grace. Both Christ and the Holy Spirit are present in this gift. Christ is present to share with us his suffering death and his victorious resurrection. The Holy Spirit is present to raise us to new life so that we can bear his fruits of love, joy, patience, faith, and hope.

The danger in this sacramental view is that we can turn it into a magical ritual. If we think erroneously of the gift of grace as a supernatural substance, then it can be manipulated by an elite priesthood. The sacrament can be perverted into a superstition that can be exploited. A story view of baptism will talk about the action and passion of persons and not the transfer of substances. Let us speak then of baptism in terms of what happens. Baptism is a new creation. To get that in perspective we must look at the first creation. And let us look at it as a story that is told. Or perhaps I should say stories, because there are several stories involved. In any case, the important thing is that I will use the language of story, not the language of the sciences or the language of philosophy. And I will use the language the Holy Spirit uses in Scripture.

In the beginning God created the heavens and the earth. The earth was without form and was void, and darkness was on the face of the deep, and the Spirit of God moved over the surface of the waters. And God said, Let there be light; and God saw that it was good.

But the goodness fell. There was rebellion in heaven when an angel, Satan, desired to be God and tried to steal God's creature. There was temptation on earth when Adam and Eve believed Satan's lie; and they too rebelled.

Now God was confronted with a problem. He could not leave his creatures in the garden he had made for them. Adam and Eve and all under their dominion were expelled, and ever after the earth and its creatures have been groaning in anguish, waiting to be delivered from this exile, waiting to be restored to God. And God waits too, because he cannot abide the rebellion and the separation from his creatures. How would God restore them?

What would you do if you were working at a problem and it did not come out right? You would start over from the beginning. You would go back to the beginning and carefully work over every step to see what went wrong. This is what God did with himself and his creature, and this is what he wants us to do with our lives. Go back to the beginning, to the start of everything before all the mistakes were made, so that you can be born anew and get a fresh start.

And what will you find in the beginning? When you started your life you were a baby in the arms of your mother. And your father was close by with his love and strength. That is the way God starts with his revelation of himself to us, with a tiny baby wrapped in swaddling clothes and sleeping in the gentle arms of his blessed mother Mary. But if you go back beyond your parents and beyond your parents' parents and back beyond and beyond, there will come a time when this world will lose form and all will become empty. There will be darkness brooding on the face of the deep before the sunrise brightened the morning, before the moonlight softened the night, before ever there was a sky in the heavens and an earth below. You will ultimately go back to the loneliness of God in the limitless seas of eternity.

And when you come to the loneliness of God you will see that it was no accident that he decided to correct all the mistakes in humanity by going back to the beginning with the sighs of the Spirit and fashioning himself as a baby.[1] Here in Christ is the starting point. It was Christ in the first beginning whose Word created the world, and the Spirit gave it life. And it is Christ again in the incarnate Word conceived by the Spirit that brings the new beginning, the new heaven and the new earth. And he begins as a baby. This is an important reason why we baptize babies, because we must all become as babies to start over again. "Except you become as a little child you cannot enter the kingdom of heaven." Christ and our baptism are the hope of our renewal, the new person in Christ who wipes clean the slate of the old person in Adam. In baptism we leave the family of Adam and enter the family of Christ. To leave an old family means to be separated from it, and that is the meaning of death, to be separated never to return. So baptism means dying to the family of Adam and rising to the family of Christ. In this we see our personal story interwoven with the story of Jesus, whose story as the Christ embraces the entire cosmos.

But in the history of salvation God did not start with baptism. Indeed he tried a couple of things before he decided to go all the way back to the beginning.

First he tried to clean up the world by means of the flood. His intention was to save a few (eight people) so that all would not be lost. This did not work, however, and so God, like a good sailor, took a new tack by electing Abraham to be the means of saving humankind. A covenant was made. Abraham and his seed were called to be a blessing to many nations, a light to the Gentiles. Henceforth God preserves Israel against his enemies. God wanted Israel to endure so that Israel could save the Gentiles. Now some endure so that all can be saved. Again, as in the flood, water is used both to condemn and to save. In the exodus Pharaoh's forces are drowned; Moses and Israel are saved; moreover, there is the saving water from the rock in the desert. The story of the flood says some are saved so that all is not lost; but the story of Israel says some have been saved in order to preserve the rest. But this failed because the Jews took their calling to be an exclusive privilege rather than a privileged task.

In the New Testament, as we have seen, the story shifts to a tale of redemption not in spite of suffering but through suffering. In the New Testament the Elect One does not endure. He dies. The old covenant, in which God promises to preserve Israel, is replaced by a new covenant, in which God neither saves some and drowns the rest nor elects some for the sake of the rest, but he slays his Elect One and indeed all the rest in order to make a new creation. Or rather I think we should say he delivers up his Elect One and all the rest to sin, and so they suffer death. The Christian story alone among all redemption stories faces up to the scandal of death as the wage of sin for everyone. Hence our story says we must give up all power and wealth and wisdom and become as little children in order to enter the new kingdom. We must die to our selves and rise to new life in the Spirit, and in that way we become alive in the family of Christ, that is, we become incorporated into the church.

These are the three dimensions of baptism. The first is dying with Christ with its visible sign of water. The font is a watery grave. And it has a cosmic scope, because it is the sign of our personal death to the old creation along with the entire world.

The second dimension of baptism is rising in the Spirit to newness of life with its visible sign of the laying on of hands. Out of death we come to life, and the new life in the Spirit brings us into a new heaven and a new earth, a whole new creation which God is fashioning according to his glorious vision with his table of times. But this new creation itself has a visible sign in the church. The church is the sacrament of the new kingdom, the visible token, pledge, promise of the final glory.

In the baptismal rite we have a sign of this third dimension in the lighted candle that is presented by a representative of the congregation. The church, as the sacrament of the new kingdom, is not a voluntary fellowship or a cultural development, although it provides fellowship and produces a culture. The church is the called assembly of the Lord, the members of which constitute, as in the great mystery of marriage, a living organism which is one, holy, catholic, and apostolic. The church is a ministry of sacrifice. As Christ was elected to be the suffering servant, so the church has been called out of the world to be sent into it to serve. Baptism is the ordination of the people of God for this living sacrifice. Baptism then makes a difference in all that we do, not that as born again Christians we can claim a special holiness for ourselves, and not that as born again Christians we can claim special gifts from the Spirit, but as born anew in the family of Christ we can suffer and serve in our daily vocations, acknowledging the ambiguity of our situation as sinners and saints in the world that is both good and evil, but always serving with love and joy and patience and faith and hope, for these are the fruits of the Spirit.

THE CHURCH

Church is story, and the history of it is the story within its larger story. Charles Williams in *The Descent of the Dove* wrote a history of the church as the story of the activity of the Holy Spirit.² The story of the church since Pentecost is the calling, gathering, enlightening, and sanctifying of the Holy Spirit as he builds anew the body of Christ from the ashes of Adam. The church is the gathering of those who belong to the Lord *(kyriakoi,* the Greek word for those who are of the Lord, from which through the creative distortion of language we get our modern words *Kirche, kirk,* and church). They are built up into a body that has a life of its own, that has a destiny filled with adventure because it has been sent out on a mission. Its destiny is the fulfillment of the quest of both God and all humankind. This phase of the story begins when the two quests, God's and humankind's, meet at the ascension of Jesus. Northrop Frye has said, "It is part of the critic's business to show how all literary genres are derived from the quest-myth."³ Stories universally reflect the natural human quest for fulfillment in various ways. In a previous work, *Story and Reality,* I tried to show how stories exhibit themes in humankind's search for resolution of evil, for satisfaction of love, for practice of holiness, for hope in a Messiah, and for meaning in human destiny.⁴ The story of the church tells how all these quests meet when God comes to his creatures with his quest, which marvelously turns us around and satisfies our deepest universal yearnings by taking them away, denying them radically, yet fulfilling them in his own way.

The Church Is Mission

God takes away in order to give. This he has done in both his creative and redemptive acts. In the continuous tradition that is called the church, God calls the elect to a suffering service in order to give them the riches of his grace. This is the mission of the church, the completion of the afflictions of Christ. The church is mission. Perhaps the ascension most sharply points up the mission character of the church in that here Jesus tells his disciples as he goes away to the Father that they are sent out into all the world, with the wonderful paradox that Matthew declares, "And surely I will be with you always, to the very end of the age" (Matt. 28:20). As with baptism, we will go back to the beginning to see how the structure of story sheds light on the doctrine of the church.

The earliest Christians remained in Jerusalem after the resurrection because they looked for the coming of the Lord to establish his promised kingdom there. Their covenant quest was rooted in the temple. Apprehensively they asked the risen Jesus, "Lord, are you at this time going to restore the kingdom to Israel?" (Acts 1:6). Daily they went to the temple because they expected the Messiah to come to this very sanctuary, thus honoring the ordinances of worship. This anticipation was based on Mal. 3:1: "Behold, I send my messenger to prepare the way before me, and the Lord whom you seek will suddenly come to his temple." Jesus answered by taking away the temple, Jerusalem, and the whole heritage of the Jewish cultus. In their place he gave them the world. With a logic of contradiction he took away the past in order to give the future.

It was Stephen who first clearly understood the kingdom to be more than a kingdom-to-Israel.[5] Stephen began the world mission of Christianity in its full eschatological sense. His work as deacon was more than serving tables. Together with Philip he was an evangelist. And his evangelism immediately aroused criticism. He was accused of talking against the holy place of the temple and the law. He was charged with replacing them with Jesus of Nazareth. And, of course, in a real sense this was true. Stephen was not against the Jewish cultus and law as such, but he certainly did declare that they belong to an outworn past and must be replaced by the living Christ as the center of life and worship. The eschatological understanding of the significance of Christ introduced a universalism which was highly offensive to the spiritually proud Jews. His eschatological insight may be seen in Stephen's last utterance. "Look," he said, "I see heaven open and the Son of Man standing at the right hand of God" (Acts 7:56). This new eschatological revelation takes the place of the prophetic expectation of Malachi. The story takes a climactic turn when the commanding character of Christ comes to center stage.

Stephen was the only one in the New Testament aside from our Lord who used the term "Son of man" as applied to Jesus. This means that he perhaps more than anybody else first grasped the significance of the universal range and bearing of the Christ event. Jesus was Son of man. This means that all human beings come under his sway. Whereas the Jews held to the permanence of their national historical privilege as chosen people, Stephen recognized that this kind of election was now withdrawn in order that salvation might also be given to the Gentiles. Whereas even Jewish Christians with all their messianic faith adhered to the temple, going up daily at the hour of prayer, Stephen saw that the Messiah was not in a building made with hands but rather was sitting upon the throne of the universe. Thus the ascension meant that the gift of the resurrected Lord was now taken away in order that a new and greater gift might be bestowed, namely, the gift of the ever-present Lord of the Christian Eucharist who graces the altar of every church around the world and in every generation. Hence the call to the church of Jesus was to leave the temple behind and go forward in the new living community centered in the ascended Lord.

All the apostles from the beginning were eschatological in their understanding of Christ's message, but at first they expected Christ to return imminently just to them. There are still Zionists and other people looking for the "rapture." Stephen understood that the church must go out and proclaim Christ to the nations. The work of those who belong to Christ was now seen to anticipate Christ's coming by announcing him to every nation in that larger world which was now included in his new dominion.

Stephen's interpretation of history sees God in this greater story constantly seeking to impel Israel toward an ultimate end in his divine plot. Beginning with Abraham, God said to him, "Go out! Leave the land of your father and seek a new home." And as long as Abraham lived, he was a landless stranger in a land of promise. So it was with his posterity too, the patriarchs and Moses. God gave Moses the command to lead his people out of bondage in Egypt, but in spite of the divine impulsion, the people always resisted. Israel was given a tent as tabernacle for worship during their wandering in the wilderness. It was fashioned after a "revealed pattern." This was brought into the land of promise by Joshua, and it was a type or figure of God's never-ceasing, never-halted appointments for his people's salvation. But the time came when Israel desired a more permanent dwelling for the Most High, and hence Solomon built the temple. But this was not the end of God's dealing with his people. It was gross error for the Jews to think so. Indeed the Most High does not dwell in a temple made by human hands. Heaven is his throne and earth is his footstool. The temple is actually no more than the tabernacle. It was not intended to become a permanent institution, halting the divine purpose for the people of God. It was only a stage prop. It was not wrong to build the temple, just as it was not wrong to obey the Jewish law; but it was wrong to rest in the temple just as it was wrong to delight in salvation by law. This is to resist the Holy Spirit, who is always a disturbing, unpredictable, innovating, iconoclastic force in our religious life.

The author of the Letter to the Hebrews draws a sharp contrast between approach to God through the law and the Christian approach through the grace of Christ. To do this he compares the experience of Moses on Sinai with the experience of Christians in the presence of the living Christ in worship in the church. It is not a tangible world to which we draw near in worship, not a world of fire and mist and gloom, with tempests and trumpets and an awful voice. This historical setting is what accompanied the law and the cultus. The Christian approaches God through the pierced veil of the holy of holies in heaven. The story lifts us through a fictional deception to a factual reality. Hence the numinous element of religious experience is described in terms of myriads of angels with the assembly of the firstborn of the church whose names are enrolled in heaven, the spirits of the saints. God is pictured as judge and Jesus as mediator with his blood effecting a better sacrifice than Abel's, because Abel cries for vengeance, historical retribution, but the blood of Christ atones for sin, resolves the historical dilemma.

The approach to God for the Christian is thus determined by a divine impulsion that drives us out from cloistered comforts to a pioneer pilgrimage, to a faithful risk in which we scuttle the settled ceremonies of this world for the harrowing holiness of heaven. Jesus is our high priest in his self-oblation on Golgotha. In this cross he nullified law and cultus and covenant, and instead he bestowed grace and Eucharist and the New Testament. It is not that the church now has no altar, but God took away the sacrifice of the temple with the one holy of holies in order that he might give us an effective sacrifice outside the camp: "And so Jesus also suffered outside the city gate to make the people holy through his own blood. Let us, then, go to him outside the camp, bearing the disgrace he bore. For here we do not have an enduring city, but we are looking for the city that is to come" (Heb. 13:12–14). Because Jesus died on Golgotha, Christians have altars in every church but yet have no holy place. Christ died in one place and at one time for all places and all times. The hidden and revealed Christ is with the Father and also on the altar. His sacrifice is done once and he is not repeatedly crucified in time. This is climactic in the story. But in all times and in different places we repeatedly share in this sacrifice because we find our place and time, our role, in this larger story.

This is the answer to all in the Christian tradition who have tried to make the church an exclusive club, whether of a Judaistic family or a monastic order or a social elite. This last is simply the modern secular expression for the same kind of spiritual pride that motivated ancient Pharisees and medieval monks.

Jesus broke that pride of exclusiveness in the cleansing of the temple. He added fuel to the fire when he spoke to the Samaritan woman. And then he showed us the way from a ritual of water purification to a Eucharist of wine when he performed the miracle at Cana.[6] Each of these three incidents in the life of Jesus may be understood if we will look at them as steps in the divine purpose for the glorification of God. The eschatological thrust in the cleansing of the temple provides a radically new perspective. Jesus did not drive out the money-changers because they were conducting a commercial enterprise in the holy precincts of the temple, as if commerce were in itself unholy traffic. This presupposes a division between the sacred and the secular, a division contrary to the whole purpose of the gospel which is precisely to make this ground on which we stand holy ground. Nor can we find here a sociological moralism which makes Jesus an indignant reformer who has set out with righteous wrath to redress the balance between a money-grabbing priesthood and a duped laity. That certainly occurs at times, but here nothing of the kind is indicated in any of the Gospel accounts. Jesus quotes passages from Isaiah and Jeremiah: " 'My house will be a house of prayer'; but you have made it 'a den of robbers' " (Luke 19:46). Without question, Jesus must have intended to say to his generation what the prophets said before him, and this was not social reform but sharp denunciation of idolatrous worship in the temple. The thievery here was the robbing of God, not the people. This is followed in John's account by a prediction that the temple would be destroyed and then raised in three days, with the explanation given that Jesus referred to the temple of his body in the resurrection.

The point is that Jesus did destroy the temple and he did replace it in three days with his risen body. The temple stood for Jewish worship which, with its legalistic sacrifices, robbed God of his glory. Jesus took this away in order to replace it with his own person as the center, both object and subject, of worship.

This is why he could say to the Samaritan woman that God is not worshiped either in Jerusalem or on Mt. Gerizim, but he must be worshiped in Spirit and in truth. He himself is the source of living water, he is the bread from heaven, he is the blood of life—Jesus in his own person replaces the Jewish rites of water purification and instead supplies the wine of forgiveness in his own life's blood, he replaces the sacrifice of the lamb with the bread of the Eucharist.

The miracle at Cana is a pointer to the hour of Jesus which is both the hour of his death and the hour of his glorification. Once again, Jesus did not satisfy a mere social amenity in changing water to wine, thus helping a careless host to avoid embarrassment. This miracle is not a quaint illustration of God's concern for little things, nor even of God's nod of approval for the jocose conviviality of a wedding feast, a nod which he must surely give away. This miracle had the high and serious purpose of manifesting the glory of God. This was done by indicating that God intends to cleanse us no longer through water ablutions, such as those of Jewish law, but henceforth through the wine purification of the Christian Eucharist as it is sealed in the hour of Jesus' death.

It follows therefore that this miracle does not lead us into a view of the church as a fellowship predominantly characterized by social feeling of friendship, but rather it requires us to see the church as a eucharistic glorification of God through the participation of the saints in the death and resurrection of our Lord.

The nature of the church's mission is not individualistic or merely historical. It is not *Heilsgeschichte* but salvation story.[7] Its story line has a proclamation with an eschatological thrust. Certainly individuals within history and history itself are profoundly affected by this eschatological mission of the church, but they are carried beyond both their personal history and the history of this world into an eternal destiny which reaches back to the beginning and extends past the end.[8]

The church is not for the individual, nor is it for the amelioration of history. Christ died as person for persons, and the cosmic Christ died for the cosmos, but only when the individual dies to himself or herself and when the world passes away will we find redemption for our bodies or freedom of creation from bondage to decay.

The holy history of Israel enters into the story of salvation with the election of Israel as God's chosen people to be the cradle for his Christ. This gift of light to the Israelites meant the withdrawal of light from the Gentiles, who were allowed in their rejection to go their own way. They were delivered up to their own sin. They shaped their own quest and wrote their own story. But God soon began to take also from Israel. In the chastisement of this holy history Israel lost its freedom, its nation, its temple. Only a remnant returned to fulfill the promised destiny. But even this was withdrawn and God left Israel without the voice of the prophets. Israel was consoled only with apocalyptic hope until finally there were none righteous, and all had gone astray. But God sent One to be the redeemer, to carry the great destiny of salvation. He alone was the whole Christian church on earth as the remnant was narrowed down to one man, the man Christ Jesus. But in him the process was reversed, and instead of narrowing, a broadening occurred.[9] As God took light from the Gentiles and gave to the Jews in Abraham, so now in Christ he took from the Jews and gave to the Gentiles. Yet he takes from the Jews only so that he may in turn show them the grace he gave to the Gentiles. "For God has bound all men over to disobedience so that he may have mercy on them all" (Rom. 11:32). Thus Jesus said, "As the Father has sent me, I am sending you" (John 20:21). And the apostles were sent into the world to build up the church until Christ could subject all things to himself. Thus the church becomes the instrument of redemption through all history with the election of a minority for the salvation of the whole.

The grab and grace cadence in the pulsing life of the church is demonstrated clearly in the chaotic condition of what we used to call "foreign missions." Our generation has watched with dismay as mission fields have been caught up in the wrenching turmoil of world revolution, originally seeded by the gospel itself, only to be cut off from the mother church. Separation has come both from onslaught of secular forces without, as in the China mission, and from indigenous forces within, as in the India mission. But the missions have been taken away from the mother church only to be given back as true members of the body of Christ. As a result, we have gained a new understanding of the church as one body with many members which contribute freely to the whole.

It was a mistake to evangelize by attracting individuals, uprooting them and wrenching them from their families and their culture, and attaching them to the Christian community. This strategy was inspired by the individualism of the past two hundred years, and the result is that we have been crossing streams by jumping from rock to rock instead of using the bridges God has provided for us.[10] We should look into the art forms, the stories, the music, the dances, and the social structures in cultures where the church is not known, and there we will find Christ already at work ahead of our coming. He will be found at the point of pain in every society struggling to release people from their bondage, their ignorance, their sickness, their poverty. The evangel of the church is to proclaim God's deliverance, not to establish institutional cells which grow alongside other institutions in the body of a society or culture. When the church becomes a cell in the general structure of society it only contributes to the sickness of that society. Cultures fight diseases in the same way the body does, by walling off the offending area. Social ostracism results and the bridge between church and non-Christian community is broken down. Sometimes such cells are welcomed as new or recovered bastions of decency and sobriety; sometimes they are tolerated as training schools for children; often they are rejected as either a threat to tradition or an obstacle to progress. The result of this misunderstanding of the nature of the church is its inadequacy to meet social problems that threaten to destroy the culture.

An adjunct to individualism is voluntaryism. The church has been falsely conceived as a voluntary fellowship of like-minded God-lovers. A feeling of friendship is supposed to result when we make a decision for Christ and join the Christian community. In common cause we now pursue the ideals of liberty, equality, and togetherness. The irony in the story is that where this feeling is lacking, no real effort is made to accept into our fellowship those who are different from us, and indeed positive effort is made to guarantee our sociological homogeneity.

The church is not a voluntary fellowship in which members choose to unite because of common ideals, least of all the outworn ideals of the Enlightenment. The church is a family in which we find ourselves to be members by election and rebirth. In a fellowship we choose our friends according to our tastes and interests, but in a family we do not choose our brothers and sisters. They are given to us and we must accept them whether we like them or not. Membership in the church is determined by the call of Christ in the Spirit. Regardless of the flatness of their noses or the accents of their voices, regardless of the things they do, whether criminal or insane, heroic or holy, all people are brothers and sisters when they have been called by the Spirit.

Another irony in the story is that we try to get social justice without spiritual community, or we try to get spiritual community without social justice, and if we do try to get them both we get them out of order. We cannot live by bread alone, nor can we live without bread; but before we get bread we must give thanks to God. So long as we think of the church as a social organization we will never have integration at the table of the Lord. When we begin to understand our election in one faith through one baptism under one Spirit, then the integration we know in our marriage with the Lamb will manifest itself in the marketplace, the school, the theater, and the voting booth. Both secular segregation and sectarian divisions violate the edifying creativity of the Spirit. The nature and enormity of this voluntaryism has been described by Dostoevsky in his penetrating picture of the Grand Inquisitor described by Ivan in *The Brothers Karamazov*.[11] The Inquisitor has become antichrist by substituting security for freedom. Ironically we freely choose our own bondage. Like the Inquisitor we choose to set up a power institution with the instruments of this world in place of the liberating, bleeding body of Christ. Only through the courage of the cross can we be the church. This means completing the afflictions of Christ by offering our homogeneous, voluntaristic congregations to the lions in the arena of this world.

It would seem then that the church will become culturally effective only when it becomes true to itself as a people movement in the establishment of a new kingdom. The church ushers in a new age under the lordship of the Spirit, who guides us into all truth. By our individualism and our voluntaryism we have allowed other spirits to rule and these are principalities and powers that are in the service of the prince of this world. If we are to be the church, we must proclaim the kingdom to be a radical renewal of both individuals and all of society.

Predestination and the Structure of the Church

We have found that the way we enter the church is through baptism by the call of the Spirit. We cannot just be born into the church, nor can we decide of our own volition to become a member. We must be chosen for rebirth. The church is the *ekklēsia,* the called assembly of the Lord. The Greek word *ekklēsia* was originally used in secular connotations for a simple gathering or assembly, but when it was used in the Septuagint to translate the Hebrew *qahal* it took on a technical meaning inasmuch as the *qahal* was the predestined elect of God called to be his assembly with the special task of being suffering servants for the Lord. It was the election of Israel to be the light to the Gentile. The whole meaning of predestination throughout the Bible must be understood in the light of this election for a task rather than election for status. The calling of God does not give us the privileged position of the saved or a sinecure in heaven. It gives us the grace of responsibility to be servants for the salvation of others by proclaiming the kingdom and showing the King's death until he comes.

A story view of reality and a narrative hermeneutic will guard against confusing predestination with predeterminism. The philosophical concept of predeterminism has nothing to do with the biblical story of predestination. Its universe of discourse is in disjunction with freedom. Predestination is a free action of God which we may freely respond to either positively or negatively. Indeed it gives us a new freedom that we did not have before the election. Israel as the chosen family was free to resist the Spirit. Judas as a chosen disciple was free to betray his Lord. Predestination means that God has chosen us to be his witnesses. Baptism is the sign of this election. God also provides opportunities for us to serve in this witness. Without this grace from God we can do nothing, but as in every story, the suspense of predestination is that we can always do otherwise. We can miss our opportunities and end in tragedy.

It was a mistake to quarrel over single or double predestination. The mistake occurred because of equivocation between predestination and predeterminism. If God predetermines some to salvation, then we are in the realm of logic, not story, and we must consistently say then that he either predetermines all the rest to damnation or he lets them choose their own salvation or damnation. Those are the logical possibilities. But they are not the real possibilities. In reality we have witnessed the actuality of God's election of some for the sake of the rest. It is not a matter of some being saved and some being damned. It is a sequential tale of some being chosen to be witnesses to the Gentiles, and then of Christians being chosen to be witnesses to the world.

During the Reformation, predestination was discussed in connection with our bondage to sin as over against our freedom before God to save ourselves. The Reformers insisted that before God we have no freedom to justify ourselves, and therefore if we are to be saved at all, it must come by the predestined grace of God. We have freedom of choice and action in matters within the created order, but with regard to redemption and our eternal destiny we have no choice or ability. This Reformation principle seems to be wholly consistent with biblical revelation and human experience. It was unfortunate that the debate became confused when a philosophical category was substituted for a narrative description.[12]

The image and description of functional election will shape the structure of the church. When we are called to engage in a common task, we find ourselves welded into a common living organism. This organism is described in the Bible with several metaphors. It is called the body of Christ, the vine and the branches, the temple of living stones, a flock of sheep, the mystery of marriage, a holy family. In every analogue the church involves life, growth, movement, work, and unity in diversity. Here in the body of Christ we find the Spirit at work creating, forming, fashioning, and transforming us to conform with the image of Christ. This is not an individualistic *imitatio Christi* or spiritual formation through personal piety. It is the power of God building us up in his church and working in us that which is pleasing to him. The church's unity is the oneness of Christ, who is both one in function and one in being with the Father. So likewise we in the church have a unity of purpose in our common task and a unity of life in finding our reality with one another and with our Lord.

It is this unity of the living organism which makes the church also a *koinōnia* ("communion"). Insofar as the members share in the oneness of Christ they share in each other. Our stories and his story meet and become a common destiny. What happens to the head happens to the members. We participate in his life as we participate in his body and blood in Holy Communion. The church is a communion of saints in that it shares in the work of Christ, who was sent from the Father to suffer for the sake of a sinful world. Christ's work is certainly finished, but the church completes joyfully what remains of the afflictions of Christ, suffering in the flesh for the sake of his body.

The image of functional election thus also becomes the basis for apostolicity in the church.[13] We have been called by God to be sent. This is what it means to be an apostle and to stand in apostolic succession. Some try to define apostolic succession in terms of ordination; others see it as continuity of pure doctrine; but the story of salvation finds true succession in the continuing drama of our calling to be sent to save others by being little Christs to our neighbors. Apostolicity derives from the mission described in Acts 2:42: "They devoted themselves to the apostles' teaching and to the fellowship, to the breaking of bread and to prayer." Continuity comes from the mission that is begun in worship.

The great cleavage in the church is between those who would make it a spiritual event and those who would make it a historical continuity. Stories can be told about both. But in the extreme those who stress the spiritual event end in sectarian divisiveness, and for them evangelism is an amoeba-like process of multiplication by division. And those on the other hand who stress historical continuity end in some kind of structural universalism, and for them evangelism is assimilation and cultural accommodation. The church cannot grow by appeal to peevish idiosyncrasies of individuals, nor can it be edified through the intimidation of a gargantuan organizational structure. Yet there is truth in Augustine's plea for the authority of catholicity: *Ego evangelio non crederem, nisi me catholicae ecclessiae commoveret auctoritas* ("I would not have believed the gospel if the authority of the Catholic church had not moved me").

Certainly the communion of saints is catholic in that it is universally continuous in space and time vertically and horizontally, and this is so because it derives its wholeness from its head who is universal and not divided. Certainly this catholicity supersedes any individual subjectivity that may claim authority. The church is not a community of pious religionists who come together because of common feelings of reverence for what they choose to be holy. But also the church is not merely a historical continuity, nor does this catholic continuity guarantee its purity and holiness. Just as Hosea had to say that the chosen people of Israel were not God's people because God has withdrawn his mercy from them, so we must say that God may constantly reject even his own church. There is always this suspense in the plot. Paul reminds us of this in Rom. 11:21: "For if God did not spare the natural branches, he will not spare you either." It is the rhythm of redemption that God chooses "the lowly things of this world and the despised things—and the things that are not—to nullify the things that are" (1 Cor. 1:28). Sometimes God must speak in history with a radical, earthshaking wrench. This he did at Pentecost.

Again he spoke at the Reformation. And both times he broke historic continuity with the fire of his Spirit. The reform of the church unfortunately falls into a pendulum swing in which abuse in one direction is countered but then often becomes abuse in another direction. A story resolution of such conflict requires a mediated tension in which the subjectivity of persons in community becomes distorted neither in the direction of a privatized sentimentality and narcissism nor in the direction of a dehumanized institutionalism.

Finally, the church is a holy mystery. The most profound insight given us in the Bible concerning the nature of the church is the metaphor of the bride of Christ. That Christ the Holy One of God should take from the sinful world a wretched bride is mystery indeed. This is the harlot Gomer whom Hosea took to wife. This is the foreign Ethiopian woman whom Moses chose to marry. The church is Rachel for whose sake Christ bears the burden. The church is chosen from heathendom, foreign and impure in itself, yet loved by Christ. The great mystery is that Christ should love the unlovable, and the only holiness the church has is the fact that it is loved by Christ.

A man loves his wife as he loves his own body. So Christ loves the church and gave himself for her. In marriage two become one flesh. So likewise in the discernment of the Lord's body in the Eucharist the bride and the bridegroom become one flesh. This is a mystery in the natural world where the beloved is chosen by her lover. She is mystified by this love and does not understand it, yet she is overwhelmed by it and renewed. So God elects us and does not ask for our intellectual cognition of his action but merely our faithful acceptance. And in this union we are renewed. We serve him who serves us.

Two aspects of the mystery of the church should be mentioned. There is a mystery of knowledge and a mystery of being. In the church the mystery that has been hid from the ages is now made known in Jesus, who was crucified. This spiritual wisdom about God was given to those who were called, but others who were not called did not receive the mystery. "Whoever has will be given more, and he will have an abundance. Whoever does not have, even what he has will be taken from him. This is why I speak to them in parables: Though seeing, they do not see; though hearing, they do not hear or understand" (Matt. 13:12–13). Once more the hiddenness and revealedness is manifest in the story, and God takes away in order to give.

The second aspect of mystery is the union with Christ described as marriage. We must be careful to distinguish this mystical union from metaphysical union which would be contrary to biblical teaching. We grow up in the body of Christ as the bride of Christ, but we never become absorbed in his deity, nor do we lose our identity as creatures. It is not growth to divinity that we experience in the church but growth to a humanity which is in the image of God.

Ministry and Government in the Church

In *The Council, Reform and Reunion,* Hans Küng says the great issue of division between Rome and its "separated brethren" is not justification by faith, nor the authority of Scripture, nor even Mariology.[14] It is, rather, authority in the church.

The problem of authority is one of the most perplexing questions of our time, and it extends into government, business, science, the arts, the family, and all of society. For nine centuries, from Gregory the Great to Luther, this was no problem, since the church was clearly the seat of authority. Freedom was the problem, however. Freedom was lacking until, at the expense of authority, this was supplied by both the Renaissance and the Reformation, however opposed these two spirits were in all other respects. The quest for freedom in every area of human endeavor characterized the centuries after Luther. The new franchise given in the sixteenth century produced a new culture with a strange wall between church and world which did not exist in the Middle Ages. We now must acknowledge the emergence of secularism as the dominant force in the modern world. For Christians who are divided it becomes imperative to settle the issue of authority so that we can speak with one voice to a world that itself cries out for authority in the midst of its free but meaningless drift. We must know where this story is leading us. What can a story view of reality tell us about authoritative ministry and government in the church?

Roughly, although this is an oversimplification in analysis, we may say there are three answers to the question, Where is the seat of authority? There are those of Peter who say authority resides in the church. There are those of Paul who say authority resides in the word of prophets and apostles, that is, in Scripture. And there are those of Apollos who say the only true authority is in the individual Christian conscience.[15] When Luther at Worms found himself at odds with the church he appealed to Scripture and conscience. This should give us a clue to proper procedure in settling this debate. If Luther spoke truly, then the Holy Spirit works in the story of salvation with several vehicles, using some to correct others when human aberrations occur, as they must necessarily do in a world being saved from sin.[16]

In the first place, then, it is the action of the Holy Spirit in the story of salvation that leads us to authority. Our question is, who or what speaks for Christ? As Christians we may agree that Christ is the ultimate authority, but in what way is his authority exerted on us so that we can act? Clearly Christ is a living person who governs with love according to the needs of the situation at hand. If we are involved in a story, he is not a feeling or a principle. He is not a proposition. He is not a constitutional structure. Yet he does work through all these things. But if Christ is the authority by which we live, we must admit that there is no absolute principle of authority that can be identified in human feelings, propositions, or legal structures. To do so would be to fall into idolatrous devotion to vehicles of grace, props on the stage, rather than a proper worship of the source of grace. We must always wait for him to say his own lines. Not the conscience, nor the Bible, nor the church can claim infallible authority. None is inerrant, yet all can claim to speak for Christ. Councils and popes have erred. The Bible is written in human words with many mistakes and contradictions. Prophets have spoken from twisted consciences. Yet the Spirit of God has been active in all these areas, and the living Word has been present giving meaning to the life of Christians through church, book, and conscience.

It seems proper to conclude that God speaks authoritatively through all these vehicles, using one as a check against the other. We can say that the Bible is God's Word only if we mean that it brings us infallibly to Christ. It is not a rule book or manual of ethics any more than it is a textbook on geology or history. It is the Word in story which brings us savingly into confrontation with the speaking Christ. The history of Protestant theology in the last century has demonstrated, to its own honest embarrassment, that the Bible itself is a historically conditioned book, although it is not a mere human achievement but truly the act and gift of God. But if this is so, it is likewise true, to the honest embarrassment of Rome, that the church is a historically conditioned institution needing constant reform and renewal, although it too is the holy body of Christ under the guidance of the Spirit, and the Spirit does not leave his church. He guides the elect into truth, but this truth is not legal, or propositional, or private; it is dramatically personal and communal. The Spirit guides us to the Person of Christ who walks alongside us and constrains each step we take, prompting us so that we edify the community with righteousness and love.

But the book and the conscience are not apart from the church. The Bible is the church's book, and the conscience of the believer is nothing but anguished sin apart from his or her common confession in the assembly of God. Thus it is only in the church that the conscientious believer gets didactic training with the Bible as guide, and it is the Spirit which brings these three—church, Bible, and conscience—into harmony. Bible and conscience have authority then only when Christ is present with his Spirit, that is, only in the dramatic interplay of the church. It should be evident now that there is no authority for any of these three except as they coinhere in each other and in the living Christ who works to save his creation. Holy Writ must find authority in holy church and vice versa as they are both realized in the conscientious witness of the worshiping community.[17]

In the second place, if the Spirit tells us where we can find authority, the nature of the church tells us what kind of authority we can expect. We have seen that the church is a living organism. The church cannot be defined or described as a democratic, representative, or monarchic political structure. None of the Aristotelian categories of political analysis apply to the church. Certainly an organism can have neither egalitarian nor monolithic behavior. Certainly also the church is not a balance of interests protected by pressure groups and elected representatives. The church has a government and at times this is mistaken for its nature, whether its form is patterned after secular governments or not. But the authority of the church on a story model does not arise either from the right of officers in a monarchic structure or from the right of laity through the transfer of their function for the sake of order. Authority arises not from rights at all, but from obligations and responsibility. So it has always been in the covenant community of both old and new Israel. The bishops do not have the right to rule any more than the laity have the right to transfer rule. Both have privileges and responsibilities according to the various functions assigned them by the Spirit. The gift of the Spirit in ordination is not an office (position, status, or place), nor an indelible character as a substantial spiritual possession, but a responsible task, an obligatory service, a role to play.

All authority derives from the work of Christ. Jesus was the Christ because he was sent from the Father to suffer for sinners and thereby glorify God. His suffering service is continued in the work of the church (Col. 1:24–25). He appointed some to be apostles with a commission to bring grace to the world and draw all people to him who was lifted up in humiliation and glory. Their positions could not be handed down. Only Peter can occupy the place of Peter as first in the living temple.[18] But their functions can be transmitted from generation to generation. They are ambassadors for Christ. Some are thus set apart for special functions, and their authority is valid when, and only when, they do the work of Christ. This work is the mission to save the world through suffering for the glory of God.

For this reason Jesus gave the authority of the keys to the apostles, and they in turn have passed this authority on to successors whom they have named (Acts 14:23). This commission gives chosen servants the authority to forgive sins and to withhold forgiveness. It is the whole work of ordained ministry that is at stake here, the shepherding work of preaching, baptizing, absolving, pastoral care, communing, and teaching. It is not an authority that can be transferred from the people. It is not an authority that can be delegated by representative legislation. It is an authority that can be given only by the higher authority of Christ since it is God who forgives sin against God, not human beings. And Christ has chosen to appoint certain ones to preach and teach and bring grace through the sacraments. This is a high view of ministry because it derives from a high view of Christ.[19]

In the third place, the specific authority of the apostolate derives from the Spirit-led coinherence of church, Bible and conscience, and the nature of authority as an obligation to serve. The apostolate was not created by the community. It was an appointment for ambassadorial service authorized by Jesus in creating the church. None of the New Testament references to the apostles indicate that they received their authority or commission from a particular congregation or community. Always an apostle represents the whole church. Paul is not the apostle from the church at Antioch, but the apostle of Jesus Christ, or of the gospel, or to the Gentiles, "an apostle—sent not from men nor by man [possibly here referring to Barnabas], but by Jesus Christ and God the Father" (Gal. 1:1).

Encounter with the risen Lord and commissioning by him define the two marks of apostleship for Paul and the early church. Many saw the risen Lord but not all were commissioned as apostles, yet Jesus appeared to all the apostles, and last of all to Paul "as to one abnormally born." The Damascus encounter is therefore not a vision but a resurrection meeting, a real encounter on the stage of history, in which Paul received his commission to proclaim this good news.

When a disciple (learner) receives apostolic authority in the name of Jesus this gives him no new rights; rather, it binds him to serve the one who authorizes him. The commission involves lowliness, not exaltation. Hence the apostolate is cleansed of all legal claims and it should be called a commission instead of an order or an office. Apostleship is like its more inclusive category predestination in that it is an election to serve and not a gratuitous sinecure. This is what is meant in 1 Tim. 4:14 where Timothy is urged not to neglect the gift that was bestowed in prophetic utterance when the elders laid their hands upon him. This is not the transfer of the gift of an office with a privileged status and an indelible character. It is the commissioning of a function. Definition of apostolic function, though not precise, involved doing exactly what Jesus himself came to do. "As the Father has sent me, I am sending you" (John 20:21). "And I confer on you a kingdom, just as my Father conferred one on me" (Luke 22:29).

It used to be said among Protestants that no unique authority had been given the apostles.[20] What authority they exercised supposedly rested on personal qualification. Adolf Harnack had taught that there prevailed at first a kind of pneumatic democracy in the church, and later, to meet the gnostic heresy, church organization became clad with divine dignity and authority. A study of the documents without this Protestant bias reveals just the reverse. The apostles had authority from the beginning because Christ gave it to them, and he gave it to them because the eschatological nature of salvation called for a suffering Messiah who gathered into his body the people of God. To accomplish this in the story of salvation the Messiah had to have fellow workers, apostles who preach, heal, cast out demons, ambassadors who can be sent with authority that comes from the Father to do Christ's work after he has ascended to heaven. Salvation is seen as the stewardship of God whereby he brings all things under the headship of Christ, and history is the theater in which this holy play takes place. Although Christ the protagonist alone does the effective work of atonement, he calls and sets apart certain ones to share in his work through preaching, service, and administration.

In the fourth place, although apostles were directly commissioned by the Lord, various other ministries of the church arose out of worship in the community of Christians.[21] This is not to imply democratic origins; rather, it means that in Spirit-led worship Christ directed his body to shape itself in a working structure that best suited its function to serve. Indeed he still continues so to direct and shape his body and its ministry.

In the beginning Christians continued to go to the temple for prayers and sacrifices, but soon it became evident that when they met in their homes for their common meal the risen Lord was also present. It was this presence with the liberating guidance of the Holy Spirit that led to a separation of Christian worship from the temple and establishment of a Christian ministry. The risen Christ came with the freedom of the Spirit. He was not bound to one place or time, but the locus of his coming was whenever and wherever Christians gathered for breaking bread. He had promised his disciples this would happen when he spoke of the destruction of the temple. In the resurrection a new body arose together with Christ the head, and this new body gets its life from the gracious presence of Christ. This body is the living church which is constantly being built up in the Lord. Such edification is its worship. No Levitical priesthood is needed to offer repeated sacrifices, because Christ has given his risen self to the Father, having been sacrificed once and for all. But now he continually intercedes for us in the heavenly holy of holies, and hence we repeatedly celebrate thankfully his victory over sin, death, and the devil. At this eucharistic celebration Christ is present creatively building his new kingdom through the hospitality of his delegated ambassadors. In the conduct of such celebrative services apart from the temple some kind of leadership had to be provided. For the variety of functions in the Christian community there arose a variety of ministries (1 Cor. 14:26).

In view of this story perspective on ministry, we must reaffirm the authority of ministry as a commission to serve which comes from Christ to apostles and their successors through the laying on of hands. But we must also reform the ministry so that there will be both a balance of authority and a structure that serves the needs of our day. The story model calls for an encounter of characters who resolve their several purposes through conflict and sacrifice. I propose that our needs can be satisfied in harmony with our biblical and traditional heritage if we establish a troika of primacy in which (1) the functions of prophecy and teaching are organized under one hierarchy as the magisterial arm of the church, (2) the functions of the sacraments are organized as the pastoral arm of the church, and (3) the functions of administration, stewardship, and evangelism are organized as the episcopal arm of the church. Each hierarchical arm should extend with authority and function throughout the entire body of the church, working for the whole at every level. Thus the magisterial arm, for example, will be responsible for teaching everywhere from nursery school to seminary. None should be supreme and each should check on the other so that the Spirit may be a living guide to all through a coinherence of authority.

While the succession of authority derives from above in all three hierarchies, primacy of the episcopal head over the other two need not be established, and indeed each hierarchical arm should be structured with collegiality so as to guard the guardianship of the head in answer to the primal question: *Quis custodiet ipsos custodes?* ("Who will guard the guardians themselves?") A further check upon abuse of authority will come from the consent of the people. While it must be clear that no authority arises from the people, on the other hand no authority can function with power without the consent and ratification of the people.

The mood of our day is one of revolt. Authority is denied in every sphere of human activity, not least of all in the church. It is very easy but false to argue therefore that authority must be earned, that no one may rule unless one can demonstrate that one deserves to rule. The fact of this cannot be denied, but the principle cannot be affirmed. We may rightly demand responsibility from bishops, pastors, and teachers, but we must remember that their authority resides in their function, not in their person. We can demand that they remain true to their function, which is to rule by serving, but we cannot say that their lead should be followed only when they win our hearts.

Yet there must be some check on leadership too, and this inheres in the general consent of the people together with the check of each hierarchy on each other. The consent of the people, however, must not be construed as a popular vote to which bishops, pastors, and teachers are responsible. The clergy in all their functions are responsible for the people to God, not to the people for God. They have been called as ambassadors for Christ and they must lead the people for Christ. They do not represent the people and reflect popular will. They represent God and reflect divine will. But as in the general principle outlined earlier concerning the coinherence of authority in church, Bible, and conscience, so in the specific authority of ministry there must be coinherence in the ordained authority through laying on of hands in the succession of bishops, pastors, and teachers together with the non-ordained authority that resides in the consent of the people.

If all this sounds like a continuing struggle with no easy solution, I do not deny it. In fact, I affirm it, because such is the nature of story, but in this plot a realistic resolution is foreseen.

NOTES

1. For a discussion of the foundation of baptism in the death and resurrection of Christ, see Oscar Cullmann, *Baptism in the New Testament* (London: SCM Press, 1950), 9ff.
2. Charles Williams, *The Descent of the Dove* (New York: Meridian Books, 1956).
3. Northrop Frye, *Anatomy of Criticism* (Princeton: Princeton University Press, 1963), 17.
4. Robert P. Roth, *Story and Reality* (Grand Rapids: Wm. B. Eerdmans Publishing Co., 1973), 77ff.
5. For a full development of eschatology and mission in the speech of Stephen, see William Manson, *The Epistle to the Hebrews* (London: Hodder & Stoughton, 1931), 25ff.
6. Oscar Cullmann, *Early Christian Worship* (Chicago: Henry Regnery Co., 1953), 66ff.
7. Perhaps the renewed emphasis on history as revelation in the work of Wolfhart Pannenberg and Jürgen Moltmann is needed as a corrective to the demythologizing and dehistoricizing of Rudolf Bultmann, but my concern is to recognize the role of history as one story in the larger story of the cosmos. Cf. Wolfhart Pannenberg, *Revelation as History* (New York: Macmillan Co., 1968), and Jürgen Moltmann, *Theology of Hope* (New York: Harper & Row, 1967). Choan-Seng Song, in *The Compassionate God* (London: SCM Press, 1982), 62, clearly refutes Pannenberg with regard to *Heilsgeschichte*. Pannenberg claims to have departed from the straight-line theology of Cullmann but universal history is appealed to after all only in the service of a narrow Judeo-Christian line. Song says: "Our conclusion is that Pannenberg's principle of universal correlation is not so attractive as it promises to be. In this day and age a Christian theology of history cannot make one giant leap from the Judeo-Christian, western history to universal history, leaving aside completely the history of the eskimos, the Australian bush folk, the Polynesians in the southern Pacific, or the Chinese-Mongolians in that vast continent of Asia." My point is that such narrowing of theology, with its concomitant narrowing of missiology and evangelistic strategy, cannot occur if we think of story, rather than history, as being ultimate. It is interesting to note that "official" historiography, whether in the historical books of the Bible or in books of other cultures such as the Confucian tradition of China, follows a simplistic formula which describes the fortune and prosperity of a ruler and his kingdom as a function of his obedience to the "Law of Yahweh" or the "Will of Heaven." When scholars want to describe the way things really happen, however, they depart from propagandistic historiography and write stories and novels such as *The Book of Jonah, War and Peace,* and *The Tale of Two Cities* in the West and *A Dream of Red Mansions, Romance of the Three Kingdoms,* and *Outlaws of the Marshes* in China. These tales give a rounded and deepened picture of the ambiguities, absurdities, surprises, and contradictions of reality.
8. This is not the same as John Dominic Crossan's "permanent eschatology" which says the eschaton is not the end of the world but a repeated shattering of complacency. This hardly differs from Bultmann's realized eschatology. Cf. John Dominic Crossan, *In Parables* (New York: Harper & Row, 1973).
9. Cf. Oscar Cullmann, *Christ and Time* (Philadelphia: Westminster Press, 1950), for a full discussion of this process.
10. Cf. Donald McGavran, *The Bridges of God*, rev. ed. (New York: Friendship Press, 1981). Song, *The Compassionate God*, 178ff., shows how Buddhists used a

method of extension, *koyi,* in the spread of Mahayana Buddhism across China and Japan which crossed over cultural bridges already in place. Instead of imposing Indian culture upon China and uprooting individuals and families from their native traditions, Buddhism extended itself into Chinese religious and philosophical thought. Ironically the spread of Christianity into the Greco-Roman world and later into barbarian Europe followed precisely this method of *koyi.* We need to learn today from Buddhists what we as Christians have forgotten from our own heritage in the theology and history of early Christianity. Song calls this a theology of "transposition."

11. Fyodor Dostoevsky, *The Brothers Karamazov* (New York: Random House, 1933), 255–74.

12. Luther was not exempt from this confusion when he wrestled with divine prescience and human free will. Cf. Martin Luther, *Bondage of the Will* (Grand Rapids: Wm. B. Eerdmans Publishing Co., 1931), 240.

13. Cf. Oscar Cullmann, *Peter* (Philadelphia: Westminster Press, 1953), 56ff.

14. Hans Küng, *The Council, Reform and Reunion* (New York: Sheed & Ward, 1962), 128ff.

15. Cf. Leslie Newbigin, *The Household of God* (New York: Friendship Press, 1954).

16. Anders Nygren has shown us how Lutherans can agree with Roman Catholics that the church is an organism, and Avery Dulles has shown us how all Christians can be edified by a diversity of models for the church. Cf. Anders Nygren, *Christ and His Church* (Philadelphia: Westminster Press, 1956), and Avery Dulles, *Models of the Church* (New York: Doubleday & Co., 1974).

17. Priesthood of believers did not mean for Luther that everyone is his or her own priest. Cf. Jaroslav Pelikan, ed., *Luther's Works,* Companion Volume, *Luther the Expositor* (St. Louis: Concordia Publishing House, 1959), 245.

18. Cf. Cullmann, *Peter,* 213ff.

19. Gerhard Kittel, *Bible Key Words,* "Apostleship," by R. H. Rengstorf (New York: Harper & Brothers, 1958), 34.

20. Anders Nygren, ed., *This Is the Church,* "Church and Office in the New Testament" (Philadelphia: Muhlenberg Press, 1952), 103.

21. Cf. Robert Paul Roth, "Ministry," in *The Encyclopedia of the Lutheran Church,* vol. 2 (Minneapolis: Augsburg Publishing House, 1965).

10

The Bible and Preaching

—the sacrament of the Word

God is the author of Scripture and our preaching. The words in both are ours, but the story we tell is his.[1]

THE BIBLE

The task of the theologian is without question more difficult and more perilous than any other task in the world. Think what is at stake. The theologian must speak for God to a yearning, sinful humanity. Theologians do not speak for themselves, nor for their family or tribe or nation, nor even for all humanity, which in itself would be an impossible task. The theologian must speak God's word to humanity. The pastor as pastor collects the prayers of the people and speaks them to God, but the pastor as theologian must hear the Word of the Lord in Scripture and in the tradition of the church, and translate and interpret that Word in language the people can understand.

Exactly what does the Bible say? Consider, for example, the passage in Genesis where Abram went to the Land of Canaan and the Lord appeared to Abram and said, "To your offspring I will give this land." Does this mean that the Jews today, who are the offspring of Abram, have a God-given right to that territory? What about Ishmael, the son of Abraham by Hagar the Egyptian; and what about Esau, the grandson of Abraham, who is the ancestor of the Arabs? It is true that the Bible also says, "It is through Isaac that Abraham's offspring will be reckoned," and this cuts off the Egyptians as Abraham's heirs; and it is true that Esau sold his inheritance for a mess of pottage, and this cuts off the Arabs. But is this the Word of God for Egyptians and Arabs and Jews today? Does the Bible say that the land of Israel, as the Zionists claim, was taken by God from the Canaanites and given to the Jews for all time, so that they have a divine right to drive out the Palestinians from their homes and occupy their land? Do the great nations of the world have the right to dispose of the "Jewish problem" that way? What kind of God is it who plays favorites with the Jews against Egyptians and Arabs?

But there is another way to read Scripture. Since the coming of Jesus Christ into the world we have a new light from God which is shed upon his Word and which, in this instance, Paul clearly explains in his letter to the Galatians. Here he says, "The promises were spoken to Abraham and to his seed. The Scripture does not say 'and to seeds,' meaning many people, but 'and to your seed,' meaning one person, who is Christ" (Gal. 3:16). According to Paul, there is a new covenant which makes Christ the heir of Abraham. And Christ is the savior of all humanity. We are all one in that we have been made of one blood by our Father in heaven. We are also all one in that we have fallen short of the glory of the Lord, and therefore God has consigned us all to sin so that he might have mercy on us all. This means that there is neither Jew nor Greek nor Arab nor Egyptian, but all are one in Christ. And no family or tribe or nation has the right to claim any territory as God-given to the exclusion of others. "The earth is the Lord's and the fulness thereof." Zionists, whether they are Jews or conservative Christians, whether they are fanatically suicidal on top of Mt. Masada or militantly oppressive in the modern State of Israel, are making the difficult and perilous claim to speak for God. If the Bible is God's Word, we will have to search the Scriptures to see what he has to say.

Ever since the Reformation, when Luther appealed to the Bible against abuse of papal authority, there has been a continuing controversy over the authority of Scripture.[2] As we have seen in the previous chapter, throughout the history of the church there have been three authorities: Paul, Peter, and Apollos. Those who have followed Paul have made the Bible the final authority for their faith. Those who have followed Peter have bowed to his successor, the bishop of Rome.[3] And those who have followed Apollos appeal to their own experience as the ultimate guide to God. Lutherans, Calvinists, and many other Protestants have generally followed Paul in their appeal to Scripture against what we consider errors of a triumphal, tyrannical church on one side and a self-righteous, anarchical experience on the other side. But within the Protestant tradition we have a running debate over what we mean by the authority of the Bible. Is it the Word of God or does it contain the Word of God? Is it God's Word to us or humankind's word about God? Is it literally true or figurative fiction?

The climate of opinion about biblical authority is confused today. We have recently experienced a general attack upon the bastions of tradition in every field. In shaky times like these both the church and the Bible give way to personal experience. Perhaps the rebellion was not so much against authority as against the abuse of authority, but the mood of our times has included a strong feeling of distrust for organized religion, and this is coupled with a nervous search for a genuine individualized "happening" which will authenticate one's relationship to God. But now on top of this revolt against authority above, there is a resurgence of concern for the literal authority of Scripture. People want to be supported by a divine Word that is absolutely true. Thus when they read in Genesis that God created the world in six days, they take this to mean six twenty-four-hour periods, as we literally measure days. When the Book of Jonah says the Lord provided a great fish to swallow Jonah, they take this to be historical fact, never considering the possibility that the story of Jonah was written as allegorical fantasy.

Why should anyone demand that every word of the Bible be accepted as literally true? And beyond this, why do these people include even the words in the margin of their particular edition of the King James Version, where, for example, it says the world was created in 4004 B.C.? Even though the Bible does not say this, because it is printed in their book they think God said it; and therefore, in their opinion, evolutionary theories about the origin of life over billions of years must be false.[4]

People yearn for literalism because in the midst of confusion they need authority, something solid and sure that they can count on. Being "born again," these people take the Bible to be God's special word to them. With an excess of zeal and little knowledge they read it in simplistic fashion, reducing the words to single, historical meanings. Yet one must observe that they also apply fantastic imagination in taking stories out of context and applying them to current events with most curious moral and political comment.

They give us the argument that if any detail in Scripture is doubted, the whole is in jeopardy. Hence every word of Scripture must be accepted as literally given. If you question one report in the Bible, where will you stop? This puts a story like Elisha's ax head floating on the water on the same level of authority with the resurrection of Jesus. This does not matter to the literalists, because both reports are believed to come directly from God. What God says in the Bible, therefore, must actually have happened in history.[5]

Indeed, this last criterion, the fact of history, is the proof of the pudding for conservative Christians who take the Bible literally. They really want to make historical all that they believe. In short, they want to believe by sight, not by faith. We believe by faith and not by sight, and this means that the Holy Spirit gives us the power to believe that which transcends our natural experience of empirical sense and rational thought; but faith is not believing in anything nonsensical or irrational; faith is not credulity or superstition. Faith is truly the mind and the senses of the newly born person. It is that new elemental power which God gives us by grace when he regenerates us in baptism. Faith cannot be described in terms of anything else, not in terms of knowledge, decision, or feeling. Faith is not reducible to cognition, courage, or trust, although when we have faith all these are shaped by it. But above all in this connection, faith is not assent to what we see in history, as if everything in the story of Christ from the virgin birth to the resurrection could be reduced to historical fact.

And interestingly at this point opposites meet, because liberal Christians are also equally interested in demonstrating their faith in terms of historical fact. Liberals will not believe anything unless it is historically verified. Both conservatives and liberals say, "You can believe this because it actually happened in history." History is the final court of appeal. History is the sacred cow of our era, for conservatives and liberals alike. Of course, their criteria for what actually happened are radically different. Liberals accept only what can pass the test of scientific criticism. Contemporary scientific, historical criticism says that since miracles do not happen today, Jesus did not actually walk on water, he only appeared to do so. Both conservatives and liberals end in a literalism that denies the transcendent dimension of Scripture which alone gives it its authority.

It appears to me that the motivation for literalism is fear, fear that if a report is not historically verified, it will be dismissed as fiction, and fear that if one report is dismissed, all will be lost. Usually when a controversy persists for a great length of time there is fear on both sides that what they hold dear will be lost. Since often there is truth in what both sides hold dear, I would like to expose the fallacies in logic on both sides of the debate, but also I would like to find the truth that each side has to contribute so that the whole truth may be known better. Obviously if fear is a factor in the controversy we will have to look at both sides with love because only love will drive out fear. No one will be convinced against his or her will.

At the outset it is a logical fallacy to require the acceptance of a single instance lest the whole be lost, because this assumes that the Bible is a syllogism or a scientific theory with mathematical integrity. Logically the domino theory will not hold water, but psychologically it is powerful because people fear it. We can eliminate the fear, however, by showing that the various discrepancies and historical inaccuracies in the Bible do not shake its basic story in the least. Actually the Bible has several historical traditions side by side, sometimes interwoven, sometimes in glaring contradiction. The dates for the crucifixion are different in Luke and John. The story of Paul's conversion is different in Galatians and Acts. The earliest Greek texts report that Mark quotes Malachi and mistakenly lumps it with a passage from Isaiah. There are hundreds, even thousands, of textual differences. While at one time it may be possible to verify some passages or smooth out differences, new evidence may arise to disqualify our judgments. In any case, since all historical evidence and scientific judgments are relative, it is never possible to find ultimate and abiding authority in the so-called facts of history. These remain only in the realm of sight, but our relationship with God depends on the gift of faith. The axis on which our eternal destiny turns has two poles, therefore, one rooted in the empirical evidence and experience of history and one reaching into the hidden and mysterious transcendence of faith. To reduce biblical evidence to history is to cut off the dimension from which all authority comes. Thus although it is good for both conservatives and liberals to insist on historical verification, it is wrong for both to claim any abiding authority in it. The authority of the Word of God in Scripture is not in isolated details but in the grand sweep of the story that is told as that story creates our salvation through our faithful response to it.[6]

Another approach, equally fearful, is the literalist's attempt to affirm the authority of Scripture by eliciting the help of commonly accepted heroes. Luther is called upon to support literalism because he advocated the plain, simple, historical and grammatical sense of Scripture. He said so, however, only to refute the "monkey tricks" of indiscriminate allegorizing which became common in the late Middle Ages. Thus Luther said: "Heretofore I have held that where something was to be proved by Scriptures, the Scriptures quoted must really refer to the point at issue. I learn now that it is enough to throw many passages together helter skelter whether they fit or not. If this is to be the way, then I can easily prove from the Scriptures that beer is better than wine."[7] Fundamentalists today have said that Ezekiel predicted the modern airplane when he saw the four wheels in the sky!

Actually all Scripture requires interpretation, and the principle of interpretation developed by the Reformation is that Scripture interprets itself. The clear and obvious passages interpret the obscure passages, and all the passages, according to Luther, must be seen in the light of Christ: "All the stories of Holy Writ, if viewed aright, point to Christ."[8] We should recognize, then, that the Bible is God's story about Christ, and that everything in it from creation to redemption concerns the action and passion of Christ. No passage may be taken out of context, and every passage must find its place in the story of Christ, who is the Word that creates in the beginning and redeems in the end.

We may say that the Bible has authority not because of a theory of inspiration or infallibility but because it is the story of a promise that has been, is being, and will be fulfilled. The Bible has authority because it can be believed. It is the story of God, who can be trusted. It is the story of God, who does what he says he will do. The story of Jesus is the fulfillment of Old Testament messianic promise. Israel was delivered from bondage and exile to become the cradle for Christ.

Devout people, however, become disturbed and fearful when the information given in the Bible is challenged as inaccurate or unhistorical. The Bible is supposed to be true. When cultural relativism skeptically rejects the truth claim of this information, people either defiantly deny the skepticism or cynically discard the Bible because they think it has nothing in it for them.

In his attempt to deal with the authority of Scripture, James Barr distinguishes three different processes of biblical study with their respective advantages and disadvantages: (1) referential, in which passages are seen to refer to entities such as real people and historical events; (2) intentional, in which an attempt is made to recover the mind of the writers; and (3) poetic or aesthetic, in which the myths and images of the text are seen as they are.[9] He finds that reading the Bible as literature has advantages in that it may thus be appreciated by non-Christians as well as Christians, and it may be read without a theological bias, but it has disadvantages in that it may become an escape from the scrutiny of historical criticism, and it suffers from the limitation of "poor articulateness of theological discussion that could be achieved if this were the only method of approach."[10] He says literary comment will improve our appreciation for the Bible but will only send us back to read it again and enjoy it more. It will not provide an outside criterion, nor will it answer fundamental questions such as: Is there a God? Did Jesus come from him? Does resurrection have existence apart from the Gospels, or does it have existence in the story in the same way that Hermione exists only in *The Winter's Tale*?

Barr points out that many Christians are not troubled by the fact that some books and stories in the Bible are fictional. The Book of Job and the Book of Jonah may profitably be read as fiction, but they do not form the central structure of faith. "This structure," he says, "appears to be formed on the basis of two things: either special events, like the birth, the death and the resurrection of Jesus, which are taken to be seminal; or passages which are unusually doctrinally articulate."[11] Barr is saying that there must be some referent outside the Bible, outside the myths and legends and parables, which can be historically determined; or, if this cannot be done, we must find some eternal message that can speak to us across the centuries. This may be an accurate description of the various current approaches to Scripture, but these approaches are wrong because they lead us to fixed ideas rather than living story. My thesis of story theology includes all three of Barr's approaches. Historical referents and authors' intentions are essential to a thoroughgoing literary theology. Moreover, in addition to historical referents nonhistorical realities must be affirmed, and affirmed not just as an idea or a message behind the story, as if the story were mere illustration or ornamental metaphor and rhetoric, but rather as ontological entities. The biblical entities do not need anything outside the Bible to authenticate them. The stories speak for themselves. Some are entirely historical, some nonhistorical, and some mixed with both immanental and transcendent dimensions. Their authority and authenticity must be judged in terms of the place they have in the total framework of God's biblical speech as he does what he says he will do.

Finally the clue to the nature of the Bible's authority must be found in the way it uses language. The Bible is neither a scientific treatise nor a philosophical essay. It is from beginning to end a story, not merely history, although it always has empirical experience as one of its poles. The ostensibly non-narrative parts of the Bible find their place in the story like stage directions or program notes. As with all stories, the Bible has movement, conflict, humor, tragedy, persons, props, and mystery, but mystery that is celebrated and never solved. The language of the Bible is therefore poetic and figurative, full of analogies and suggestive images. There are three kinds of analogical uses of words: similes, metaphors, and symbols.[12] Similes are explicit comparisons, as when Jesus said, "This is what the kingdom of God is like. A man scatters seed on the ground" (Mark 4:26). Metaphors are comparisons with direct identification, as in Psalm 23: "The Lord is my shepherd." Symbols are words of comparison in which the comparison drops out of sight, as in the prologue to the Gospel of John: "The Word became flesh." None of the words in these passages can be taken literally. The kingdom of God is not a seed, the Lord is not a shepherd, Jesus Christ is not a word. Yet by means of this analogical, suggestive, and indirect language we cross over from the literal to the transcendent, and thus communication by image-making brings us to God.

Let us look at the way stories make images for us that lift us into a new world. Shakespeare's *A Midsummer Night's Dream* is a story that weaves together two worlds, the world of the people of Athens and the world of fairies. Each of the two worlds has within it a hierarchy of characters. The people of Athens have their Duke, who is betrothed to the queen of the Amazons. There are among them the prominent citizens who provide the chief plot for the play with their mixed-up love affairs. And there are the lowly craftsmen who bring humor and surprising connectedness to the play. The fairies also have their king and queen, and at the bottom of their ladder is the mischievous Puck, who provides the action that brings the two worlds together. But although the actions of the fairies influence the destinies of the people, the world of the fairies is always unseen. Only Bottom, the lowliest of the craftsmen, directly encounters the queen of the fairies; and then it is when he has been transformed by Puck into a monster with an ass's head and she is under the spell of a magic potion. When we watch the play we are lifted out of our monodimensional world of cities and suburbs into a new realm which has these two worlds that intermix. What is otherwise absurd and impossible now becomes intensely and delightfully real. And it is interesting to see how the two worlds interact. The effect of one upon the other is real, but it is never coerced and the results leave us with the feeling that we are always free and responsible for whatever happens. These are not causal connections that can be isolated and verified, but in the story they are real connections nonetheless. Another example of this is *The Tragedy of Macbeth* where the three witches predict Macbeth's future, but in fact he shapes his own destiny by his vaulting ambition. He is told by these supernatural wraiths that he will be king of Scotland, that no one born of woman can harm him, and that his castle will stand secure until Birnam's Wood comes to Dunsinane Hill. With such fortunetelling coupled with his insatiable desire for power Macbeth fulfills the prophecy of the witches by his own actions. What we attribute to fate is thus portrayed in the play to spring from our own nature. In short, we make our own luck—as does Macbeth.

These are small stories, and the world is full of stories, but the Bible is the story that includes and embraces them all. In the Bible we see many worlds. As Jesus said, in his Father's house are many rooms. And the mystery, the surprise, the delight of the divine drama is that it is all played out on the stage of freedom. God is free and we are free, yet paradoxically he has won the victory in the conflict of his story and his will is done in heaven and on earth, not deterministically in details but in the cosmic sweep of things, in the denouement of the play.

With this understanding of the nature of biblical language, we can now answer our original questions about the Bible as the Word of God and whether it is literally true or figuratively fiction. We can say that it is true that the Bible is the Word of God, but when we speak this way we do not speak literally. We speak figuratively in a metaphor, but the figure is not fiction. And to speak in a metaphor does not make the Bible less authoritative, because, as Aristotle said, "Metaphor is by far the most important language in poetic diction."

Far from losing the authority of the Bible, this recognition of the nature of its language gives us the freedom to go beyond the literalism of the flesh to the dynamism of the Spirit. But the freedom of the Spirit also bespeaks the responsibility, the constraint, the orderliness of the Word. The Spirit never acts without the Word. With the Father the Word and the Spirit constitute the Holy Trinity, and the Trinity is never divided.

This brings us back to the beginning where we said there are three seats of authority: the church, the Bible, and faithful experience. As God is Father, Son, and Holy Spirit, each serving the other in the Godhead, so we have on earth the church, the Bible, and the faith of believers, each serving the other and providing a troika of authority. The Bible does not stand alone. It is the book of the church and the inspiration of its members. Its authority must always be interpreted by the magisterial arm, the teaching office, of the church in the light of the believing consent of its readers. With that kind of check and balance in three seats of authority, there is both a process of self-correction at work in the area of interpretation and a process of growth in revelation as the Holy Spirit brings new life to each new generation. This too is part of the new birth that occurs when we are lifted into God's new heaven and new earth to become players in his holy drama.

Thus the Bible gives us new life. It is no dead letter. But in one sense it certainly is a letter. As Kierkegaard said, the Bible is a love letter on which the lover tells his beloved to come at once because he wants to hold her in his bosom. But suppose we do not act on the message but stop and consider the date, the style of penmanship, the grammar and vocabulary. Suppose we spend years wondering about the authenticity of the letter, wondering and hesitating, wrestling and worrying, even quarreling among ourselves about its meaning, and never, never act on the message!

PREACHING

Preaching is God's way of telling us about himself and our destiny through words that are intelligible and moving.[13] Preaching does not add any grace beyond what we receive in baptism, but it helps make us conscious of it. Both preaching and baptism are happenings, prevenient and irresistible, in which we receive a gift that comes to us before we come to it (prevenient), and a gift that is given to us without our choosing it (irresistible). We are chosen. We cannot choose to be chosen, and we cannot resist being chosen, although we are always free to throw away the gift. Thus infants receive baptism, and the baptism of infants is the norm, because in baptism we receive a person. The Person of Christ comes to us and he brings with him to the infant the multitudinous members of his body, the church. Infants can receive this Person and his members because baptism is not by our choice or effort but by God's election and grace. But the election and grace are not automatic, or mechanical, or coercive. God is free and we are free. God does not revoke that freedom which he gave us in his image, not in his providential care for us according to the creative order of things, nor in his predestinating salvation of us according to the redemptive order of things. God never violates our freedom. Thus he does not cause our salvation. He calls us to salvation, and we are always free to reject him. This is the excitement of preaching. In it we are aware of the drama of a free struggle in which minds are opened, decisions are made, emotions are felt. Human consciousness and intelligibility are manifest in the sermon as we wrestle with the power of the Word to liberate us.[14]

In an ecumenical age we should be grateful for what we can give, not fearful of what we may have to give up. Certainly one great contribution of the Reformation has been the revival of the preached word, but we have gone through a period recently in which sermons have not been in vogue. Faddish substitutes for sermons were tried, and perhaps the electronic preachers have filled the vacuum created by our loss of confidence in preaching. But our Christian faith can never discard its Word of God theology. The sermon has gotten into trouble because it has not been understood in its true sacramental sense.[15] Just as the Eucharist is the nonverbal proclamation of the Lord's death until he comes and is therefore a "sermon," so also the sermon is the verbal proclamation of the Lord's death until he comes and is therefore also a "sacrament." The living Lord is present in the preached word.[16] Preaching tells us the good news that

Christ rose and is with us. The sermon is always interpretation of Scripture, nothing but Scripture spoken, come alive in the current idiom. Preaching is the story of the Bible with power to give us new birth for the coming kingdom. It is disastrous when preaching abandons that story for pious poems. The sermon is not a maudlin Mother's Day mouthing of vacuous platitudes, nor does the sermon supply the sentiment desired to support our status quo culture. The sermon is a prophetic message calling us to judgment. It is the critic of our culture. And also the sermon is a hopeful message promising mercy and release from sin and really working in us a creative reconciliation. Gospel preaching is always prophetic. It sends out both warning and hope.

Sermons require both preachers and hearers. They will fail if the preachers say only what pleases and if the people in the pews listen only to what they want to hear. Preaching then becomes spouting water over a host of narrow-necked bottles. Not many of them get very full. What we need is revolutionary preaching which will communicate the power of the Spirit to nurture the new birth that is begun in baptism. Jesus began his preaching by renewing the Spirit as he spoke through Isaiah, to feed the hungry, to free the prisoners, to uplift the oppressed, to heal the blind. He did not talk to people about pie in the sky; he did not talk about the condition of their souls, not even about their prayer life. He told them about love, joy, peace, community, freedom, freedom from tyranny, and freedom from fear, especially freedom from fear.

We have a marvelously, terrifyingly rich field today for the planting of the gospel. The social stress and political turmoil of our world are ripe for revolutionary preaching which will renew us both for this life and the next. The gospel we should preach is Christ and him crucified, Christ is risen working among us, Christ will come again in glory. But how will we tell the many stories that precede, surround, and follow from this story of Christ?

There is a story that points to this problem. A little boy went to Sunday school and learned about Moses and the exodus. When he came home his mother asked him about the lesson, and he began to tell her with great excitement that Moses was told by God to go behind the enemy lines and rescue the Israelites. He brought them to the Red Sea and there he commanded his engineers to build a pontoon bridge, and the Israelites all crossed over to the other side. But now Moses saw the army of the Pharaoh coming with his tanks, so he quickly radioed headquarters through his walkie-talkie, and they sent some bombers which came and blew up the bridge just in time to save the Israelites. "Well," said the mother "did your teacher tell you that story?" And the little boy said, "She told me a story, but if I told it to you the way she told it to me, you would never believe it!"[17]

To tell the story of Christ in such a way as to get people to believe it should not be the main item of the homiletical agenda. We certainly do not want to get in the way of their believing, but also we do not want to change the story to make it palatable to its hearers. If we change the story, it will lose its power to transform, because it is constantly being transformed to suit every audience. No, we must let the gospel be the gospel. To change it to suit our ears is the unforgivable sin against the Holy Spirit, because when the Spirit comes to us in the Word we must accept that Word and let it work its wonder in us, and we must not substitute for it some twisted, softened, sweetened human word. The little boy did not tell the story of Scripture. He told a different story about a man who used his wits and cleverly outmaneuvered his enemy. This is an interesting story too. It shows how modern people interpret history. The story in Exodus shows how one ancient people, the Israelites, saw their history. They saw God intervening on their behalf in accordance with his covenant to preserve Israel against his enemies. This was a supreme instance in which God acted in history as a deliverer from tyranny, as the shaper of a nation's destiny, and as the judge against oppression. The story as we have it is told by the Jews. It is supposed to be true, because as a part of the canonical literature the claim is made for it that God inspired the telling. But how would this story have been told by the Egyptians? It is difficult to recover this. Perhaps the Egyptians would have said, "Our God abandoned us because we did not bring enough offerings," or maybe they would have said, "We lost because God plays favorites and he chose Israel against Egypt." In any case, whether they read history in terms of their sin or God's whimsy, the Egyptians would not have told the story as the Jews did. We are Christians, neither Jews nor Egyptians. And we will read the story in the light of the Christ of the New Testament. The New Testament says some things about God and history that radically change our perspective on everything. In Christ through the Spirit we will not read the story of the exodus the way either Jews or Egyptians read it. The New Testament clearly says God is no respecter of persons. He does not play favorites. He sends the light of his sun on the wicked and the good alike. If a tower falls on some people in Siloam, it is not because they are more wicked than the people in Jerusalem. If Pilate is a scourge to some Galileans, it is not because they were worse sinners than those who were spared. If a man is born blind, it is not because he sinned or his parents sinned.

All this is astonishing because it means that we have a terrific paradox on our hands. We must not water down the gospel or change its story to suit our fancy. Yet God's own book is full of changes. Jesus says, "You have heard it said of old, but I say unto you . . . ." We must not change the story, yet a literalistic retelling of the story is impossible too. Let us state the paradox positively: We must tell the story without twisting it, and we must interpret it in the light of Christ. We do not have to choose between literalism and interpretation. That dilemma is false. We can reject both an acrid fundamentalism and an arid liberalism. The truth of the gospel which we preach is that we have this treasure in an earthen vessel. This means that every word has the infallible authority of the Spirit in it, and every word has the limitation and the mortal decay of our humanity in it. It does not mean that we can pick and choose some words of Scripture and reject others. If Scripture is inspired and authoritative at all, then the work of the Spirit in it is consistent throughout, since the Spirit does not run out of breath. The gospel we preach from Scripture does not lie or contradict itself. It is this certainty which we need to proclaim from our pulpits. All the uncertainties, inconsistencies, and shifting interpretations come from the human, earthy side of the biblical vessel. We preach no tentative, wobbly word of human beings. As Paul said, "I did not receive it from any man, nor was I taught it; rather, I received it by revelation from Jesus Christ" (Gal. 1:12).

Consider what this certainty means for our preaching.[18] Certainly the gospel does not deal with probabilities as does science. This is not so clearly understood today because the successes of the sciences attract and beguile us.[19] Regardless of this success, science does not deal with absolute truth, but rather with workable guesses about mathematical probabilities. These are always subject to change, and indeed whole systems of science can be scuttled for new systems. The gospel, on the other hand, proclaims an absolute certainty which does not depend on the accumulation of evidence or the addition of experiences. We do not wait breathlessly for the facts to be gathered in and tested in a laboratory to see if Jesus really rose from the dead. Can't you imagine our misery in such uncertainty, with the scientists frantically calculating on their slide rules and the lower management punching their computers while the multitudes clamor for an answer?

Paul proclaims an absolute certainty in his preaching which is not dependent upon changes in his personal experience, for he can imagine that someday he himself might distort the gospel. He can even imagine that an angel from heaven might come and preach a false gospel. He is not sure of himself and he is not sure of angelic visions; but he is sure of the gospel revealed to the church, so sure that he will put himself and the angels under a divine curse if they distort the gospel. This is the certainty and conviction with which we must preach. Our age has become so enamored of the compromising spirit of Erasmus that we forget that we can stand in the company of the undaunted Luther.

Nowhere is the certainty of the gospel stated with such convincing clarity as in the first chapter of Ephesians: "Praise be to the God and Father of our Lord Jesus Christ, who has blessed us in the heavenly realms with every spiritual blessing in Christ. For he chose us in him before the creation of the world to be holy and blameless in his sight. In love he predestined us to be adopted as his sons through Jesus Christ." This is the gospel we must preach. Our salvation is certain and unconditioned so far as our election in

Christ is concerned. We have the sure and certain sign of it in our baptism. We have the sure and certain proclamation of it in the preaching. This certainty does not depend upon Paul or any of us, nor upon our experiences. It depends on the election of God. This is predestination, not predeterminism. It is the free act of God whereby he chose us in Christ before creation. All that happens happens in accord with the plan of God, and nothing can frustrate his sovereign will. We call this providence. But now I am speaking of predestination according to which our names are written in heaven for a destiny to come. This is what we mean when we say Christ died for you. Christ lived and died two thousand years ago in the purpose of God for you personally even before you were born. And this purpose of God follows a plan that governs all history unto the fullness of time. Nothing happens by chance, but also nothing happens according to blind laws of fate. Everything happens according to the loving and intelligent purpose of God. There is therefore no question about the outcome of history or our personal lives. This destiny has been won for us beforehand by the riches of God's grace in his beloved Son. And it is all done freely—no programming, no interruption, no thunderbolts from heaven. And as in every good story with love and conflict and mystery, it all can be otherwise.[20]

That is the great paradox. This absolutely certain good news comes into a world of uncertainties and miseries, a world that is fraught with sickness unto death, in bondage to decay. And this must be understood in its fullest implications, for it means that everything in our world has been separated from God—everything, the ground on which we walk, the time in which we live, our bodies, minds, and spirits—everything is uncertain. This is part of our very creatureliness. The psalmist says, "The earth is the Lord's and the fulness thereof.... He has founded it upon the seas, and established it upon the rivers." A sea is a rolling, moving, unpredictable thing; a flood is a raging torrent. This is hardly a picture of certainty. But in a far more disastrous way, because of the fall of Adam everything under him and everything after him is under the curse of God's wrath. Adam's sin was that he would rather be God than under him. Because of this sin, we who are all earthlings in Adam, and that includes the entire world as we know it, must suffer the pain of death.

This is the condition in which preaching must occur. We are all under the sentence of death. This death manifests itself physically in the termination of our bodily functions, but it is manifest in many ways long before we stop breathing. We are already dead but we just won't lie down. As the author of Ephesians said, "God ... made us alive with Christ even when we were dead in transgressions" (Eph. 2:4–5). Our death is manifest emotionally and mentally and socially and sexually and nationally and radically in the manifold separations that disrupt our lives. All flesh is grass, and the life of human beings is like a tale that is told. But the final word came from Jesus:

"Heaven and earth shall pass away!" This means there is a limit on everything in creation. And more than this, there is hostility between everything in creation. There is a war of all against all. Man who was given dominion over the earth must struggle against the elements of the earth and earn his living by the sweat of his brow, and the woman must bear her children in anguish. Yes, and the whole creation groans as in travail. There is enmity between fathers and sons, mothers and daughters, there is strife between brothers and sisters. The family is bound together by nature but torn asunder by sin. There is strife between worker and employer, who are by nature dependent upon each other but by sin driven to mutual rivalry and hatred. There is bitterness between the sexes, who must cling to each other for life itself but who live together in a mysterious bond which often is broken and more often only tolerated. There is struggle for power and wealth among the nations, whose limits have been set by God but whose ambitions are akin to the devil's. There is suspicion, distrust, and fear between the races, which were made of one blood to dwell on the face of the earth but which have turned the beauty of variety into the ugliness of exclusion. And not only is there external separation between individuals and groups but also there is an inner division in the human soul. There are fightings without, but also fears within. The flesh lusts against the spirit and the spirit lusts against the flesh. As Paul says, "For what I do is not the good I want to do; no, the evil I do not want to do—this I keep on doing" (Rom. 7:19). The whole world is out of joint.[21]

But the paradox goes deeper. The person in the pew can plant a garden. We preach to people who sing the magnificent chorales of Johann Sebastian Bach. Before us are children whose smiles light up the day. We live in a world in which rain falls like laughter and lilacs kiss the air. Lovers catch their breath with lissome, liquid grace. The wax white arbutus trails down the moss bank and gentle stings of snow die upon our cheeks. The man with furrowed brow puts his trembling hand on the wrinkled cheek of the woman who has given him a lifetime of love. Our cities flourish with burgeoning wealth. Our nation lives at peace on this continent with both of its borders undefended. We go forth in history lifting our destiny to greater and greater heights. This too is our condition, and our preaching must address it with both gratitude and careful concern. Always our blessings are mixed. We are beset with ambiguities. Our fortunes are fraught with perils and possibilities. Shakespeare said it most wonderfully in *Hamlet*:

> What a piece of work is a man! How noble in reason! how infinite in faculties! in form and moving, how express and admirable! in action, how like an angel! in apprehension, how like a god! the beauty of the world! the paragon of animals! And yet, to me, what is this quintessence of dust? Man delights not me—no, nor woman neither, though by your smiling you seem to say so. (Act 2, sc. 2)

We preach to men and women engulfed in a mysterious paradox of sin and saintliness. But the gospel we preach has no ambiguity. The gospel is sure and certain and single but it becomes a two-edged sword because of our duplicity. The tension between the certainty of God and the uncertainty of his creatures, however, is resolved in the real presence of Christ in Word and Sacraments. Christ is the living Word whose Spirit makes our wavering spirits strong, comforted, and sanctified. In preaching and sacraments the certainty of election and the uncertainty of faith meet and find their resolution.

By taking us into himself in Holy Communion, Christ takes us out of this world of sin and separation and hostility and death, and he takes us into a new world of life, the world of God's peace and heavenly rest. This life in the new world is God's life. It embraces the span of time from beginning to end. This means that in our worship, in both preaching and communion, we do what is otherwise impossible, we re-create a moment in time, we are born anew, we go back to share in the suffering of Christ's cross, indeed we share in the entire passion of God's life, and we are carried forward with him unto his glory. For us the present moment is fleeting; it slips into the past and is never recovered. Insofar as that moment is corrupted by our sin, we are left with regret concerning it. We wasted it, we did violence to it, and we cannot undo the damage we have done to God's creature. Once the moment has passed, it has died and we have died to it. But it is not so with God. In his life he loses no moments; they keep building up gloriously, although, to be sure, he suffers the sin of every moment we corrupt. But he takes the spoiled moment and turns it into a glorious triumph according to his plan of salvation. See what he did with the moment of Judas' betrayal. My every act and thought, my whispers and my dreams, my fears and my confidence, God takes them all unto himself and with groanings of his Spirit he makes alive what I have lost. This is how we are born anew, this is how God dwelled with the fullness of his deity in Jesus bodily and how through preaching and the sacrament we are built up with the fullness of God's life in Christ's body, the church.

How then will we preach to effect this new birth? As did Paul, who spoke about his preaching to the Corinthians: "We put no stumbling block in anyone's path, so that our ministry will not be discredited. Rather, as servants of God we commend ourselves in every way: in great endurance; in troubles, hardships and distresses; in beatings, imprisonments, and riots; in hard work, sleepless nights, and hunger; in purity, understanding, patience, and kindness; in the Holy Spirit and in sincere love; in truthful speech and in the power of God; with weapons of righteousness in the right hand and in the left; through glory and dishonor, bad report and good report; genuine, yet regarded as impostors; known, yet regarded as unknown; dying, and yet we live on; beaten, and yet not killed; sorrowful, yet always rejoicing; poor, yet making many rich; having nothing, yet possessing everything" (2 Cor. 6:3–10).

Preaching must find its place in the liturgical service. It will tell the story of the church year. Preaching must be embedded in repeated rituals, regular as well as festival, thereby telling the story of the living tradition. In this way stories have power to re-create the past and prepare for the future. Preaching thus becomes part of the life-giving energy of *worship*, a sacramental means of grace which brings Christ really present into the lives of believing Christians.

NOTES

1. Cf. Amos N. Wilder, *The Language of the Gospel* (New York: Harper & Row, 1964); also Karl Rahner has an interesting theory on God as author but not writer, *Inspiration in the Bible* (New York: Herder & Herder, 1961).

2. Cf. James Barr, *The Bible in the Modern World* (London: SCM Press, 1973), 13ff. Barr would abandon both inspiration and authority of Scripture as being no longer fruitful in theological discussion. In place he advocates description of the function or use given to the Bible in the church and for faith. See also Hubert Cunliffe-Jones, *The Authority of the Biblical Revelation* (London: James Clarke & Co., 1945).

3. Cf. George H. Tavard, *Holy Writ or Holy Church: The Crisis of the Protestant Reformation* (London: Burns, Oates, & Washbourne, 1959).

4. Cf. Arthur G. Hebert, *Fundamentalism and the Church of God* (London: SCM Press, 1957).

5. Barr, *The Bible in the Modern World*, 168ff. Barr shows how ultraconservatives are really more concerned with the infallibility and harmony of Scripture than they are with literalism. Thus the issue is authority.

6. Ibid., 24–25.

7. Martin Luther, *WA*, vol. VI, 301.

8. *American Edition of Luther's Works*, vol. 22, 339.

9. Barr, *The Bible in the Modern World*, 65ff.

10. Ibid., 74.

11. Ibid.

12. Cf. Owen Barfield, "Poetic Diction and Legal Fiction," in *Essays Presented to Charles Williams*, by C. S. Lewis (Grand Rapids: Wm. B. Eerdmans Publishing Co., 1966).

13. Cf. Karl Barth, *The Preaching of the Gospel* (Philadelphia: Westminster Press, 1963).

14. For an excellent treatment of the humanness of the authentic preacher, see Frederick Buechner, *Telling the Truth: The Gospel as Tragedy, Comedy, and Fairy Tale* (New York: Harper & Row, 1977).

15. Cf. Gilbert E. Doan, Jr., "Preaching from a Liturgical Perspective," in *Preaching the Story*, by Edmund A. Steimle, Morris J. Niedenthal, and Charles L. Rice (Philadelphia: Fortress Press, 1980).

16. On the presence of Christ in preaching in a sacramental sense, see P. T. Forsythe, *Positive Preaching and the Modern Mind* (Grand Rapids: Baker Book House, 1980), 348.

17. This story is a modern folk tale version of a nineteenth-century rationalization of the exodus. The J document reports that the Lord drove back the sea with a

strong east wind. Edward Robinson in 1856 called this a miracle of *timing* in which Moses chose the right moment to cross and the Egyptians were inundated because they were too late. "The Israelites were probably on the alert, and entered upon the passage as soon as the way was practicable." Cf. Edward Robinson, *Biblical Researches in Palestine* (Boston: Crocker and Brewster, 1856), 1:57. For a warning against softening parables or modifying their secular tone for moral or ecclesial reasons, see John Dominic Crossan, *In Parables* (New York: Harper & Row, 1973).

18. For a full discussion of certainty, see P. T. Forsythe, *The Principle of Authority* (New York and London: Hodder & Stoughton, 1912).

19. Cf. Nathan Scott, *The Broken Center* (New Haven: Yale University Press, 1966).

20. On the freedom and surprise with which God deals with his creatures see Robert Farrar Capon, *The Third Peacock* (New York: Doubleday & Co., 1971).

21. For a discussion of irony that heals, see Morris J. Niedenthal, "The Irony and Grammar of the Gospel," in *Preaching the Story,* by Steimle, Niedenthal, and Rice.

11

Eucharist and Service

—liturgy and the action of Christ's passion in the global city

The liturgy of the church has been fashioned by the drama of salvation. It includes prayer, and we shall discuss the meaning and function of prayer in an interlude, but because worship is dramatic our liturgy involves encounter of persons which goes beyond the conversation of prayer. Liturgy is not only where God comes to give grace to his creatures; it is also where church and world meet. There is a double motif of incarnation and resurrection in worship, producing a double climax at distribution and dismissal. And then the action of Christ's passion is carried into the global city, where we offer ourselves as living sacrifices, holy and pleasing to God—our spiritual worship.

Israel's cultus was developed out of a consciousness of themselves as the elect covenant people, an election which was sealed by circumcision as the sign that God gave Abraham the satisfying ram instead of Abraham giving God the sacrifice of Isaac. This covenant consciousness, with incorporation into the family of Israel by circumcision, was articulated in the life of the family by means of the celebration of the mighty acts of Yahweh with his people. Each festival was a recounting of the divine-human drama in history. The exodus was seen to be God's *deliverance*. The law from Sinai was seen to be God's *demand*. The feeding and protection in the wilderness wandering was seen to be God's *providence*. For each of these divine actions a feast was celebrated in grateful response—Passover, Pentecost, and Tabernacles. In contrast, Canaanitic, Egyptian, and Mesopotamian religion was centered in the nature cycle, with worship offered as petition and gratitude for fertility. Israel had to come to terms with this, and they did so by recognizing that the God who acted in deliverance and demand was also the God who provided crops and children. They therefore combined Passover with the barley harvest of first fruits and made it the Feast of Unleavened Bread. Similarly they combined the wheat harvest with Pentecost or the Feast of Weeks, and the final harvest in September-October with Tabernacles or the Feast of Tishri.

Then a new act of God came with Jesus. Instead of remembering Passover Christians remember Jesus and his victorious resurrection which delivers us from sin and death, a universal deliverance that goes beyond national destiny. Hence we celebrate Easter. Instead of remembering the law Christians remember the descent of the Spirit at Pentecost. And instead of remembering Tabernacles, Christians remember the incarnation at Christmas. In the north there was great concern for the winter solstice in the nature cycle and that seems to have been determinative in setting the date for Christmas.[1] The new covenant was sealed by baptism, which replaced circumcision. But if the story is understood properly, none of these changes in worship are replacements. They are really advances on earlier acts in the drama which are proper preparations in both Hebrew and Gentile backgrounds.[2] The Christian changes with their radical shift of consciousness in worship were established by the resurrection appearances of Jesus, first at mealtime in the miraculous form described in the Gospels and then in the sacramental form which we continue to experience to this day. It soon became evident to the early Christians that the Levitical priesthood and temple sacrifices were no longer needed in the drama of this new worship.

Christian liturgy is the action of the people in petition for and grateful response to the gracious action of God in Christ Jesus. It is sacramental. Sacraments are outward signs of inward grace. They communicate mysteriously through visible metaphors the hidden reality of God's saving activity. They realize for us in the present a token of what will come in glory in the future. They are more than communicators or revealers; they are effective means or realizers of God's grace. In them God really comes to us and gives us life out of death. They are God's means by which he puts us in his service, not our means by which we appropriate divine favor. It is grace that uses sinners in the service of God, not we who use grace in our own service.

The Sacrament of Holy Communion is so rich in meaning it is impossible to embrace its mystery in words. It has many names: the Breaking of Bread, Holy Communion, the Lord's Supper, the Eucharist, the Mass, the Liturgy, the Service, the Sacrament of the Altar. These names indicate some of the various meanings. They tell of dimensions such as the victorious presence of Christ among his people and at his altar, the sacrifice that God offers to effect forgiveness and new life in sinners, the participation and communion which we share because of this godly passion, the good news we proclaim as we remember this gift, the thanks we return as we anticipate the future fulfillment when the story comes to its end, and the service we carry to the world as resurrection Christians before this end.

What was the origin of our rite? Most likely Oscar Cullmann is right in saying that Communion had its origin in the resurrection appearances of the Lord at the meals of the disciples between Easter and his ascension.[3]

This means it did not have its origin in the common meals of Jesus with his friends (the *chaburah*) during his ministry. This would have shaped our worship as human fellowship, and it would be difficult to distinguish between the providence of Christ as he is present at breakfast and the redemption of Christ as he is present at the Eucharist. Nor were there two types of Eucharist as Hans Lietzmann thought, an earlier Jerusalem meal of joyful thanksgiving and a later Pauline meal of sad sacrificial remembrance on the model of the mystery cults.[4] In all accounts from the beginning we detect both joy and sadness. There was realized joy in the presence of the risen Lord as well as hopeful expectant joy in his coming at the last day. There was also solemn remembrance of the death of Jesus with its terrifying significance. And there was deep sorrow for the great weight of sin. It was the presence of the living Word of Christ together with the guidance of the Spirit which brought the early Christians away from their worship in the temple and established a new worship centered in the risen Lord.[5]

The victorious presence of Christ at mealtime instructed the disciples concerning the enigmatic meaning of the last meal Jesus enjoyed with them at the approach of the Passover season.[6] His words and actions were recalled in the light of his death and resurrection, and it was now recognized that his death was a sacrifice for them. When he took bread and broke it he dramatically foretold the breaking of his body, and when he poured wine he foretold the shedding of his blood. This sacrifice is once for all, yet as he broke bread once and fed five thousand, so he gave us bread to distribute to many in all generations. The broken bits of bread join with the flesh of each believer and are taken up into our life, becoming a guarantee of the restoration of our real self with the presence of the real Christ. The flesh and blood of Jesus in his incarnation conveyed the living Word to his contemporaries. This was the function of the flesh. Now we do not have the incarnate Jesus but we have the bread and wine of the Eucharist. They function for us as did his flesh and blood for his contemporaries. We do not have the baby in the manger, but for us Christ is born in the cradle of our hands when the communion bread is placed there.

Jesus could therefore say, as it were: "This is my body . . . this is my blood . . . you have seen me in the flesh but now I am going away and you will no longer see me, but I will leave with you this sacrament. You will see the bread and wine as you see me. It will do for you what I have done, but as flesh and blood did not reveal this grace so also the Spirit must come with the bread and wine."[7]

In this story construct there is no need for metaphysical speculation on the change of bread to the substance of Christ's body. The concern of the Bible is to proclaim what God has done, is doing, and will do in the sacrament, not to give us a rational explanation of the mystery. Also in a story view action really occurs and continues to occur, and therefore we cannot reduce the doctrine of the Eucharist to a mere memorial. This might falsely stress what we do and not what God does. And if it speaks of God's act at all, it does so only as a remembered act in the past, but the sacrament involves not only a past act but also the present and future service of God. Once more we perceive the reality of time necessitated by the story model.

It is true for communion, as it is true for the sermon, baptism, and confession, that God effectively works his grace unconditioned by the officiant or the receiver. In the medieval view this grace was conceived as spiritual substance which when infused into the believer gives him or her merit to journey into the presence of the faraway God. The biblical view tells another story about God coming in the presence of Christ the Word who becomes known to us by intercession of the Spirit. Instead of grace taking the sinner to God, God brings himself in grace to the sinner. Hence a new testament is established in which Christ gives himself to us in the seal of his death. We receive this guarantee in bread and wine which function for us just as his flesh and blood did for his disciples. Hence he re-presents to us the sacrifice which he gave once on Golgotha, and which he continually presents to the Father in heaven.

This is not a magical operation, because the work of God does not automatically save. It is a sign revealing the hidden mystery of God. It must, therefore, as signs in the sermon and other sacraments, be received in faith. Consequently when it is not received in faith it works condemnation. As the Word is a two-edged sword, the sacrament can cure or curse. All depends on discernment in faith by the Spirit. It should be clear that this discernment comes by testing in the Spirit, and not by cognitive exercise. The significant words used by Paul in this connection are test *(dokimazetō)* and discern *(diakrīnon)* (1 Cor. 11:28–29). Neither can be construed in any intellectual sense without making the sacrament an exclusively esoteric rite limited to those who have the correct gnosis. The sacrament is a monstrance, a public placarding of the Lord's death before the world. It is not a secret ritual but a proclamation. It is true that it is not offered promiscuously, but it is openly declared that here the Lord is victoriously present, and the Lord is blessed life for those who believe but terrifying death for those who reject the gift of the Spirit. Receiving Christ worthily does not mean in good behavior or right cognition but in Spirit-led faith. Such reception brings forgiveness and with it healing and victory over death. Unworthy or faithless reception brings the separation of sin and its consequent sickness unto death.

Therefore there can be no compromise or mixing with the ways of the world. In ancient times Greek people believed their gods could be appeased by offerings and rituals of bread and wine. They believed their gods influenced their own behavior too. There is tragic irony in this as, for example, in the myth of Phaedra, who was provoked by Aphrodite to betray her husband Theseus by seducing her stepson Hippolytus. When Hippolytus rejected the advances of Phaedra, and when Theseus heard of the betrayal, Theseus prayed to Poseidon for revenge. This is accomplished when Hippolytus is dragged to death by his chariot. Phaedra kills herself and Theseus learns the truth too late.

Here tragedy is fateful, and illicit behavior is provoked by the gods. Paul does not deny the reality of this mythical truth. He fully apprehends the force of the pagan gods, but he brands them devils (1 Cor. 10:20; also cf. Lev. 17:7; Deut. 32:17; Rev. 9:20). The stark, horrifying anguish of this is the realization, too late, that the very gods that people have worshiped have brought them moral collapse and fateful nemesis. These gods, or devils with different names, still rule and provoke, but the cup of the Lord is not to be mixed with the cup of devils. It is the victory of Christ that such fate is overcome, and the new life brings conduct rich in gifts of the Spirit.

Finally the Sacrament of Holy Communion is a foretaste of the messianic banquet. It is an eschatological feast which proleptically carries us beyond the last day into the heavenly communion with the coming Lord. Hence while it is rich in remembrance of things past and overflowing with joy in the Person present, it is also pregnant with hope for things to come. It is truly a celebration.

A SUPPLICATORY INTERLUDE ON PRAYER

Our English word "worship" comes from an Anglo-Saxon background originally referring to the *worthship* which we receive from the grace of God in his presence at Holy Communion; and also the *worthship* which we give to God as we acknowledge him and celebrate him in prayer, praise, and thanksgiving. Thus we do not make ourselves worthy, but we proclaim the worth that God gives to us and we give glory to God in our praise of his worth.

Another word commonly used for communion is "service." In our worship we serve God, who first serves us; we then bring our service out from the church into the streets, where we serve our neighbor. The Christian faith begins and ends with service; it begins with the suffering servant Jesus who died that we might live, and it ends with our living sacrifice which is our reasonable service, our continuing worship, on behalf of our neighbor.

Still another word is "liturgy." This word comes from the Greek. "Service" comes from Latin and means bondage, the work that is done by a loyal slave for his or her master. "Worship" comes from Anglo-Saxon and means giving worth. But "liturgy" comes from two Greek words: *leitos* and *ergon*. *Leitos* means people; we have our word "laity" from it; and *ergon* means work or action; we have our word "energy" from it, the capacity to do work. Liturgy then means the work or action of the people. When we gather in church as the people of God we enact, put into effective, dynamic action, a celebration of his presence. Actually liturgy is the response of people in action to the grace of God in the sacrament. Holy Communion is the sacrament that is central in our Sunday worship, but there are many kinds of worship besides communion: baptism, daily prayers in morning and evening, occasional prayers such as litanies, compline, rituals for confirmation, for burial of the dead, and for marriage.

In worship we pray, but prayer and worship are not the same thing. Worship may include our prayers, but primarily worship is a response to what God does when he gives us his grace. Worship is thanksgiving for God's forgiveness, for his victorious presence in communion, his renewal of life in baptism, his healing in sickness, his comfort in death, his blessing in marriage. First and foremost in worship we celebrate what God does, not what we do. There are things in a story world that we do and things that God does. What we do is always a response, a thanksgiving, a derivative of the author's prompting. We have been made in his image. We love only because God loves us first. We worship only because God calls us to gather in his presence. As Luther said, we believe that we cannot by our own reason or strength believe in Jesus Christ our Lord, or come to him but the Holy Spirit calls us by his Word.

Prayer must not be confused with worship. Our worship includes prayers; but prayer is what we do, and it does not do for us what the sacraments do. Prayer is the believing heart's conversation with God. It is our word to God, and the word that we bring to God may be a word of thanks, confession, repentance, lament, praise (often we sing our prayers or recite them as psalms), or a word of petition. But when it is a word of petition we must be especially careful that we do not try to use prayer as a lever, as if it could do work, as if it could manipulate God. Luther explains the petitions of the Lord's Prayer in his catechism, and with each one he says the petition will be granted without prayer: the name of God is indeed holy of itself without our prayer but we pray that it may be hallowed by us; the kingdom of God will come without our prayer, but we pray that it may come among us; the good and gracious will of God is done without our prayer, but we pray that it may be done by us; God gives to the wicked and to the good their daily bread, but we pray that we may receive it thankfully. Always the difference that prayer makes is upon us, that we may be changed, not that we may have some special power over God to make him do our will. Thus prayers in worship always thank, praise, and ask that we may do God's will or that his will may be done among us.

Conversation is a two-way street. If we speak to God in prayer, how does he speak to us? Obviously we must not do all the talking. We must give God room, a place and time for his response to our thanks and laments and confessions and supplications. The psalmist says, "Be still before the Lord and wait patiently for him" (Ps. 37:7), and, "Be still, and know that I am God" (Ps. 46:10). Indeed, if we pray in the presence of the holy God, we will be stunned into silence. Isaiah in the temple stopped short and said,

"Woe is me! For I am lost; for I am a man of unclean lips" (Isa. 6:5). The prayer of silence is perhaps more important than all the words we utter. John the baptizer went into the wilderness to prepare for the Messiah apart from the noise of the city. Jesus walked in the mountains alone to listen to his Father, and he told his disciples to closet themselves when they pray. Quiet stillness alone can penetrate the depths of interiority. God does not always speak in resounding rumbles from the echo chambers of eternity. He speaks as Elijah heard, in a "still, small voice." But as the brooding breath of God moved over the deep in the beginning, so the silent Spirit changes each of us in the depths of our being when we are still before God in prayer.

The conversation of prayer can take place anywhere, but in worship we come to church where a holy people gather in a holy place. What does it mean to pray in the Kyrie for "this holy house, and for all who offer here their worship and praise"? This space is sacred; we come into it and at once we are hushed. It is different from any other place in the world. Because Jacob saw God in his dream he built a shrine there and called it Bethel, the house of the Lord. And when he wrestled with the angel he saw the face of God, and so he built a shrine there and called it Peniel, the face of God. Sacred places are different. They declare the transcendent. Paradoxically they show power in the fragile presence of the divine. Prayers, on the other hand, can and should arise anywhere and anytime.

Prayers of praise and thanksgiving clearly glorify God, and we have no question or confusion about them. But prayers of petition and intercession need clarification. There is much confusion about them.

A basic presupposition for prayer in a story construct is that God is a free person and he has created us free persons. There is no room for any kind of determinism in the theater of prayer. God as a free agent cannot be manipulated or coerced in any way. We too are free agents; we likewise cannot be manipulated or coerced even by God. He is not an idol who can be bought or influenced by our prayers, offerings, sacrifices, gifts, good behavior, obedience, or anything we do. We are not puppets or marionettes dangling on divine strings from heaven. God is free and we are free.

If there is freedom, how can our prayers do anything for us? If God cannot be changed, why should we pray? And if God can be changed how can he remain God? Does he then become our puppet? Does prayer have power? Can I get what I want by praying, assuming of course that I pray hard enough and that I pray correctly with a good heart? Or maybe that is a selfish way of asking the question. Let me change it: can I get what God wants by praying? And do I fail to get what God wants by not praying?

If my prayer does get for me what God wants, then I must know how to pray correctly and I must muster all my strength and courage to pray. With this point of view people often use the illustration that prayer is plugging in to the power of God. This means that God is powerless without my prayer.

Freedom seems to require that God is powerless; yet, on the other hand, freedom does not require that I have power over God. We can conclude then that these questions are all wrong. Prayer is not a lever that moves God. Prayer is not the energy that I draw out from God when I want to plug him in. Prayer does not do work for me. All of this would be striking down a straw man if popular religion were not replete with this kind of prayer piety. The story category will avoid both mechanical and electrical metaphors for prayer.

Then if prayer is not such a power machine, what is it? We have said that prayer is conversation of the believing heart with God. Conversation is free speech. Conversation does not coerce. Conversation may inform, remind, admonish, thank, praise, request. Prayer is not just any conversation. It engages in some of these kinds of talk but not all. We have already said that prayer conversation thanks and praises God. Can we give God information he does not already have? That is absurd. We are talking to the God who knows us in our inward parts, better than we know ourselves. Can we remind God? Does he forget? Can we admonish God? We are talking to the Holy One. What about our requests? When we ask for something the answer can vary from a flat no to a not yet, or a never, or a maybe, or a yes if conditions change, or a partial yes, or an all-out yes. When we come to God with our petitions we should expect this spectrum of answers. That is the way it is in free conversation. This means that all prayer is contingent upon God's will for us.

In a story view, prayer as conversation accounts for the freedom of a struggle between contending persons. The wrestling with God in the laments of Old Testament patriarchs, prophets, and psalmists indicates the need for us to work out our problems through the expression of prayer. It does not suggest that God can be persuaded to change his will to suit ours. Jesus' teaching about persistence in prayer is also directed to our need to trust in the promise and grace of God. It does not suggest that God is slow to hear (Luke 18:8).

But the persistent question still is this: Does our prayer do anything to change God? Is God moved by our prayer or are we changed?

In one sense we can certainly say that God is changed by prayer. He is pleased, he is glorified, by our praise and thanksgiving. Mary said, "My soul praises the Lord." When God blesses his creatures he is glorified, magnified, by their response, just as any parent is uplifted by the good behavior of children.

But is God's action reversed or in any way turned because of my prayer? Does God provide me with my request because I pray, and does he fail to provide it because I do not pray? Listen to the blasphemy in those questions. Where is God's mercy if he gives me only what I want and not all I need? And where is his power if he needs to be reminded of what I need? No, our God is both merciful and powerful, and he provides for my needs long before I even think to pray. He sends the sunshine on the good and on the wicked alike, with or without their prayers. So in this sense prayer does not change God.

What then should we pray for? Should we pray for victory in war, or in sports, or success in business when it means the defeat of our competition? We have heard prayers for victory in wartime, but consider the God to whom we are talking. He is the creator and father of both contestants. He plays no favorites. He died for us all. But if in any conflict or competition one side is more worthy, can we not say that this value will prevail because God wills it? Yes, but then our prayer must bring us to the side of God and not bring God to our side.

Should we pray for bread, for livelihood, if God provides it without our prayer? We said we pray to receive these blessings gratefully. We pray always that we may do God's will in our petitions. In other words, we begin to see that our prayers are meant to change us. We are the ones who are affected by this conversation we are having with God. When we pray we see that our requests are wrong or badly timed. Or we see that they are right, or rightly timed. The Holy Spirit either corrects our bad prayers or confirms our good ones. So God is not changed in this sense by our prayers, but we are.

Finally, should we pray for healing or success or power? What do we mean by such prayers? We know that many people are healed without praying. Success and power do not come only to the pious. Do we mean that we are asking God to step in with a special kind of help where medicine leaves off, or where our natural powers fail? Is God a God of the gaps who fills in the power when we find our own power to be insufficient? Is he the *deus ex machina* of the ancient Greek plays? Is he out on the periphery of our lives to be appealed to as a last resort, as insurance when we are in desperate need? These are the rhetorical questions that Dietrich Bonhoeffer asked many years ago, and their blasphemy is so obvious we should not have to ask them again were it not for the current mood of prayer piety inspired by fear and exploited by faith healers and charlatans. But if it is God's will that we should be healed or that we should prosper in any way, then our prayers may indeed create in us conditions that will open the way for the godly will to work in us. For this reason we should pray for ourselves and for one another, but we should not try to make prayer do the work of work. Prayer should not be used in place of medicine or any human energy. There is a time for work and a time for prayer, and that means there are times we should not pray. What about the injunction to pray without ceasing? This means we should never cease to live in the attitude of prayer. It does not refer to the literal form of saying prayers all the time, like Jerry Cruncher's wife, who was always flopping on her knees at the least provocation. There are times when we should work, and times when we should rest, but always we should be open to the prompting of

God so that we do not miss the chance to say our lines. And then consider the assurance and the beauty of talking with the Holy One with the confidence that he will listen!

LITURGY—WHERE CHURCH AND WORLD MEET

Let us now return to the story of worship.

> Listen, I tell you a mystery: We will not all sleep, but we will all be changed—in a flash, in the twinkling of an eye, at the last trumpet. For the trumpet will sound, the dead will be raised imperishable, and we will be changed. For the perishable must clothe itself with the imperishable, and the mortal with immortality. When the perishable has been clothed with the imperishable, and the mortal with immortality, then the saying that is written will come true: 'Death has been swallowed up in victory.'
> 'Where, O death, is your victory?
> Where, O death, is your sting?'
> The sting of death is sin, and the power of sin is the law. But thanks be to God! He gives us the victory through our Lord Jesus Christ. (1 Cor. 15:51–57)

There has been a running debate down through Christian history between those who think the gospel is good news about the last day as a literal cataclysm of cosmic proportions and those who think eschatological language is figurative poetry for an ever-present process. This passage from Corinthians leaves no doubt that Paul expected a real and imminent end which would bring final victory for the glory of God. Yet Paul is neither a literalist nor merely a futurist, for he speaks often of the present reality of regeneration. That is why he concludes this passage with a "therefore": "Therefore, my dear brothers, stand firm. Let nothing move you. Always give yourselves fully to the work of the Lord, because you know that your labor in the Lord is not in vain." Paul says the same thing in the twelfth chapter of Romans where he describes spiritual worship as a living sacrifice, an acceptable use of the talents God has given us. God gives us the victory in the end. Resurrection is our hope. But in the meantime we have work to do in the world. Because we do not have to worry about death, neither to store up riches nor to make religious peace with God, we can be free to serve our neighbor and even love our enemy.

It seems to me this is what our communion service is all about. Liturgy is where church and world meet. It is the celebration of God's victory in the risen life of Jesus, who is present now to give us this new life and make us free to serve in the world. The separation of communion from service, *leitourgia* from *diakonia,* is demonic on both sides. It is just as wrong to think we can worship without social action and reduce Christianity to suburban religion as it is to think we can serve society without worship and reduce Christianity to inner-city politics.

The Two Motifs of Incarnation and Resurrection in Worship

As in all stories, there are motifs or themes with variations and repetitions running through the action of worship. According to one motif, liturgy is incarnational, pertaining to Jesus' birth and death, and according to another motif, liturgy is anastasial, pertaining to his resurrection. In subtle ways the same structured form may have phases of both motifs, just as a sermon is both law and gospel. Liturgy is an exchange, an action in which God gives us himself in Christ through the forms of bread and wine, and we give ourselves to God in the forms of offerings and service.[8] Actually, of course, God gives us his righteousness and life, and we have nothing to give him but our sin and death. That is indeed the unmerited exchange. The doctrines of *sola gratia* and original sin apply; but we are also baptized Christians who are regenerate in the Spirit, and we bring with us the new person, hidden in our flesh, growing in grace. While we may not look any different empirically to the world, or even to ourselves, we believe in faith that we have been transformed, and because of this we do things strange to the world and to ourselves, things that are holy and acceptable to God although they may be absurd and obscene to the world. Therefore in liturgy we give to God not only his world in sin and death but also his redeemed world in the righteousness and new life which we have received in Christ through baptism. Moreover, both motifs, incarnational and anastasial, are active in this exchange. When God gives himself in liturgy he makes himself known as present in the breaking of the bread both as the crucified and the risen Lord. He is the God who took on sinful human flesh and then rose from death to glory. Likewise we give ourselves with suffering sacrifice in the flesh under the cross and at the same time as transformed, regenerate spirits in joy and peace and hope.

Let us examine more closely the incarnational phase. Incarnation has traditionally meant the coming of God to his world in the flesh of Jesus of Nazareth. Since *space* was the basic counter in the game of metaphysics in the ancient world, Christian theology defined this encounter between God and his creatures in terms of substance. Somehow in Jesus this substance of God and man became one. Hence in the sacrament the substance of bread and wine became transubstantiated into the substance of God. Tillich, as we have seen, found this to be contradictory, so he rejected the incarnation. Bultmann and others who take *time* to be the basic category of existence define the incarnation in terms of an event in which God comes to his creatures. In this view it is not necessary to say that God became human, only that he came *to* human beings. At first this seems in accord with the biblical view, but there is danger of limiting the event to the realm of meaning and thereby subjectivizing it.

In my view, regardless of the metaphysical counters we use, the reality of the action of God coming to human beings as *human* must be affirmed. Furthermore, the coming of Jesus, which was once for all, is repeated in his coming in bread and wine of the liturgy. Indeed the bread and wine function for us incarnationally just as the flesh of Jesus did for his contemporaries.[9] Empirically they did not see God. They saw the son of Mary and Joseph, who was a mortal sinner like anyone else. We do not see God on our altars either. We see dry bread and fragrant wine. But God was there in Jesus bringing that which is holy to that which is unholy. This was the fulfillment of the promise that was made to Abraham and renewed in the covenant with Moses, the burning bush being the prolepsis of the virgin birth. In the bush that was not consumed by fire the holy God came and changed the cursed earth into holy ground. He did not destroy it, he renewed it from above. And in the birth of Jesus he did not take what was natural and sinful and make it supernatural and holy; rather, as we have seen, God took what was holy and transcendent and entered into that which was unholy and terrestrial. Yet the sinful flesh of Jesus was not consumed, but instead it ran its course unto death and then was raised in glory as the fulfillment of what was begun in Jesus' conception. In the same way God is present in the bread and wine, not destroying it or us but consecrating it and us in the mysterious action of liturgical incarnation.[10]

I think it is possible to avoid the troubles of both Thomas Aquinas' substantialist metaphysics and Bultmann's meaningful-event subjectivism if we think of the incarnation in terms of an operation or function of God. We then describe a storied action or happening. It is true this happening occurs many times, and in one sense is repeated, but not as an unbloody sacrifice repeats a bloody sacrifice. Actually, if time is real, nothing is ever repeated. Rather, the repetition is in the fact that it is the same God who comes to us many times. He came only once in Jesus, but he comes often to every generation in the Eucharist. Yet his coming is always new and the effects are open-ended. The work that is done in this divine operation suits each generation. God is truly all things to all people. That is the way of story. The same story is told over and over, but each time it is fresh and new.

As we have said many times, this view takes the reality of time seriously. Time is an aspect of the life of God, and instead of seeking transcendence in a static timelessness we find it in the future. All religion is concerned with the impact of the transcendent on the immanent, and biblical revelation has this concern also, but it especially emphasizes future transcendence. And our future is both near and far. That is to say, it is open-ended for immediate change and it is also rich in the possibility of cosmic transformation. Natural religion is like Faust, who sees contentment and wants to stop time, seize it, and live forever in a static heaven. Precisely this religious contentment robs Faust of his soul. Christianity is different in that it rejoices in change. This is why it is so painful. There is no other way in incarnation than the way of death. The old forms must be cast off, we must die to them, so that the new forms may be assumed, and in this way we rise from glory to glory. There is a progress in grace, there is a destiny to which we rise, for "no eye has seen, no ear has heard, no mind has conceived what God has prepared for those who love him" (1 Cor. 2:9).

The incarnational motif in liturgy expresses and reenacts first sacramentally and dramatically and then as extended service in the world all the things Jesus did when he was among us. As he wept over Jerusalem, we confess our sorrow for sin; as he lifted his heart in thanks for the fruit of the earth, we sing our thanksgiving for all the blessings of life; as he preached to the multitude, we read and proclaim the word of promise and hope; as he showed compassion on those in distress, we extend benevolence in the offering; as he died at the hands of cruel men, we worship amidst the mockery of the world; as he sent his disciples to baptize and teach, we are dismissed to witness and serve. In liturgy God and church together meet the world, because in doing the work of incarnation together we go the way of the cross, completing the afflictions of Christ (Col. 1:24). Over and over again we tell the story of salvation in liturgical action.

Just as the reality of the incarnation is hidden but climaxed in the elevation of bread and wine, so the reality of resurrection is hidden and climaxed in the dismissal. Also as there are incarnational elements in all the parts of the liturgy—in the confession, prayers, hymns, lectionary, preaching, creed, offering, Eucharist, fraction, distribution, dismissal—so there are anastasial elements throughout. As we are *simul justus et peccator,* so in our prayers we both die and rise with Christ. Our prayers are sinful and we must die to them, be separated from them, and they must be made holy and acceptable to God by the intercession of the Holy Spirit. So also with our confession, our preaching, our offerings, and all we do. The incarnational phase of liturgy must therefore be matched with the anastasial phase, for just as the Gospels do not end with the crucifixion but with the resurrection, so liturgy does not end with the distribution but with the dismissal. This is indeed a great mystery, because it seems that we have reached the end when we all go away, but it is really the beginning of the action of the people as they go into the world. And again, as the incarnational phase is a great mystery because through the essentially trivial elements of bread and wine the great God comes to us, so in the dismissal the apparent emptiness and absence of God is mysteriously coupled with the compulsion to sacrifice and serve in the world with joy and abandon. Christ is really present also in our work.

Suffering Service in the Global City

Christ came to free us from sin and death. In liturgy we reenact this liberating drama by eating bread and drinking wine. We take them into the prison of our bodies and make them our flesh. We take God in the incarnate Jesus into our sinful human flesh so that he shares our death. But as Jesus rose on the third day, so we rise in the mystery of faith with him and live as liberated new spirits even before the last day.

We Christians know about this healthy renewal through death in the regenerate life of faith. If the world is a story, we should expect an antagonistic motif running counter to it throughout the plot. And indeed the demonic counterpart to this healthy death and resurrection which we know in liturgy may be seen everywhere in the world, near and far, on all levels. Take, for example, the history of our own beloved America. From the beginning we have had a struggle between containment in the law and rebellious liberation from the law. America has a heritage that vacillates between Puritan, Cromwellian authoritarianism and noisy, blasphemous revolt. We began with the ethic of Plymouth's flinty theocracy, a style of abstinence and constriction. Our politicians have been Franklin, Adams, Lincoln, Wilson, Coolidge, Eisenhower. This has been on the lawful side of our character, but on the other side we have always had a certain rowdy fever, an anarchic romanticism, a demonic exuberance that rages gleefully and voyages fiercely into dark currents of mystery. Our poets have been Poe, Melville, Twain, Wolfe, Hemingway, and Tennessee Williams. Notice that both of these processes are demonic. The process of law, due process, is the process of materialization—incarnational, but demonic. It brings the incarceration of order, the prison of institution. The process of materialization begins in the idea and becomes incarnate in persons and institutions and then becomes mechanized and dehumanized in what Lewis Mumford calls "the Pentagon of Power."[11] This is simply the modern expression of the biblical beast, the original worm. There is in all human history an incarnational process that seeks itself in profits, progress, publicity, piety, and power. We have seen it in the Third Reich, in Japan, in Holy Russia, in ancient Rome. Furthermore, the Leviathan always bursts of its own weight because there is a counterprocess of etherealization—anastasial, but demonic. This process begins with the breakdown of institutions when a counterculture challenges the rigid power structure and casts off all custom and decency, law, order, and respect. Then black becomes white and heroes become heels. Chaos is king and anarchy is his mistress—for he could not have a wife; that would be too lawful.

We can clearly see these two processes at work in history: the legalistic process, which begins with an idea and incarnates itself in persons who then become incarcerated in institutions that mechanize and materialize in the rigor mortis of bureaucracy; and the mystical process, which begins in idealistic visions with the breakdown of law and institutions and etherealizes itself in the absurd and obscene not only to the law but also to God, because, unlike the foolishness and scandal of the gospel, this worldly revolution is counterproductive and nihilistic. These are the pulsebeats of human history, both cosmic and personal, a history that is sick with sin. It is into that raucous rhythm that we have been dismissed to serve.

We have heard a great deal about the celebration of the secular.[12] To be sure, there is God-given goodness in secularity. Perhaps the threat to our environment and the newly awakened sensitivity to ecological balance have influenced this new theology, but we should have known it all along from our understanding of the first article of the creed, from our perspective of the cosmic Christ, and from the revelation of the true incarnation in which Christ not only shares our sin and death but also affirms our humanity. It is true that the secular in itself is not evil. We are not Gnostics or Hindus who give matter a pejorative sense. Also, forms are not in themselves good, and therefore new forms may be welcomed from time to time as they show themselves to be edifying for the community. Change of form does not necessarily destroy the substance of the creature. But we must never forget when we celebrate the secular, both in its matter and form, that the demonic, dual process of materialization and etherealization is constantly trying to frustrate the divine destiny of the world. And the irony of history is that even the people who seek the ideal of goodness get caught perpetrating the greatest evil.[13] So the incarnational and anastasial dimensions of liturgy have demonic counterparts in the materialization and etherealization of false worship, the worldly devotion to the idols of the marketplace, the school, the home, the government, the gallery, and the temple.

But alongside human history is church history, from the first promises and covenants given to Abraham and Moses to the fiery descent of the dove in our present age. Alongside the pulsebeats of human history and hidden with Christ in the mystery of God is another pulsebeat. Alongside the world is the church, and we do not shut out the world when we go to church. We do not escape the world when we worship. Indeed the world comes into the church every time we worship, because we are there. But the great mystery of our faith is that here in liturgy, world and church meet, and through this conflict emerges, not by evolution but by peaceful revolution, a new creation. There is therefore beside the sin-sick human beat a healthy, holy beat, a beat that also knows law and death, but a beat that prevails because it sings the reconciling peace of resurrection.

The church is the called and sent people of God. As we celebrate the things of God's creation in our ebullient secularity, so also we celebrate the people of God's redemption in our sanctified ecclesiality. But just as we found the presence of the demonic warring against our divine destiny in the secular, so also there is a demonism of the institution and a demonism of the ethereal warring against the holiness of the church. Indeed the demonism prevails in both sectors, the secular and the ecclesial, whenever we celebrate either the things of creation without the Creator or the people of redemption without the Redeemer.

What is the reason for the contrapuntal dual demonism of materialist idolatry and ethereal mysticism? It is greed. It is a flaw in our character. We have believed the serpent's lie and grasped at being God. And greed immediately produces fear. The earth is the Lord's, but we try to make it ours. When we have grabbed for the world, fear of losing it seizes us. Our confidence slips away because we have forgotten who we are. This was the anguish that rent the soul of Biff Loman in Arthur Miller's *Death of a Salesman*. Biff was the son of a salesman who tried all his life to be someone other than himself. His life was therefore a gossamer veil of deceit. At the end when the world was breaking in pieces about him, with his father's fraud exposed for all to see, the young man cries out from the depth of his soul: "All I want is out there, waiting for me the minute I say I know who I am! Why can't I say that, Willy?"[14]

He could not say who he was, because he was alone and did not belong to anyone. He had no vocation, no stewardship, no evangelism, because he wanted the world to be his instead of giving himself to the world. His life was bound to the insecurity of time with all its mendacity, and time was forever slipping away without his getting anything done. We must work, but our work must be a giving, not a taking. Our Eucharist will help us find ourselves when we lose ourselves in loving service for God to the world. Our role will be Kierkegaard's paradoxical knight of faith. He knows what it means to be a Christian. He knows that to be a Christian will make a subtle difference in the way he walks through the park. He may go to the same theater and see the same play as before he came to this self-understanding and this Christ-understanding, but now he will see the play with different eyes because now he is a different, new man. He may work in the same office or the same mill, but now he will respond to every moment from the new vantage point of the moment before God. He is not the fearful man of greed. He is now the liberated man of grace.

Tolstoy gives poignant testimony to this paradox in the experience of Levin in *Anna Karenina*. Levin slowly moves from skeptical agnosticism to a second naiveté, a wondering faith that overwhelms without solving. He finds that after he can no longer disbelieve, the expected solutions and behavior do not come. He thought he would now be in control of himself, affable to his friends and loving to his wife, Kitty, but instead the outward change was unnoticeable. The final paragraph says it all: "I shall go on in the same way, losing my temper.... I shall still be unable to understand with my reason why I pray, and I shall still go on praying; but my life now, my whole life apart from anything that can happen to me, every minute of it is no more meaningless, as it was before, but it has the positive meaning of goodness, which I have the power to put into it."[15]

Levin discovered the meaning of goodness from a peasant who talks to him about the difference between people, about some who live for themselves and some who live for God. This is a difference which "cannot be explained by reason—it is outside it, and has no causes, and can have no effects. 'If goodness has causes it is not goodness; if it has effects—a reward—it is not goodness either. So goodness is outside the chain of cause and effect.' "[16]

A merely naturalistic view of reality must have causes and effects for everything; a merely mystical view must have no causes or effects; but a story view will find causal meaning in some things and mysterious freedom in others and coherent integrity in all things.

Dom Gregory Dix provides an excellent coda to this chapter in his introduction to *The Shape of the Liturgy*:

> Over against the dissatisfied "Acquisitive Man" and his no less avid successor the dehumanized "Mass Man" of our economically focused societies insecurely organized for time, Christianity sets the type of "Eucharistic Man"—man giving thanks with the product of his labors upon the gifts of God, and daily rejoicing with his fellows in the worshipping society which is grounded in eternity. This is the man to whom it was promised on the night before Calvary that he should henceforth eat and drink at the table of God and be a king. That is not only a more joyful and humane ideal. It is the divine and only authentic conception of the meaning of all human life, and its realization is in the eucharist.[17]

NOTES

1. Oscar Cullmann, *Noel dans l'eglise ancienne* (Paris: Delachaux & Niestlé, 1949).

2. Hans Lietzmann, *Messe und Herrenmahl* (Berlin, 1955), and Rudolf Bultmann, *Theology of the New Testament*, 2 vols. (New York: Charles Scribner's Sons, 1951), argue for Hellenist origin, but Krister Stendahl, ed., *The Scrolls and the New Testament* (1957; reprint Westport, Conn.: Greenwood Press, 1975), shows Hebrew and Essenic background.

3. Oscar Cullmann, *Early Christian Worship* (Chicago: Henry Regnery Co., 1953), 14.

4. Lietzmann, *Messe und Herrenmahl*.

5. Robert P. Roth, "Meaning and Practice of Communion in the New Testament Period," in Robert P. Roth and others, *Meaning and Practice of the Lord's Supper*, ed. Helmut T. Lehmann (Philadelphia: Muhlenberg Press, 1961), 3–14.

6. Joachim Jeremias, *The Eucharistic Words of Jesus* (New York: Macmillan Co., 1955), 14ff.

7. Ibid., 139ff.

8. Dom Gregory Dix, in *The Shape of the Liturgy* (London: Dacre Press, 1945), lends support to the notion that liturgy is structured action, therefore the enactment of a story.

9. This incarnational view of Eucharist is propounded by Wilhelm Stählin, *The Mystery of God* (St. Louis: Concordia Publishing House, 1964).

10. For a discussion of the parabolic enactment of the words of institution and Jesus as parable of God, see Jeremias, *The Eucharistic Words of Jesus*, 145ff.

11. Lewis Mumford, *The Pentagon of Power*, vol. 2 (New York: Harcourt Brace Jovanovich, 1970).

12. Harvey Cox, *The Secular City* (New York: Macmillan Co., 1965).
13. Cf. Reinhold Niebuhr, *The Irony of American History* (New York: Charles Scribner's Sons, 1952).
14. Arthur Miller, *Death of a Salesman* (New York: Viking Press, 1949), 132.
15. Leo Tolstoy, *Anna Karenina* (Norwalk Conn.: Easton Press, 1975), 935.
16. Ibid., 911.
17. Dix, *The Shape of the Liturgy,* xviii.

12

Into the Ages of the Ages

—the inevitable sequel

We come to a conclusion. Every story has an end. But the end is a new beginning. There is always a sequel.

To begin the end it might be well to recapitulate with a summary statement of the thesis. God made the world as a story. Reality is dramatic. The world is the theater of God. The metaphor of story is intended to carry us to an understanding of reality that is categorical, that is, universal and all-embracing. Other metaphors that have been suggested for this purpose in the history of culture, such as idea or substance or impression or process, are rejected because they are inadequate and reductionistic. While story is not simple but is compounded of many elements, it nevertheless cannot be reduced to something other than itself, and therefore it can rightly serve as a category. Everything that is is storied reality, and even things that are not, in the sense of the old ontologies (both essential and existential), have their story.

There are many kinds of stories, short and long. There are parables, short stories, tales, legends, myths, sagas, novels, and plays. There are fables, fictions, fantasies, autobiographies, biographies, and histories. There are farces, burlesques, satires, comedies, tragedies, and tragicomedies. There are ballads, lays, elegies, and epics. The richness of form is indicative.

And the Bible is God's story for us. Not only is the Bible full of stories, some historical and some not, but the Bible itself is a grand and cosmic story. Everything in it has its story setting. The Gospels are integral stories but they are also set in the greater story of Israel and they extend into the Christian mission to the world. The Deuteronomic code is not itself narrative, but the Mosaic sermon with its statutes and ordinances has a meaningful place because it belongs to a narrative about the deliverance of Israel, the story of the wandering Aramean told in Deut. 26:5–9.[1] The same may be said for the wisdom literature, the psalms, the prophecies, the epistles, and the Book of Revelation. Every psalm, whether it is a lament or a praise, tells a story of dramatic relationship. Every epistle is occasional and eventful.

But beyond and behind these literary forms, all nature and all history is narrative. Every quark, electron, and molecule has its life story; every planet, sun, and galaxy; every plant, animal, and person; every family, tribe, and nation. Even God lives and moves and enters into the plot, although as author of the story he is both a part of it and apart from it.

All stories have certain things in common. Stories have a beginning and an ending with a climax and a denouement. Stories have a plot with characters in conflict and community, in tension and resolution. Stories have a place with props. Stories have a time or sequence. Stories have stage directions or instructions from the author about the setting or about his intention for the characters, and sometimes these directions are written into the story as a Greek chorus. Stories have internal integrity or meaningful continuity. And stories have freedom or surprise within a meaningful context. Indeed God's story for us has the freedom of the theater of involvement in which the characters participate in writing their own lines.

This thesis is a grand counterrevolution because it restores God and his people to the center of the stage. The ancient world had a place for God in the center of things. For Plato and Aristotle, God was prime mover or first cause. For Homer, God was the father of the gods and the manipulator of human destiny. In this ancient view all nature is a series of secondary causes and all history is actually the result of God's puppetry. The world is determined by a system of causality which ultimately derives from an impersonal Nemesis. Stories with a happy ending are a Christian repudiation of this ancient divine determinism, and Western determinism has its counterpart in the Oriental council of *karma* and the Muslim *kismet*.

The modern world removed God from its scientific equation, and so all nature is understood to be *sui generis,* and all human events are chronicled on a behaviorist model which in the extreme denies freedom and responsibility. The ancient and Oriental world found reality to be timeless and ideal. Aristotle had a place for time within his system, but the system itself was static. He also had a place for matter, but matter is not the same as substance, and for him reality was not material but substantial, that is, rational and formal. The ancient world chose to follow the tradition of the Parmenidean stasis. The modern world sees reality to be temporal and material. Modern people follow the Heraclitean flux. In such a world of changing relativities there is no God and people are epiphenomenal.

This thesis, which is neither ancient nor modern, Western nor Oriental, restores God to the center of the stage, and people in his image are there with him. *Imago Dei* means that among God's creatures people have been given the freedom of the Spirit of God, the intelligence of the Word of God, and the uniqueness of God the Father. The biblical story of creation is different in this respect from all other creation stories. Instead of the gods being conceived in the image of creatures—human beings, animals, forces of nature, males or females—human beings are disclosed to be formed in the image of God. And although the masculine metaphor is consistently used to render the character of God in both Testaments (this means we can never refer to the biblical God as "she"), nevertheless we do not see this masculine character as a human male.[2] What is revealed about God in the biblical story is that he is unique. There is only one God and there are no other gods like him. Likewise, in our image of God each of us is unique and there is no other like any of us. For this reason God is center stage and we are there with him.

Creation in a story theology is by Word and Spirit. Creation does not involve a causal connection. It is, rather, an imaginative communication. God is the author of a story. We are his brain children. The scenario is a theater of involvement. Author and spectators are all actors in the cosmic play. The God who is center stage is not there as Nemesis or Moira but as a loving, laughing, crying, teaching, disciplining, imaginative person.

In a story world, nature is the stage with its props, but there is more to the theater than the stage. There are also flies and wings and orchestra that surround and support the stage. Behind the stage is the green room. There are many rooms, many places. "There are more things in heaven and earth, Horatio, than are dreamt of in your philosophy" (Hamlet, Act 1, sc. 5). We do not have a dualism of nature and supernature but a multiplinity. The problem of naturalism is that it cannot account for freedom and imagination, mysteries that image God. The problem of supernaturalism is that it despises places and times, creaturely commonplaces that come from the loving hand of God. Both naturalism and supernaturalism are reductionist, but the Christian story is neither merely materialistic nor merely gnostic.

In a story world, history is in the plot but not all of the plot. Again we must not reduce everything to either mere historical empiricism or mere timeless value and meaning. During the twentieth century most biblical hermeneutics and attempts at constructive theology have been limited to historical and empirical parameters. Bultmann's demythologizing was prompted by his gratuitous statement that in an age of electricity and radio no one can believe in a world of spirits and miracles.[3] A text, to be true, must be historically and empirically credible. Gerhard Ebeling did not depart from this historicism when he developed a "new hermeneutic" which proclaims the power of language to create a world. The language event (*Sprachereignis*) is not some supernatural, otherworldly word that breaks into the natural, human order of things. It is ordinary human language which discloses salvific truth.[4] Wolfhart Pannenberg also contends that the truth of revelation does not come to us directly from above but is written indirectly in history, not in a special strand of holy history but throughout all of history.[5]

In the past few years, however, many scholars have become uneasy with this historicism. Ironically some of the ammunition used against it comes from observations by Ludwig Wittgenstein, who is best known for his logical positivism, an analysis of language which restricts truth under a principle of empirical verification. Wittgenstein's later modification of this principle does not deny the original restriction but it does allow us to talk of language as meaningful according to accepted usage. Language is likened to playing a game in which the players not only understand and accept a common set of rules but they can act upon them in pursuit of a common goal. We can talk about meaningful religion, even though we cannot claim its truth, if we have a community that uses a common faith language.[6] This functional and social use of language is supported by Hans-Georg Gadamer, but when Hans Frei picks it up he neglects the historical verifiability of a text in favor of the realistic rendering of the identity of an agent.[7] Frei's agentic ahistoricism asks us to read a text without reference to its historical setting because its narrative reality is self-authenticating.

Strangely, but not uncommonly, extreme opposites meet. The demythologizing of Bultmann left him, in the interest of historical and existential verifiability, with a timeless message or kerygma which has no historical referent. When all is said and done, the cross of Jesus is not determinative. All depends on the decision of the believer for the message of justification by grace. The danger of gnostic arbitrariness is as great in this hermeneutic as it is in the agentic hermeneutic of Hans Frei. The historical approach in the extreme meets the literary-linguistic approach at the same point of error. We would be wise, therefore, as Amos Wilder says, to get a better understanding of both.[8] The diachronic trajectory of historical study must inform and be informed by the synchronic analysis of literary criticism.

We are saying that we cannot have truth without meaning, nor meaning without truth. While a truth claim is needed to go beyond meaning, nevertheless truth cannot be reduced to historical evidence. There are many kinds of truth: empirical, rational, theoretical, hypothetical, historical, traditional, mythical, personal—and the story truth which I am describing. This story truth cannot be defined completely, because the nature of story includes the ultimate inscrutability of God. Empirical truth includes documentaries, chronicles, and all the taxonomies of scientific systems. Rational truth embodies deductive systems, whether legal or scientific. Theoretical truth refers to speculative interpretations of any set of human experiences. Hypothetical truth refers to useful, working guesses or hypotheses in practical human endeavor. Historical truth brings meaning and understanding to the sequence of human experiences. Traditional truth is the accepted customs of a community. Mythical truth is the explanation given to the ultimate mysteries of communal life. Personal truth is the trust we give one another in personal encounter. Story truth includes all of these and more. The "more" refers to truths about such realities as creation, resurrection, and final consummation—realities which can be verified only by the presence of the Holy Spirit as he works in the community of faith.

The criteria by which to evaluate this truth of the Spirit are the gracious gifts of faith, hope, and love as they function in the community of believers. In a story view we deal with characters in relationship. The characters are both individuals and communities, and both have distinctive personalities. And every personality operates with memory, imagination, and understanding. All persons in the drama act and are acted upon in the line of time. Faith orients us to the past through memory. By faith we are sustained and we repeatedly recover our identity. Faith is the gift of the Spirit which makes it possible for us to confess that Jesus is Lord. Hope orients us to the future through imagination. Our hope in the promise of the Spirit creates us anew and thrusts us forward to meet our destiny, which is shaped by our heritage and a free range of new possibilities. Love orients us to the present through understanding. In love we understand ourselves in a belonging relationship. The identity that we know from the past through faith and the identity that we hope for in the future become edified in the present through dramatic testimony and confession, that is, *worship*.

Paul Ricoeur says some things that support this narrative criterion of truth when he talks about a "hermeneutics of testimony." He seeks to form an experience of the absolute not by example or symbol but rather by testimony. Examples, in the tradition of the *analogia entis,* become norms, and hence legalism destroys the absolute. Symbols lack historic closeness. Meanings then are not tested by historicity and we end in free-floating arbitrariness. "The example," he says, "is historic but is obliterated as the case before the rule. The symbol is not obliterated so easily; its double meaning, its opacity, renders it inexhaustible and causes it never to cease giving rise to thought. But it lacks—or can lack—historic density; its meaning matters more than its historicity."[9]

But when truth is seen to be a witness, a testimony, a living confession, then idolatries of legalism and arbitrariness are avoided. When, for example, we read the Gospel of John as a message it reverts to ideas about God, which tend to become humanly small or capricious. But when the Gospel of John is read as a story it becomes the witness of Jesus—and also the witness of the Baptizer, the disciples, God, and the Spirit. And this witness is more than mere history or symbol; it is testimony in the cosmic trial between God and Satan. And the ironic reversal in this story is that the earthly defendant becomes the cosmic judge in the eschatological trial.[10] The revelation of this reversal brings to us an understanding that produces in us a testimony which bears the scrutiny of the faithful community. The signs of faith, hope, and love are manifest as we see ourselves built up in the growing body of Christ (Ephesians 1—2).

As we move toward the final curtain, and beyond, a proper understanding of time and times is necessary to get the story straight. Periodicity and sequence necessarily characterize time with occasional kairotic moments that are once-and-for-all. Time describes the life of God. Its passing is his glory. Each moment, each age, brings riches to the growing story of his life. Time itself does not need to be redeemed. We can speak of periods in the life of God that are past, but they do not need to be recovered, because they were never lost. We have an intimation of this in the celebration of the Holy Eucharist when we pray the great thanksgiving prayer and recount the mighty acts of God. We look back to when God spoke to Abraham, and this speaking is alive for us today.

But apart from the grace of our worship, time for us as sinners is not cumulative and edifying. Time in our fallen condition is erosive and disintegrating. The very thing that makes both time and space glorious in the life of God and his creation, discreteness, becomes a curse to us. As Kierkegaard said, there is a *discrimen rerum,* a discreteness in all things which because of sin has become a divisive discontinuity.[11] Discreteness originally, and in God, makes possible variety, change, growth, novelty, surprise, all the glorious wonders that time can bring. But sin has made us fearful of the gaps between things and between moments. Now everything is broken apart. We therefore grab the land and seize the day. We build up our treasures on earth, where the thief comes and the moth destroys. Like Faust we cling to the moment of contentment and dare not take the risk of faith that in the next moment God will give us a new heaven and a new earth. The Christian story is precisely this promise: "Do not be afraid, little flock, for your Father has been pleased to give you the kingdom" (Luke 12:32). But human religions and all sinful endeavor have been prompted by our refusal to believe that. Human societies organize themselves on the conservative principle of law, and this is necessary and good because without it there would be chaos and anarchy; but invariably they absolutize the law and bring disintegrating tyranny. They rigidly conserve a status quo that is replete with sin. Human religions quest for goodness, truth, beauty, and the transcendent, and they lift us to heights of discipline, insight, magnificence, and serenity; but inevitably they create idols through their quest and the best of human endeavor becomes the worst. Human religions celebrate the past and try to recover origins through rituals, telling the story of what happened so as not to lose it, but they only repeat and time is thereby disallowed renewal. Biblical revelation is the story of God's quest, not ours, and it truly provides through grace all that law and religion seek because everything is superseded by the promise of the future. This makes a difference in the way the past is celebrated and the present is acted.

Paul Ricoeur contrasts the "It is" of the *Proem* of Parmenides with the "He is coming" of the Bible. The Parmenidean "It is" effects an ethic of the present. The biblical call effects an ethic of hope. The Parmenidean caution was *Nec spe—nec metu* ("Do not hope—do not fear"), which is much like the Hindu and Buddhist "Do not desire—do not suffer." But the Bible speaks of the Coming One. The resurrection of Jesus is not the end of the promise but the first fruits. Hence there is from the promise of the Coming One a linkage of freedom and hope, and the *promissio* involves a *missio*.[12] It is the Judeo-Christian thrust into the future that makes all the difference.

Stories may be told in various ways and the sequence in the telling may not always be the same as the sequence in time. We can begin the story in the middle and with flashbacks go back to the beginning. Good stories also have adumbrations of the future. Obviously we know our own story, both as individuals and as a race, only from the middle; but there is enough integrity in the story known to us to make it possible to reconstruct origins and anticipate destinies. It is essential, however, to get the proper sequence and not to leave out any of the periods. The error of liberal historicism is its neglect of the ultimacy of the future because of its legitimate concern for the present. The error of literalistic fundamentalism is its neglect of historical injustices because of its proper projection of hope beyond history.

We must know what time it is for us. We must know which chapter of the story we are living in. There has never been a synchronous age in which all people walk together in the same time. Some nations are centuries behind others. Or they may be behind in some things and ahead in others. America is behind in health care delivery but ahead in medical technology. Some individuals are disjointed in time. Children try to do before their time things only adults can do. Older people try to recover their youth by acting like children.

We must know the story in its proper sequence. We began with creation and then came the fall. With temptation came the loss of both innocence and the promise of maturation in communion with God. Fall into sin is the dramatic tragedy in which we freely and responsibly chose to believe the adversary's lie and thereby entered into his treacherous trap. We are both rebels and victims, guilty and caught. The story continues, after this tragic beginning, with the historical phase of our painful struggle to build the city of earth, because we have been expelled from the Garden of Eden. And the tragedy of history is that we confuse Cain's city with the city of God. The truth is that the story goes on, and into the historical phase of the story comes a new time. We cannot go back in time to the beginning. There is no reversibility in time. The loss and destruction we experience in time tempts us to seek escape through mystical ecstasy. We try to stand outside time.

Because of time's erosion there is a quest in all stories.[13] Some stories tell of the quest in terms of hopeful dreams. Others sink into cynical despair. Experiments with reversibility by storytellers such as T. H. White and Kurt Vonnegut show that knowledge of the future, if we could have it, only results in tragedy because we freely choose not to use it. The young Arthur in White's *The Once and Future King* does not avail himself of Merlin's wisdom.[14] Some quests project into the future; some try to recover the past. Gilgamesh enters upon a hazardous journey seeking a future that will preserve his past. With regard to the past, Marcel Proust sought to remember it all. A truly realistic view of time will not seek to fixate on either past or future.

Our quest should not try to preserve the past, because the past needs not recovery but resurrection, which is a radical renewal and re-creation. Our quest should not try to discover the future as if the future were fixed and discoverable, because if that were the case, then the future would not be future; it would be a past into which we move sequentially. In reality the future is not fixed. Only its possibilities can be known, and their actualities wait upon the free choice of God and his creatures. In this sense it must be said that even God does not know the future, because the future is not something that can be known.

Time and place can never be separated. Hermann Minkowski discovered this for the physical measurement of time. Poets have often observed this for our psychological perception of time. Sometimes place is maximal and time is minimal in that time appears not to move or it moves in fits and starts rather than smoothly and inexorably. Tragedy moves inexorably in time as fateful destiny crowds in upon the characters, as in *Macbeth* and *King Lear*. Comedy moves in fits and starts or sometimes hardly moves at all because we are lost in love, as in *Twelfth Night*. Places are therefore temporary. A particular place is for the passage of a particular sequence of time. The place of *A Midsummer Night's Dream* is a wood near Athens. In *As You Like It* the action occurs in the forest of Arden. In *The Tempest* everything takes place on Prospero's island. These places are places set apart. They are places where mistakes are made which make things worse before they get better. From the mistakes we learn. By misunderstanding we come to understanding; from telling lies we learn the truth. The tragic occurrences become a process of redemption. After the action and passion of the play are resolved, the characters leave the place that had been set apart. That old place has done its work of healing. The characters come to the place like refugees fleeing from the unjust torments of an unkind world. They are cast out of the garden by an angel with a flaming sword. They are cast overboard into the jaws of a great fish. The characters go to these places—the forest, the island, the belly of the fish, the city of the earth—not for punishment as to a prison, but for healing. The forest revives the players, the island releases those under a spell, the big fish spits Jonah upon the beach. These places are places of refuge. They are places of exile, wandering in the wilderness, a long march, an exodus that leads to a new genesis. They are not places of escape but places of renewal for a new turn. The place of this world with its age of history is a place set apart for such redemption in preparation for a new heaven and a new earth. And when this world has fulfilled its function, when the comedy is ended, like Eden, it will be swept away by an angel with a flaming sword to make room for a new stage setting.

The city of earth with its historical phase is a *via dolorosa*. We must go the way of the cross to arrive at the glorious conclusion of resurrection. On the way we do not solicit the sympathetic weeping of bystanders. That was the way of the pagan hero. His tragedy evoked pity. The biblical hero in God's story stirs in us a mysterious awe. We are drawn to his suffering with reverential love. We look up to his painful death with worshipful joy, and we take up our cross. We do not seek to suffer but we go forward in our pilgrimage turning every torment into a triumph. This place becomes a time of discipline, a schooling and training in which we grow strong in faith by fixing our eyes on Jesus, "the pioneer and perfecter of our faith" (Heb. 12:2).[15] The tragic victory of Christ produces in our tragic story a resolution of grace, not one of success or one of escape.

William F. Lynch says the trouble with modern tragic plays is that they are romantic. The hero faces the facts with courage and the solution is self-reliance. Or with some playwrights there is no solution at all, for example, with Jean-Paul Sartre or Jean Genet or sometimes with Eugene O'Neill. When O'Neill is theological his plays have a leap of escape.[16] The Christian story, in contrast, delivers a tragic victory, a final *eucatastrophe* through suffering.

There is no romantic reversibility. We cannot restore Eden and innocence. That period is finished. But we can go forward into a new period, a new age that is already beginning in the midst of the old age. We can only go forward, as Kierkegaard said in *The Concept of Dread*, through the gracious gift of repentance to faith.[17] The opposite of sin is not virtue but faith. When sin is taken from us by the grace of forgiveness and the renewal of baptism we do not return to an original righteousness. We move forward through repentance and faith to a life of witnessing in love. From the promise comes our mission.

The sequence, as Paul tells the story, involves a succession of sin, wrath, law, and death which are met, again in sequence, with Christ's suffering on the cross, the grace of mercy, the Spirit giving life, and the resurrection.[18] Sin is met with forgiveness, not punishment. We are invited to start over again and the past is forgotten. Wrath is met with the grace of mercy, not angry petulance. God does not send a thunderbolt from the sky. He delivers us up to our sin. He lets us freely go our own way (Rom. 1:24). If in sin we want to be independent of God, he allows us our uniqueness, because he never violates our freedom and the image in which he made us. Law is met with the life-giving Spirit, not with killing judgment. In the new age we are guided not by rigid rules but by a Person who shows us the way. Death is met with resurrection, not resuscitation. Death is not sent to us by God; it is our doing and the devil's as we separate ourselves in sin. Death is not annihilation but our separation from God, and as such it is suffered by him as well as by us.

Resurrection begins with Jesus' rising from the tomb and it leads, as the first fruit, to the final consummation. The risen Christ has ushered in a new time which pulses in secret alongside the old time of this world. The old time is still the same; it is doomed, yet there is a difference now. It is not a difference that can be seen or measured, but it can be experienced in faith, and it produces both love and hope. We know by faith in the victory of Christ over sin, death, and the devil that he is bringing all things into subjection under himself. This new time of secret work is full of anticipation. The story of the old world is coming to an end, but a new story is beginning. Reality is a repertoire. Before the curtain goes down in the last act a new play has already begun. The action of the old play is being carried forward and is drawing to a close. We have an expectation that is double. We can see signs of a cosmic cataclysm and we can see signs of a new heaven and a new earth. The final judgment is not merely historical, nor does it restore us in history, nor can it be seen in any way from evidence in history, neither through sophisticated erudition nor by crude and deluding popular speculation. The future is not fixed; it is unpredictable. The end will come as a thief in the night, in a moment when we least expect, in the twinkling of an eye. No one will know the time of the end, but this is not the end of time. There is no biblical support for an end of time. The time of the end brings a new time, and it comes with a surprise ending. It goes beyond history, however, and therefore we cannot describe the furniture of the new heaven and earth. With hope and imagination we simply take the holy risk and respond to the call that draws us through death to life into the age of the ages—*aiōn tōn aiōnōn*.

NOTES

1. Cf. George W. Stroup, *The Promise of Narrative Theology* (Atlanta: John Knox Press, 1981), 147.

2. Cf. Dale Patrick, *The Rendering of God in the Old Testament* (Philadelphia: Fortress Press, 1981).

3. Rudolf Bultmann, "New Testament and Mythology" in *Kerygma and Myth,* ed. Hans Werner Bartsch (New York: Harper & Row, 1961), 5.

4. Gerhard Ebeling, "Word of God and Hermeneutics," in *Word and Faith* (Philadelphia: Fortress Press, 1963), 325.

5. Wolfhart Pannenberg, *Revelation as History* (London: Macmillan & Co., 1969), 123ff.

6. Ludwig Wittgenstein, *Philosophical Investigations* (Oxford: Basil Blackwell, 1967), 8ff.

7. Hans-Georg Gadamer, *Truth and Method* (New York: Sheed & Ward, 1975); Hans W. Frei, *The Eclipse of Biblical Narrative* (New Haven: Yale University Press, 1974).

8. Amos N. Wilder, *Jesus' Parables and the War of Myths* (Philadelphia: Fortress Press, 1982), 32.

9. Paul Ricoeur, *Essays on Biblical Interpretation* (Philadelphia: Fortress Press, 1980), 121–22.

10. Ibid., 140.

11. Søren Kierkegaard, *The Concept of Dread* (Princeton: Princeton University Press, 1944), 45.

12. Ricoeur, *Essays on Biblical Interpretation,* 161.

13. Cf. Edward H. Schafer, *The Divine Woman: Dragon Ladies and Rain Maidens in T'ang Literature* (Berkeley and Los Angeles: University of California Press, 1973).

14. T. H. White, *The Once and Future King* (New York: G. P. Putnam's Sons, Berkeley Medallion edition, 1966).

15. Cf. Reinhold Niebuhr, *Beyond Tragedy* (New York: Charles Scribner's Sons, 1937).

16. Cf. Willaim F. Lynch, S.J., *Christ and Apollo: The Dimensions of the Literary Imagination* (New York: Sheed & Ward, 1960).

17. Kierkegaard *The Concept of Dread,* 97.

18. The sequential themes of sin, wrath, law, and death and their conquest by forgiveness, mercy, Spirit, and resurrection follow the analysis of the first eight chapters of Romans in Anders Nygren, *Commentary on Romans* (Philadelphia: Muhlenberg Press, 1949).

Index of Scriptural References

OLD TESTAMENT

Genesis
1—59
1—11—9
2:7—59
32:25—12

Exodus
29:17-18—84
31:1-5—105
35:31—105

Leviticus
17:7—160

Deuteronomy
26:5-9—174
32:17—160

1 Samuel
16:13—105
16:14—82

Job
13:15—73

Psalms
37:7—161
46:10—161
90:4—38

Proverbs
8:22—103

Isaiah
6:5—162
42:1—105
61:1—105

Amos
2:6—75

Malachi
3:1—120

DEUTEROCANONICALS/APOCRYPHA

Sirach
24:9—103

NEW TESTAMENT

Matthew
4:10—82
8:29—85
12:26—82
12:28—106
13:12-13—130
28:20—120

Mark
2:7—98
10:45—84

Luke
1:35—101
4:5-6—82

4:22—98
6:37-38—97
10:18—83
12:32—179
18:8—163
22:29—134
31:1—82

John
1:18—99
6:42—98
8:44—82
15:22—33
16:8-11—107
20:21—125,134

Index of Scriptural References

Acts
1:6—120
2:36—88
2:42—129
5:3—82
7:56—121
12:24—82
14:23—133

Romans
1:3—100
1:24—182
1:29—5
6—15, 79
7:19—152
8:14–15—79
8:21—82
8:23—101
8:38—41
11:32—125

1 Corinthians
1:27—100
1:28—129
2:9—168
5:7—78
10:20—160
14:26—135
15:24—38
15:51–57—165

2 Corinthians
4:18—46
5:19—90
5:21—100, 101
6:3–10—154
11:14—82

Galatians
1:1—134
1:12—150
3:13—100

3:16—140
4:3—82
4:4—100

Ephesians
1:3–5—150
2:2—82
2:4–5—151
3:19—5
5:2—84
6:12—41, 82

Philippians
2:6–11—88, 100

Colossians
1:24—168
1:24–25—133

1 Thessalonians
2:18—82

3:5—82

1 Timothy
4:14—134

Hebrews
2:14—82
13:12–14—123

1 Peter
4:12–13—72
4:12–14—81
5:8—82

2 Peter
3:8—38

Revelation
9:20—160
20:2—82
20:7—82

Index of Names

Aeschylus, 66, 114
Albee, Edward, 71, 104
Alexander, Samuel, 45
Altizer, Thomas J. J., 18
Anselm, 24
Apollinaris, 90
Aquinas, Thomas, 32, 46
Aristotle, x, 2, 21, 24, 46, 55, 70, 97, 146
Arius, 103
Asch, Sholem, 96
Athanasius, 107
Augustine, 33, 41, 110, 129
Ayer, Alfred J., 5

Barfield, Owen, 154
Barr, James, 144
Barrett, C. K., 114
Barth, Karl, 7, 108
Barthes, Roland, 8, 12
Beckett, Samuel, 14, 71
Bergson, Henri, 34, 43
Bierce, Ambrose, 36
Black, Max, 35, 39, 63
Bosch, Hieronymus, 71
Braque, Georges, 36
Brentano, Franz, 25
Brontë, Emily, 67
Brunner, Emil, 7

Bruns, J. Edgar, 104
Buechner, Frederick, 154
Bultmann, Rudolf, 7, 20, 166, 176
Bunyan, John, 80

Campbell, Joseph, 54
Camus, Albert, 68
Cappadocian Fathers, 107
Capon, Robert Farrar, 155
Chekhov, Anton, 71
Chemnitz, Martin, 90
Childs, Brevard, 7
Chisholm, Roderick M., 43
Choan-Seng Song, 137
Chomsky, Noam, 8, 58
Chuang Tzu, 44
Cobb, John B., Jr., 18
Come, Arnold, 107
Conrad, Joseph, 67
Crossan, John Dominic, 43, 137
Cullmann, Oscar, 37, 157

Dante, 80
Darwin, Charles, 56, 62

De Quincey, Thomas, 33
de Saussure, Ferdinand, 8
Descartes, x, 23, 94
Dilthey, Wilhelm, 8
Dix, Dom Gregory, 172
Doan, Gilbert E., 154
Dostoevsky, Fyodor, 67, 126

Ebeling, Gerhard, 7, 176
Eckhart, John ("Meister"), 34
Eichrodt, Walther, 7
Einstein, Albert, 25
Eliade, Mircea, 15, 21
Eliot, Alexander, 63
Eliot, T. S., 51
Euhemerus, 16
Euripides, 66

Faulkner, William, 67
Fichte, Johann Gottlieb, 93
Forsythe, P. T., 154
Fraser, J. T., 44
Frei, Hans, 177
Frye, Northrop, 54, 77, 120

187

Index of Names

Frye, Roland M., 87
Fuchs, Ernst, 7

Gadamer, Hans-Georg, 43, 177
Genet, Jean, 182
Giles, Herbert A., 76
Goethe, Johann Wolfgang von, 80
Gregory of Nyssa, 90
Guellelmin, Victor, 63
Gutiérrez, Gustavo, 7

Haeckel, Ernst, 56
Hammerton-Kelly, Robert, 76
Hanson, Paul, 10
Harnack, Adolf, 134
Hatsopoulos, George N., 63
Hayes, Zachary, 62
Hazlitt, William, 70
Hegel, Georg Wilhelm, 45, 92
Heidegger, Martin, 8
Heisenberg, Werner, 57
Holmes, Roger W., 43
Hopkins, Gerard Manley, 113
Hume, David, x, 25, 93
Husserl, Edmund, 8, 94

Ibsen, Henrik, 5, 71
Ionesco, Eugene, 71
Irenaeus, 101, 103

Jacobi, F. J., 94
Jenson, Robert W., 111
Jeremias, Joachim, 20
Jülicher, Adolph, 20

Kandinsky, Wassily, 69
Kant, Immanuel, 23, 93
Keenan, Joseph H., 63
Kierkegaard, Søren, 14, 69, 70, 93, 96, 99, 146, 171, 179, 182
Kirk, Geoffrey, 19

Küng, Hans, 131

Langbaum, Robert, 77
Leach, Edmund, 19
Leibniz, x, 28
Lévi-Strauss, Claude, 8
Lewis, C. S., 12, 16, 49, 53
Lietzmann, Hans, 158
Luther, Martin, 131, 143, 161

Manson, William, 137
Mao Tse-tung, 17
Marlowe, Christopher, 66, 80
Maruoka, Daiji, 76
Marx, Karl, 17
McFague, Sallie, 87
McGavran, Donald, 137
McKnight, Edgar V., 8
Melanchthon, Philipp, 1, 89
Melville, Herman, 67, 69
Miller, Arthur, 171
Moltmann, Jürgen, 7, 110, 137
Mondrian, Piet, 69
Mumford, Lewis, 169

Newbigin, Eugene, 182
Newton, Issac, 24
Niedenthal, Murray J., 155
Nietzsche, Friedrich, 68

O'Neill, Eugene, 182
Otto, Rudolph, 99

Pannenberg, Wolfhart, 7, 137, 176
Patrick, Dale, 183
Pearson, Karl, 63
Pelikan, Jaroslav, 113
Pepper, Stephen, 63
Picasso, Pablo, 36
Pinter, Harold, 71

Plato, x, 2, 24, 25, 33, 46, 55
Prenter, Regin, 40
Propp, Vladimir, 19
Proust, Marcel, 181

Rad, Gerhard von, 7
Rahner, Karl, 109
Ricoeur, Paul, 8, 10, 21, 178
Robinson, Edward, 155
Rothe, Richard, 110
Rudin, James, 18
Rudin, Marcia, 18

Sartre, Jean-Paul, 182
Schelling, F. W. J., 93
Schleiermacher, Friedrich, 94, 101
Scott, Nathan, 70
Stählin, Wilhelm, 172
Shakespeare, William, 33, 66, 67, 71, 75, 97, 145
Skinner, B. F., 58
Soelle, Dorothee, 7
Sophocles, 66
Strauss, David Friedrich, 20
Strindberg, August, 71
Stroup, George W., 183
Styan, J. L., 71

Tavard, George H., 154
Tertullian, 103
Tillich, Paul, 7, 92, 166
Tolkien, J. R. R., 53
Tolstoy, Leo, 17, 171
Toynbee, Arndt, 15
Trible, Phyllis, 63

Ujinobu, Zenchika, 68

Via, Dan O., Jr., 77
Vonnegut, Kurt, 180

Wherry, Joseph H., 54
Wicker, Brian, 19

Index of Names

Wilder, Amos N., 21, 42, 177
Williams, Charles, 80, 119
Williams, Tennessee, 99
Wingren, Gustaf, 114
Wink, Walter, 7

White, T. H., 180
Whitehead, Alfred North, x, 7, 15, 26, 45, 115
Wittgenstein, Ludwig, 23, 43

Xenophanes, 15

Yoshikoshi, Tatsuo, 76

Zeno, 34

Index of Subjects

A Midsummer Night's Dream, 11, 145
Anna Karenina, 171
As You Like It, 33

Baptism, 116
Bible, 3, 139

Causality, 6, 25, 27, 38, 49
Church, 119
Creation, 6
Creation stories, 51, 59
Creationism, 58

Endgame, 14
Entropy, 58
Epic of Gilgamesh, 50
Eucatastrophe, 64, 73, 182
Eucharist, 156
Existential philosophy, 8

Hamlet, 152, 176

Image of God, 61, 175
Inspiration, 3

Language, structural analysis, 8, 13
Laughter, 72
Liturgy, 156

Measure for Measure, 6, 22, 97
Metaphor, 10, 21, 26, 78, 97
Ministry, 131
Mystery plays, 71
Myth, 15, 19, 20, 103

Narrative hermeneutics, 6, 9
Narrative ontology, 20
Noh drama, 68
Northwest Indians, 51

Orestes, 102

Paradox, 34, 36, 149, 171
Perception, 23

Phaedra, 159
Phenomenology, 8
Philosophical metaphors, 57
Prayer, 160
Preaching, 147
Predestination, 127

Reality, 22, 40
Redemption stories, 64

Scientific models, 57
Service, 168
Sisyphus, ix
Space, 65
Structural analysis, 13

The Tempest, 75
Tragedy, 64
The Tragedy of Macbeth, 145
Tragicomedy, 71
Time, 16, 25, 33, 64, 179
Trinity, 2, 105

Uncertainty principle, 57